I0542976

ཚོན་མོ་ངས་འདོད་ཆགས་ལམ་བྱེད།

Tantric Path of Desire

A Unique Presentation of How to Practice
The Quintessence of The Genuine Tantra Path
Embracing Sexuality
And Other Skillful Means for Reaching Immutable Bliss

Shar Khentrul Rinpoché Jamphel Lodrö

Translated by
Rimé Lodrö (Ives Waldo)

Edited by
Lobsang Dorjé (Rafael Nassif) and Rimé Lodrö

Dzokden

©2023 Dzokden

All rights reserved. No part of this book may be reproduced electronically, digitally or by any other means, including photocopying, recording, or any system of archiving, without written permission from the publisher

Author: Shar Khentrul Jamphel Lodrö
Translator and Editor: Rimé Lodrö (Ives Waldo)
Editor: Lobsang Dorjé (Rafael Nassif)

First Edition
ISBN (Paperback): 978-1-958229-75-0
ISBN (ePub): 978-1-958229-76-7

Published by: DZOKDEN

This work was produced and published by Dzokden, a not-for-profit organization. This organization is devoted to propagating a non-sectarian view of all the world's spiritual traditions and teaching Buddhism in a way that is completely authentic, yet also practical and accessible to Western culture. It is especially dedicated to propagating the Jonang Tradition, a rare jewel from the remote regions of Tibet which holds the precious Kālachakra teachings.

For more information on scheduled activities or available materials, or if you wish to make a donation to support our work, please contact:

Dzokden
3436 Divisadero Street
San Francisco, CA 94123 USA
www.dzokden.org
office@dzokden.org

[This book contains adult language and mature themes.
It is suitable for adults 18+ only.]

In tantrayāna that produces the path of bliss,
As defilements are washed away by defilements,
Conceptions are purified by conceptions themselves,
Saṃsāra is abandoned by saṃsāra itself.

Just as fire may be kindled from a fire,
It can also be extinguished by a fire;
Thus, what is kindled by the fire of desire,
Can be extinguished by the fire of desire.

Padmasaṃbhava
The Path of Means, the Essence of Great Bliss

Contents

Suchandra from Śhambhala who requested the
Buddha to impart the Kālachakra Teachings

The secrecy of secret mantra[1] is the secret
Of true, eternal reality, which is a natural secret.[2]

If direct perception of that secret absolute,
And the merely imputed imagined,[3] are not well known and
distinguished,
And are not competently analyzed, from error and confusion,
Knowledge, experience, and realization will be explained,
As being something other than what they really are.

By your receiving this gift of teachings bestowed by me,
Enjoy your share of the Dharma of the Golden Age!

Khentrul Rinpoché

---

1 "Secret mantra," *gsang sngags,* is the most commonly used term in the Tibetan version of this book to refer to the Buddhist tantric teachings, *rgyud.* "Secret mantra" says explicitly that these are secret teachings, while with "tantra" this is just implicitly understood. That said, in this English version of this book we use "tantra" in most cases to avoid misunderstanding and to reflect the author's preference. More details in Part Two chapter 1. (*All footnotes were added by the translator and editor*; when "Rinpoché" is mentioned, it is referring to the author of this book as a reference for us writing the footnote or a specific part of the footnote.)

2 The absolute truth realized by secret mantra or tantra is naturally secret because ordinary beings can apprehend only the dualistic delusions imagined by conceptualized relative truth.

3 Absolute truth is beyond complete and precise description by the conceptual language of the relative, and so it can be realized only by direct perception.

Translator's Preface:
Problems and Possibilities, an Introduction

First, this book presents a *problem*. In the author's original Tibetan version of this book, written by a Tibetan for other Tibetans, the problem was presented as the degradation of Tibetan religious and secular culture in ethnically Tibetan countries dominated by renunciate monks, which is certainly unfortunate, but what is the relevance for people in other countries? This English version of the book presents the essence of that Tibetan problem as a psychological one that is relevant to people everywhere. It is a problem of personal and cultural being stifled by the strict values of people who reject ordinary life in the name of values they see as of higher value, whether these are religious, political, or scientific.

For example, many authorities in different religions of the world say that renunciation of the pleasures of ordinary life, and in particular celibacy, are required for any genuine religious attainment. Doubtless, many have made significant spiritual progress by such means, but a great deal of guilt and misogyny results from ordinary people being infected by the idea that only these ascetic holy men are living as people ought to live.

Such values hinder more approachable forms of religious expression that find religious attainment at the heart of ordinary life. There is always a higher spiritual or even ultimate reality to connect with, but attaining it in a way that solves the problem of the difference between renunciant and ordinary life just stated depends very much on the possibilities of the human mind and spirit. Therefore, in presenting this problem and its solution, I shall refer to passages from many religious traditions. In doing this I am not arrogant enough to think I can understand all that they have to say at a glance. I know that much of it will escape me. It is more like reading books or seeing TV shows about different families in diverse parts of the world. Many aspects of their experience are hard or impossible to understand, but some spontaneously resonate on a deep level and give insight into what I have experienced with my own tantric Buddhist family.

Taking renunciate Buddhism as an example of the problem, when a son was born to the Buddha early in his life when he had ascetic, renunciate values, he said,[4]

> "A rāhu is born, a fetter has arisen." Accordingly, the child was named Rāhula, meaning a "fetter," or "impediment."

In a similar manner, Buddhist monks who are constantly struggling to repress temptations of sexual desire can easily fall into the strategy of personifying their disgust with *saṃsāra* by displacing it onto women. Nuns may do the same with men:[5]

> For the most part desire for women rises
> From thinking that a woman's body is clean.
> The bodies of women in reality
>
> Have nothing clean about them whatsoever. [...]

---

4   T. W. Rhys Davids tr., p. 79.

5   Nāgārjuna, *Ratnāvalī*, D5148 Tengyur, spring yig, ge, 2:47, 112B:1.

Like a person, not knowing what it is,
Craving an ornamented pot of filth,
Such are deluded, ignorant ones of this world,
When it comes to their attitude to women.

The same psychology commonly occurs in other renunciate traditions. Within Christianity, Saint John says of the 144,000 men of the elect who will enter Heaven:[6]

These are the ones who were not defiled with women, for they are virgins.

This approach is so unreflectively patriarchal that it did not seem necessary to mention the final abode of females, however saintly or profane. An obvious implication, even if it was unintended, is that since women are not among the elect, they cannot enter Heaven, and so they must be destined for the other place.[7] Certainly consorting with them is enough to disenfranchise men who would otherwise be among the elect.

I visited the cave on the Island of Patmos where Saint John wrote the book of *Revelation*. One of the main attractions is an immense rock in the wall of the cave. Many people who touch it feel a powerful sacred energy even today. Undoubtedly the visions of this Saint John carried measureless blessings at the time they occurred. However, 2000 years later, might not some reconsideration of his seeming contempt for consorting with females in that verse be in order? Saint John takes a more compassionate approach in *John 2* when he describes the day that Jesus, at his mother's bidding, revealed

---

6   Revelation 14:4. *Holy Bible*, King James Version. Christian Art Publishers, PO Box 1599, Vereeniging, 1930; RSA: Printed in China, 2016.

7   Hell, for those unfamiliar with Christian doctrine.

his divinity to the world by turning water into wine at a wedding feast:[8]

2:1   And the third day there was a marriage in Cana of Galilee; and the mother of Jesus was there:

2:2   And both Jesus was called, and his disciples, to the marriage.

2:3   And when they wanted wine, the mother of Jesus saith unto him, 'They have no wine.'

2:4   Jesus saith unto her, 'Woman, what have I to do with thee? Mine hour is not yet come.'

2:5   His mother saith unto the servants, 'Whatsoever he saith unto you, do it.'

2:6   And there were set there six waterpots of stone, after the manner of the purifying of the Jews, containing two or three firkins[9] apiece.

2:7   Jesus saith unto them, 'Fill the waterpots with water.' And they filled them up to the brim.

2:8   And he saith unto them, 'Draw out now, and bear unto the governor of the feast.' And they bare it.

2:9   When the ruler of the feast had tasted the water that was made wine, and knew not whence it was: (but the servants which drew the water knew;) the governor of the feast called the bridegroom,

2:10 And saith unto him, 'Every man at the beginning doth set forth good wine; and when men have well drunk, then that which is worse: but thou hast kept the good wine until now.'

2:11 This beginning of miracles did Jesus in Cana of Galilee, and manifested forth his glory; and his disciples believed on him.

If you are still wondering about the significance for this book of the mirac-

---

8   *Ibid.*

9   A firkin is equivalent to the Hebrew bath of about nine gallons. Even six pots of two firkins would be 54 gallons. Quite a party!

ulous wedding feast that launched Jesus' ministry, tantra in any culture is an extraordinary affirmation of ordinary life. Thus, a little later, *(John 10:10)* Jesus says,[10]

> I am come that they might have life, and that they might have it more abundantly.

That is what we are talking about. The *Chāndogyopaniṣhad, 8.7.3,* presenting a Hindu approach to renunciate yoga, says,[11]

> They dwelt there for thirty-two years, practicing brahmacha-rya.[12] Then Prajāpati said to them: 'For what purpose have you both been living here?' They said: 'A saying of yours is being repeated by learned people: The self which is free from sin, free from old age, free from death, free from grief, free from hunger, free from thirst, whose desires come true and whose thoughts come true. That it is which should be searched out...'

Though limitless saints and sages have gained spiritual attainment from turning away from seeking external things that appear to gratify the false self of ordinary life to pursue union with ultimate reality as it is revealed to them, this is a problem for most of us who are unable to follow their heroic example. This passage seems to imply that people who

---

10   *Ibid.*

11   *Upaniṣhads the, Taittirya and Chhāndogya,* by Swami Nikhilananda, Volume IV, Harper & Brothers: New York, 1959, p. 377.

12   Brahmacharya, *tshangs spyod*: restraint from seeking fulfillment outside of one's true inner self, the nature of Brahmā. Since the nature of Brahmā includes everything, this could conceivably be done without giving up anything. However, it is usually accomplished by renouncing gratification from external phenomena in the world, particularly sex. Therefore, the term is commonly used to mean renunciation, and celibacy in particular.

cannot give up ordinary life must also give up the best of being human. Devout Tibetans, especially, feel terribly guilty about that, and often in their hearts, they cannot help regarding marriage as a terrible defeat. Therefore, an ongoing theme of this book will be the unintended, collateral damage that arises from the religious ideal of renunciation. Such a serious problem requires a serious solution.

In seeking such a *solution*, the main subject of this book, we should pay attention when others in all cultures who are knowledgeable about how to live, say that the highest ideal can be reached in ordinary life as well, or even better than by renunciation, formalized by monasticism or otherwise. They claim that, in the attainment that all great religions seek, everything in heaven and earth is revealed as holy. Ordinary Hinduism reveres the love of Kṛiṣhṇa and Rādhā, whereof it is said,[13]

> Darkness can never drive out darkness, only light;
> Hatred can never drive out hatred, only love.

Another branch of yoga is associated with the Śhivaliṅga and the source of phenomena as the male and female cosmic principles. More about that later.

In Islam, even the Prophet Mohammed was married. The fourth chapter of the Holy Quran, Surah an-Nisa, addresses the mutual rights of human beings, laying the foundation for a sound family life. The opening verse urges mankind to acknowledge that all human beings share the same roots as descendants of Prophet Adam and his wife Eve, and thus may Allah be pleased with them:

> O mankind, fear your Lord, who created you from one soul and

---

13   https://feedingtrends.com/radha-krishna-love-quotes-eternal-love-story-radhe-radhe-devotion. The original verses are in Hindi. We changed the English ones a bit to fit this book's metrical pattern.

created from it its mate and dispersed from both of them many men and women... (Quran, 4:1)

Also,

And one of His signs is that He created for you spouses from among yourselves so that you may find comfort in them. And He has placed between you compassion and mercy. Surely in this are signs for people who reflect. (Quran, 4:30:21)[14]

In Judaism, Chasidic mystics and Rabbis have wives as a matter of course. Here is a miraculous story about the founder of Chasidism, the Baal Shem Tov, and his wife:[15]

One year on *Simchat Torah*[16] in Mezibuz, many members of the inner circle of the sixty most advanced students of the Baal Shem Tov were dancing into the night with great joy, while consuming large quantities of wine. The wife of the Baal Shem Tov, Leah-Rachel, was concerned that there would not be enough wine left for *Kiddush*[17] the next day and *Havdalah*[18] in the evening at the end of the festival. She went over to her

14 Quran.com.

15 https://www.chabad.org/kabbalah/article_cdo/aid/4134428/jewish/Repercussions-of-Wine-and-Dance.htm. See also Buber, Martin, *Tales of the Hasidim*, Schocken Books: New York, 1991.

16 "Rejoicing with the Torah," a holiday that celebrates and marks the conclusion of the annual cycle of public Torah readings. *Simchat Torah* is a component of the holiday of *Shemini Atzeret* ("Eighth Day of Assembly"), which follows immediately after the festival of Sukkot (harvest festival of booths celebrating the protection of the Children of Israel during the exodus from Egypt).

17 (Hebrew: "Sanctification,") Jewish benediction and prayer recited over a cup of wine immediately before the meal on the eve of the Sabbath or a festival.

18 ("Separation" in Hebrew,) this is the sabbath's closing ritual, when three stars appear on Saturday evening. With blessings over lights, wine or grape juice, and spices, *Havdalah* is an inspiring way to end the sabbath and start the new week as a family.

husband and said,... 'I think you should tell them to please stop drinking so much. Otherwise they will keep dancing and drinking, drinking and dancing, until we do not have any wine left for Kiddush and Havdalah.'

The Baal Shem Tov smiled broadly. He replied, 'Good point! You may go tell them to stop. They will listen and go home.'

The Rebbetzin[19] turned to go to the nearby room where the chasidim were dancing and celebrating. She opened the door...and froze in the entrance in shock. Her husband's followers were merrily dancing in a tight circle and she saw flames of fire surrounding them and hovering over them like a wedding canopy!

She did not take another step towards them or utter a single word. Instead she turned around, went down to the cellar of their house, took as much wine as she could carry and silently placed it on the table of the enthusiastically dancing chasidim. ... Surely the *Shechinah* — the Divine Presence — was dancing together with them!

Note the suspicious coincidence that this story too is concerned with wine and weddings. In many later teachings of the Buddha, and in many Hindu teachings as well, such a life-enhancing approach is called "tantra." According to the biographies of the eighty-four *mahāsiddhas*,[20] any aspect of life, however exalted, humble, or even degraded can become a tantric path to enlightenment. Some of these *siddhas* are ordinary working people, like fishermen, arrow makers, butchers, soldiers, and prostitutes.

For example, once a wandering yogī asked a shoemaker for alms. He gave what he could, saying, "Pray for me, as I must spend all my time mak-

---

19 Rabbi's wife.

20 See footnote 47.

ing shoes to support my family. I am not free to wander everywhere seeking religious truth, as you do." The yogī replied, "Truth is already within you, and nothing around you fails to speak of it. You need not change your way of life. As you sew the upper parts of shoes to the soles, think 'I am sewing enlightenment above to delusive, fallen existence below. I am bringing all things together in a single perfection.'" Following only that simple instruction, the shoemaker attained a realized state.[21] It was some time before he realized he was a mahāsiddha because the outer form of his life had not changed at all.

The Kalkī Kings and Queens of the *Kālachakra Tantra*[22] are the epitome of enlightened expression by bodhisattva spiritual warriors like that yogī in more exalted walks of life. They seek enlightenment not only for themselves, but for all beings, all countries, and all worldly phenomena as well so that our world manifests as a peaceful land in a Golden Age of enlightened activity that is not exclusively Buddhist but can be participated in by all cultures.

As explained later in this book, they teach that this Golden Age will be brought about by spreading tantric teachings. These will allow ordinary people to overcome the selfish, negative emotions — *kleśhas* in Sanskrit — that are the source of the endless suffering of this "fallen world." Advocates of self-denial tell us that those of us who cannot eliminate them by renunciation must abandon hope. However, the tantric path allows

---

21   Recounting from memory details of a story taught in a translation meeting by Trungpa Rinpoché. I do not know his source, but a similar story of a shoemaker mahāsiddha named Chamaripa can be found in pp. 69-71 of Robinson tr., *Buddha's Lions*. Chamaripa, as *Chamaru*, wrote the *Thabs dang shes rab brtse ba lnga pa, Prajñopaya-viniścaya-samudaya-nāma*, Toh 2381 *Tengyur* 2381, rgyud, zi, 13a4-14a2.

22   This tantra speaks of Dharma Kings and Kalkī Kings of Śhambhala. Khentrul Rinpoché reports visions and transmissions of future female bodhisattva Kalkīs, as in his own text *Empowerment Liturgy of the Dharma Kings and Kalkīs of Śhambhala in the North, along with the Kalkī Princes and Princesses*, entitled "The Heroic Courage of Spiritual Warriors of Great Power."

XXII   TANTRIC PATH OF DESIRE

us to make our emotions into friends; this is accomplished by *the kleśhas becoming aspects of the path* to spiritual transcendence of the fallen ordinary world. Both these negative teachings about destructive emotions and these positive teachings of transcending them depend only on perceiving human nature. Though the teachings taught here were preserved for many centuries in Tibet, what they teach does not depend on any particular qualities or limitations of Tibetan culture.

In particular, when we are affirming life in this world, sexual desire, rather than being regarded as a guilty pleasure of indulgence in the foulest degradations of fallen existence, can be revealed as the most sublime means of liberation. As such, it is known by Tibetan Buddhists as the *Path of Desire*. However, there is nothing intrinsically Tibetan or Buddhist about this insight, and people everywhere have come to similar conclusions. The Englishman William Blake says, in his *Little Girl Lost*:[23]

> Children of the future age,
> Reading this indignant page,
> Know that in a former time
> Love, sweet love, was thought a crime.

As a presentation of Sufism, mystic Islam, the *Rubaiyat* of Omar Khayyam of Persia, as translated by Edward FitzGerald, says,[24]

> Here with a Loaf of Bread beneath the Bough,
> A Flask of Wine, a Book of Verse — and Thou
> Beside me singing in the Wilderness —
> And wilderness is Paradise now.

---

23 Blake, William, *Complete Writings with Variant Readings*, ed. Geoffrey Keynes, Oxford University Press: London, Oxford, New York, 1969, p. 219.

24 *Rubiyayat of Omar Khayyam*, p. 3. The verse here differs from the better known later version.

That simplicity is indeed enough. These recurring references to wine in the context of love are metaphors for love's ability to intoxicate us into the experience of the divine at the center of our ordinary world. However, for some, a more exuberantly elaborate approach is even better. The *Song of Songs* in the *Torah* or *Old Testament*, chronicles how the love of the Israelite King Solomon and the Ethiopian Queen of Sheba brought them to realization of the divine, beginning in the King James translation:[25]

> Let him kiss me with the kisses of his mouth!
> For your love is better than wine;
> Your anointing oils are fragrant;
> Your name is oil poured out; [...]

The Tibetan Gendün Chöpel, whose verses appear at the Appendix I of this book, became disillusioned with the self-imposed "torture" of monastic renunciation and plunged instead into the intoxicating delights of the Path of Desire. Rather than stopping at the simple savor of bread and wine, he writes the equivalent of a gourmet cookbook, detailing how sexual enjoyment so enhanced becomes a vehicle for attaining "enlightenment."[26]

> By this merit, may all companions of the same family
> Traverse the misty gloom that conceals the path of passion,
> Until, from the peaks of the mountains of the sixteen joys,
> They see the cloudless sky of true reality.

> Yutrön, Gangā, Asali, and the rest of you,
> You ladies I came to know, as we made free with our bodies,
> Continuing on our path that goes from bliss to bliss,

---

25   *Song of Songs*: 12:8, *Holy Bible*, KJV, op. cit.

26   Verse 584, as translated below from the author's Tibetan text.

May you reach Dharmakāya, the ultimate great bliss.

Embracing desire appears as an outrage to self-appointed guardians of the traditional morality of tortuous denial because they know nothing of pure desire. The mahāsiddha Saraha's *Songs of the Inexhaustible Treasury* reminds us that Buddhist yogins at a tantric feast engage in the "outrageous" directness of their practice because it is a direct path to enlightenment:[27]

> Sometimes, entering charnel grounds, the 'lamps'[28] are practiced.
> With a fearless mind, sleep in places haunted by ghosts.
> Associating with outcasts, invite a circle of corpses,
> Grasping no limits to practice of 'this is done, this is not.' [...]

> Having fully performed the mad activities of the great secret,
> By spontaneous acts without 'to be done' or 'not to be done,'
> Like a drunken elephant blissfully plunging into a lake,
> We are freed if we practice outrageous teachings, says Saraha.

In the same vein, the *Guhyasamāja Tantra* says,[29]

> All the activities that we desire,
> If we indulge them just the way we like,
> By our performing these activities,
> We shall quickly attain the state of Buddhahood.

---

27   As cited in the translator's own unpublished translation of: *Longchenpa, The Great Chariot, A Commentary on The Great Perfection: The Comfort and Ease of Mind*, electronic MSWord file, p. 763. Saraha, *Dohākoshacharyāgīti*, D2264 Kangyur, rgyud 'grel, zhi, 31a.

28   Indulging in what is normally considered forbidden or disgusting, these indulgences are called lamps that reveal ultimate reality. See footnote 460.

29   *Guhyasamājamahākalparāja*, D442 Kangyur, rgyud, ca. chap. 2, 100a1, as cited in *op. cit*, p. 773.

I know from experience that this kind of language raises entirely reasonable doubts and fears in many hearers. Did not the great religious figures of history take great care to be good and compassionate? Therefore, it is essential to point out that Saraha was talking about the appropriate state of mind for experiencing absolute reality at a sacramental vajra feast. Before this practice is done, protective barriers are created to isolate practitioners' minds from all selfish, "demonic" thoughts of passion, aggression, and ignoring the sacred value of others. Only after this bubble of divine purity is established, may the mind be released from conceptual limitations to experience it fully and directly. The hearers' fears above would be justified if practitioners were to ignore these protective preliminaries. Rather than pure, selfless perceptions leading to the essence of enlightened bliss, they would then be indulging in ordinary cravings that sent them straight to the lower realms. That discernment makes the difference between success and failure in tantra.

The Path of Desire is a literal outrage only if love and human life itself are the crimes that so many deniers of life say they are. For those who aspire to be Buddhist tantrikas, this book presents a way of liberation through joyfully embracing ordinary life. Its goal is the same enlightenment the Buddha attained, and which he first taught was to be attained through monastic renunciation. For those of us who seek only to experience ordinary life at its best, that goal can also be attained. However, when we seek the dividing point between these ordinary and extraordinary goals, there is nothing in particular to find; thus, like the shoemaker, we may go farther than we think at first into the single intoxicating reality beyond conception. In any case, that indescribable reality of the Buddha's tantras, like the bliss of a maiden on her wedding night, must be experienced to be known.

[Technical note: I'm told that many readers skip the footnotes, appendices, and glossaries in books they read, as a matter of course. That's your personal standpoint, but if you do that with this book, you will miss many supporting examples, explanations, and colorful easter eggs.]

Rimé Lodrö (Ives Waldo), Denver, Colorado USA, early 2023.

Editor's Preface

The profound tantra path is the path of limitless continuity that never stops. Here, everything we experience should be integrated as part of our practice. As sexual desire is something extremely powerful and natural for us who are born in the desire realm, it is more than obvious that it is important for tantrikas to learn how to integrate it into their path. It is a terrain of great possibilities.

In general, saṃsāric sex is often controlled by ignorant craving, self-ishness, self-gratification, and so forth. Indeed, the essence of sex is the perfect union of masculine and feminine principles. Though in sex their blissful union is obvious, it pervades all existence; it represents the profound truth of non-dual reality and points us in its direction. Rinpoché guides us step by step on how to gain insight through the means of actual practice.

While learning how to transform sex into a sacred experience is one focus of this book, Rinpoché also teaches us how to properly use any of our kleśhas, such as anger, jealousy, and so on, rather than rejecting, repressing, or concealing them. Thus, even if your experience of these kleśhas or other desires is stronger than your experience of sexual desire, or if you have heavy physical limitations preventing you from any sexual practice, you can still benefit from reading this book. There is also no reason why bliss achieved through other experiences such as through art, connecting with nature, or devotion and so forth could not be brought onto the path.

For Rinpoché, it is clear that all people, including lay devotees, monastics, and non-religious persons are capable of practicing tantra. This book can be seen as their "empowerment" for learning that. Although it is obvious that spiritual realization naturally depends on the degree of the practitioner's preparation, there is no doubt that anyone can benefit to some extent from the practices presented. Though, as with everything new in life, we will make mistakes in the beginning, but we will improve over time, as long as we do not give up.

It is important to place this work within the context of Rinpoché's long-term aspirations. He took as his life goal to help create conditions for a second Golden Age to manifest on our Earth as prophesied in the *Kālachakra Tantra*. Being in the presence of Rinpoché's unwavering compassion to present this book in English in the best form, it is difficult to describe the spiritual inspiration we received from working with him. It is impossible to repay the gratitude we have for his writing this necessary book and supporting the translation and editing processes. We pray that his altruistic intention will be fully accomplished.

How this Book Was Written and Edited

A book on the Path of Desire is a long-standing aspiration of Rinpoché. As of 2019, he began to work concretely on drafts in English, with the support of Yeshé Wangmo based on extensive sketches written in Tibetan. After resuming the work alone in Tibetan with periods of breaks between work phases, he finished writing it in early 2022. Rimé Lodrö finished a completely new Tibetan-English literal translation in mid-2022. Rinpoché requested Jamphel Tsultrim, a native speaker of Tibetan who is fluent in English, to read his translation and send us feedback. Moreover, an earlier draft translation made by Rinpoché himself, summarizing some chapters, was taken as a reference for comparison.

Although Rinpoché often addresses Western practitioners in the book, as it was originally written in Tibetan, he automatically shaped the content and its presentation for his Tibetan audience. One of our main concerns when editing this book in English was to reformulate its expression in a way that is relevant and comprehensible for a diverse Western audience. Furthermore, since this book presents various controversial topics, it is important to avoid misunderstandings. Rinpoché strongly supported us in that regard and allowed us to shift, cut, reduce, expand, add, and reformulate passages and add footnotes where it would result in better understanding for most readers. What is most important in his approach to translation and the editing processes is that the meaning is clearly presented rather than being a "correct," literal translation.

Since the first draft translation was completed, we met with Rinpoché for extensive meetings for a period of nine months. Rinpoché was incredibly patient and generous with our avalanche of questions and gave us extended explanations which we then implemented in this English version, either directly in the main text or in the footnotes. When this new version of the book was completed, he instructed us to share the manuscript with different readers to support the book's finalization process. We are thankful to Jatun Risba, Sarah Perry, Shylton Dias, Venus Gravagna, Vanessa Mason, Adrian Hekel, Ravi S. Kudesia, Kerstin Rotter, Merilyne Waldo, Yeshé Wangmo, Shoshana Shapiro Adler, Tanya Gyatso, and Prabha Ng for providing feedback. Afterward, once again, we compared the final version with the previous literal translation and Rinpoché's own abridged translation, and the remaining questions were clarified with him. We completed the final proofreading phase thanks to the contribution of Philip Bralich, Vanessa Mason, and Adrian Hekel.

The Path of Desire is a short title used by Rinpoché when working on his first English sketches. When it is said in the subtitle that it is a "unique presentation" of tantra, we need to understand the intended meaning. Tantric teachings and their explanations go back to the Buddha's time, but what is said to be unique or unprecedented here is his direct explanation of tantric practice in terms lay people can understand and apply and the attempt to reform contemporary Tibetan Buddhism on that basis.

His reasons for doing so are presented in the first part of the book and elaborated in an extended manner in its second and subsequent parts. The third and fourth parts present direct instructions preceded by introductions with the fourth part being the central part of the book. The fifth part features various concluding chapters and advice on how to move forward upon the book's completion. The verse passages at the end of each chapter were all composed by Rinpoché to facilitate a poetic and conclusive summary of the topic. Extensive quotes from Gendün Chö-pel were added by him in Appendix I. We added selected passages of the *Kālachakra Tantra* in Appendix II, and for the benefit of those without a background in Buddha-Dharma, we included a glossary. The few terms that appear only once in the book are mostly not included in the glossary but are explained in footnotes, except for lists (see Glossary Lists). The bibliography of works in Tibetan was provided by the translator. All explanatory footnotes were added by the editor and the translator. As Rinpoché suggests, you may want to skip some parts and open the sections that speak more directly to your own current reality.

Rafa Lobsang Dorjé (Rafael Nassif),
Dzokden Kalapa in Garanas-Austria, early 2023.

Author's Homage

Namo Guruve!

Embodying all the Victorious Ones combined as one,
This treasure of compassionate wisdom without extremes,
Exists as the intention of the holy Guru,
Who is inseparable from the yidam Kālachakra.
Assembly of Kalkī Bodhisattvas of Śhambhala,
And compassionate root and lineage Gurus, take care of us!

Prajñāpāramitā, ḍākinī of great bliss,
You who are absolute goddesses, Marīchi and so forth,
All of you within the assembly of ḍākinīs,
Who arise in pure fields, in tantric practice, or naturally,[30]
And the treasury of companion yogins, heroes, and heroines;

This treasure of goodness and happiness, the nature of
   Sugatagarbha,
Is a wondrous, gradual path that joins us to reality,

---

30 Three different types of ḍākinīs: 1) manifesting in pure lands, 2) manifesting as the tantric consort of a human being, and 3) manifesting directly out of realization. See "ḍākinī" in the glossary.

Through both changing and changeless passion, peace, and bliss;
Eliminate all obstacles to presenting this sacred subject!

By the inferior merit of beings of this dark age,
With wanton behavior and battles of logic, this tantra path
Was polluted; unable to bear it, I am writing about its essence;
All yogins, Kalkīs, and sages, please assist me in this!

I appreciate corrections from unbiased, sagacious persons,
But, I have no time to hear the jealous verbal complaints
Of arrogant, selfish, short-sighted ones; for those so deluded,
What can I do, aside from shedding tears of compassion?[31]

If this meaning is known, it is right for all;
If this meaning is realized, it is good for you and others;
If this meaning is received, all accumulations of goodness
Need not be sought elsewhere, apart from your own nature.

My book has few scriptural quotes to make me seem to be
    learned;[32]
There are no accounts of miracles to give me a holy veneer;[33]

---

31 He is distinguishing short-sighted scholars who know only conceptual words of sectarian doctrine from the competent wise who have realized the meaning beyond words, and so are also beyond biased attachment to the dogma of any particular school.

32 It is common for Dharma books to have many supporting scriptural quotations. Rinpoché says here that this formal method can in fact be used as a lucrative strategy to make average scholars appear as great learned ones. Rinpoché does not follow this approach and chooses to address topics directly throughout the book, avoiding adding quotations as much as possible.

33 Instead of presenting stories about his own accomplishments in order to give him a "holy veneer," Rinpoché presents himself as no more than a simple wanderer who keeps the three vows, and focuses on his subject.

Leaving behind all pretense of righteousness and shame,
I present just direct instructions on how to do actual practice.

Shaven-headed monastic literalists attached to words,
With a narrow focus on their habitual outer conduct,
Fathom no depths of meaning beyond what is on the surface;[34]
We should be very careful of obsessive fools like these!

You who have exhausted your merit for tantrayāna,
And lack the union of male and female in this life,[35]
First, having looked at just the table of contents and summaries
That you read, just what is right for you is quite important.[36]

---

34 This criticism applies *not to all* monastics, only those who are too attached to study, not being able to go beyond an arrogant intellectual approach. These monastics look like the Buddha, because they shave their heads; but they are far from realizing the profound meaning of his teachings. It is good for them to study reasoning but bad to focus on this alone because they will never attain enlightenment by that approach. This verse also criticizes nuns and monks who develop a superficial, fundamentalist, or close-minded approach, neglecting deeper aspects of the teachings.

35 Those whose circumstances do not allow them to practice the literal path of sexual union, because they are too old, isolated, hindered by vows, and so forth, can skip sections on explicit technique and focus on general principles that do apply to them.

36 Some parts of the text were written primarily for specific groups, like elaborations on vinaya for monastics, logical proofs for those educated in Buddhist logic, and Tibetan customs for Tibetans. General readers may want to skip these sections.

PART ONE

Ten Reasons Why This Book
Had to be Written

1

The Need for Re-evaluation of Present Day Understanding and Practice of Tantra

Though India was the original source of tantra, self-declared Indian *tantrikas*[37] are a small percentage of the total number of contemporary Hindus.[38] Still, when we consider the practices of Hindus, which constitute about 80% of Indian religious practitioners, their elaborate offering liturgies and mantra recitations, their devotion to their deities and *Gurus*, and their view of an all-pervading ultimate self have many resemblances to the corresponding features of tantra. Unfortunately, those in this wider population who can interpret tantric texts well enough to practice according to authentic instructions, do not seem to be many.

Usually, ordinary Hindus do not keep their practices secret as Tibetan tantrikas traditionally did, and still do in many respects. Most deny that they are practicing tantra, reserving that word for practices involving

---

37   See the glossary at the end for this and other specific terms.

38   André Padoux, *The Hindu Tantric World*, an Overview, pp. 154-165, discusses various recent tantric groups and individuals throughout India.

malevolent mantras and sexual indulgence.[39] Nevertheless, the extent in the world of Indian practice systems whose style resembles or is based on tantra is much greater than the extent of Buddhist tantra. For example, the dissemination in the world of body training[40] and yantra yoga[41] exercises of Tibetan tantra is quite limited, but different kinds of physical yoga whose origins are associated with Indian tantra are found in many cities of the world even if in a fragmentary or non-authentic form.

Moreover, though most Tibetans have participated in tantra to some extent, if we think about the relatively small percentage of them who now practice tantra genuinely, and think carefully about their practice in relation to what was done in the past, it is easy to recognize the degree of corruption that has been introduced. Therefore, the need for a serious consideration of how to renew tantric tradition is urgent before its essence is lost altogether.

A new Western understanding of "tantra" as concerned *only* with sexual technique has spread everywhere on the internet. Tibetan Buddhist tantra does include sexual concerns,[42] but it is important to know that it goes far beyond that. In my observation, in terms of study, contemplation, and practice, no other kind of tantra on this Earth is as vast and elaborate as Tibetan tantra. Vast and powerful though it may be, how much realization is it producing nowadays? Unfortunately, it is not accomplishing as much as it could, so we need to reflect carefully on how this deficit might be remedied. The time has come to go beyond mere scholarly explanations and the superficial chanting of tantric liturgies to actually restoring the practice tradition that has been corrupted and rejected in recent centuries. To do that, the full scope of tantra's real mean-

---

39   Padoux Op. Cit., pp 153-154 has a section, "Tantra: Pervasive, but not (or hardly) Perceived as Such."

40   *Lujong, lus sbyong.*

41   *Trulkhor, 'khrul 'khor.*

42   As the later passages by Gendün Chöphel will eloquently attest.

ing must be re-introduced.

If you wonder what the path of tantra is like, rather than consisting of causes that produce realization of fruition that we can experience only later on as done in the sūtric paths, *in tantra, the experience of the fruition itself is pointed out in the practitioner's mind.*

In that way, experiencing aspects of the fruition is made into the essence of the path from the beginning. Moreover, *the kleśhas, and in particular, desires evoked by all the qualities of the senses,*[43] *without being rejected, are made into aspects of that path.* Tantric scholars and genuine tantrikas know with certainty that these are powerful forces driving spiritual practice, and that is not disputed.[44]

The gate for entering into tantra is empowerment with the associated tantric *samaya* or commitments. Most Tibetans have attended such empowerments, and therefore have entered tantra in the superficial sense of having attended an empowerment ceremony. However, few have recognized the true meaning of those empowerments and samayas in their minds. Moreover, the authentic practice of these teachings requires that all parts of practitioners' lives must become aspects of the tantric path. It seems evident from observation that most Tibetans have not entered into tantra in these deeper senses.

Those of the Land of Snow may know theoretically that all the *kleśhas* are to be made into the path. However, if, as said, they are not actually doing that in their lives, is not their practice of tantra mere wishful imitation and lip service? Yes, it is. Therefore, now there needs to be a re-evaluation and renewal of tantric practice. Motivated by the compelling knowledge that these teachings are being lost day by day, I concluded that

---

43   Here, desire is the most important kleśha to be brought to the path though other kleśhas must be brought to it as well as explained in detail in Part Three of this book.

44   For beings like us who were born in the desire realm, the most pervasive kleśha is desire; common people know from experience that desires are the main force driving ordinary life.

a book like this had to be written in order to give practical guidance that would allow tantrikas to renew their genuine tradition.

2

The Need for Tantra to be Integrated with Daily Life

In twelfth-century India, Muslim invaders destroyed Buddhism including the teachings of Buddhist tantra. However, Hindu tantric and tantra-like teachings were not eradicated at that time. Historical tradition gives many reasons for the disparity.[45] One important reason why Buddhist sūtra and tantra were destroyed was that, mostly, very erudite Buddhist teachings were being practiced by highly educated individuals; less educated, ordinary people, could not acquire, understand, or practice these teachings.

---

45 Buddhist tantras, such as the *Kālachakra*, describe how tantric groups in villages would arrange to meet for tantric offering feasts using secret signs as you can see in Appendix II. The picture of Buddhist tantrikas painted there suggests that, far from being integrated with their society, they were afraid of being persecuted by it. Hinduism was integrated into Indian society from the start. Traditionally, Hindus are born by caste into certain stations in life, whose duties or Dharmas they are expected to carry out to the best of their abilities. Some Hindu tantrikas, like their Buddhist equivalents, had some trouble with the social disapproval of their activities; and, like them, they tended to give up the activities that caused the trouble over time. However, where the Buddhist tantrikas tended to merge into the lifestyle of monastics who renounced ordinary society, the Indian ones merged with ordinary society and even received royal support for centuries.

Therefore, the number of Buddhist practitioners could not increase, and the monastic class to whom the teachings were primarily entrusted remained a small one.[46] When these scholarly monastics were eradicated, the sustainable practice of Buddhist sūtra and tantra disappeared among lay Buddhists as well.[47]

According to the historical account generally accepted by Tibetans, due to ninth-century sectarian disputes within Tibet, Dharma institutions of the Buddhist sūtra tradition, monasteries, and so forth, were destroyed

---

46 Dependence on monastics as the ultimate authorities on Buddhist doctrine and practice made it difficult for tantrikas to continue after monastic Buddhism disappeared in India. The difficulty was only increased by the fact that the same problems ensured that their communities were able to develop only in small parts of India to start with. True, the ideal in the *Kālachakra* was a peaceful and harmonious unbiased society, but that ideal became widespread only when tantrikas migrated to ethnic Tibet where there were Buddhist countries open to these teachings. Moreover, any tantrikas who migrated out of India only thinned the ranks of those who remained there.

47 There was a popular tantric lay movement, consisting of yogīs and yoginīs like the eighty-four mahāsiddhas which attempted to integrate tantra with ordinary life. Some of these tantrikas were highly educated like Nāropā, the former abbot of Nālānda University, but others held various ordinary stations. In this movement, there were few hindrances due to caste, wealth, and social status. Additional note on patriarchy: Of the eighty-four mahāsiddhas whose life stories are presented in *Buddha's Lions*, only four, Lakṣhmīnkarā, her sisters Mekhalā and Kanakhalā, and Maṇibhadrā were female. However, if we look at depictions of the eighty-four, there are females in about half of them. By the non-dual nature of the Path of Desire, the female consorts of Ḍombipa, Ghantāpa, Babhaha, and so forth, are said to share their partner's realization. Thus, after Ḍombipa's death, Ḍombi Yoginī became an independent female tantric teacher, famed for dancing on the water of a lake. Both Ghantāpa and his consort could fly in the sky. One day, Saraha met a woman arrow-maker and was mesmerized by her meditative concentration while she made the arrows. She accepted him as a tantric consort and transmitted oral instructions to him. Tilopa learned the meaning of suchness by acting as the servant of the prostitute, Dharima, for many years, according to the *Life of Tilopa* by Wangchuck Gyaltsen, an early electronic draft of a translation by the Nalanda translation committee, pp. 21-25. There was less patriarchal bias among them than in the monastic Saṅgha, but as only a few female tantrikas like Yeshé Tsogyal, Niguma, and Machik Labdrön are well-known in their own right tells us that patriarchy was and is alive in India and Tibet.

as they would later be in India by order of King Lang Darma, who ruled from 838-41.[48] In that case, when the institutions of sūtric Buddhism were destroyed by Lang Darma, tantric teachings persisted. One reason was that in Tibet, unlike India, Buddhist tantra was not dominated by leaders of the highest classes. To destroy tantric Buddhism, Lang Darma would have had to extinguish most of the Tibetan people.

Tibetan tantric practices were preserved at that time because they were integrated into the lives of ordinary people.[49] Such people were drawn to tantra because its teachings enhanced all aspects of their lives. Therefore, its teachings were well-suited to them, and they wanted to learn them. As a result, Tibetans who were willing and able to practice tantric teachings were very likely to be taught how to do so. The same must be true if we want to keep these teachings alive at the present time. However, this is no easy task. Even highly educated *Lamas* with considerable personal realization can go wrong trying to teach tantra in modern cultural situations. It is clear that this topic requires careful consideration, like that provided below.

If tantra is a path of knowing how to make the kleśhas we constantly encounter into aspects of the path, *tantra must connect with all aspects of daily life.* Kleśhas manifest naturally in all human beings, even realized ones, in whom they manifest as aspects of wisdom. Since that is so, there is no one whose daily life is not mixed with them. If that were not the case, the tantric path would be invalid. However, it is valid, because, as the kleśhas are present in us all, the prerequisites of tantra are present in us

---

48 After he converted to the *Bön* religion, he became king by assassinating his brother, King Ralpachen, who prioritized giving power and resources to Buddhist monasteries. Lang Darma was assassinated in turn by the accomplished Buddhist tantrika Lhalung Pelgyi Dorjé. Subsequently, the famous monk Atiśha was invited to come from Sumatra to restore Tibetan sūtra practice.

49 To a certain extent, but surely much more than nowadays when Tibetan lay people have practically no access to the higher stages of the practices for which they have received only symbolic empowerments as described below in chapter 10.

as well. People constantly deal with their kleśhas in some way. What they need to know is how to relate with their kleśhas *properly*.

Many practitioners of Tibetan Buddhism mistakenly believe that, since tantra is fruition practice, only very advanced practitioners who have realized the fruition can practice it. If that common fallacy is not rectified, most people will continue to be discouraged from entering tantra. Then the genuine experience of the essence of tantra will become increasingly rare. In that case, it will be difficult for tantra to endure for long. Therefore, the idea arose in me that a book like this had to be written to correct the misapprehensions that make ordinary people think that this precious path is unavailable to them.

3

The Deterioration of Genuine Tantric Practice in Tibet

Outside and inside Tibet, some monastics who could not keep their *vinaya* vows abandoned them in despair, and then said that they were now tantrikas. Some of them cultivated long hair with a topknot to look like tantric yogins of bygone times. The essence of tantra is actually concerned with inner practice. Therefore, these lapsed monastics' emphasis on their hair and clothing suggests that they were more concerned with justifying giving up their monastic vows than with liberation.

If we try to evaluate the significance of these people who are as odd as they look, it is enough to view their foibles as eccentricities of individuals. However, we can also consider the motivations and the larger environmental factors that led them to do as they did. Is not their desire to continue Buddhist practice even after they failed at being monastics a good thing? Though long hair and a topknot do not make a tantric yogin, their problem is less that they want to look like former tantric yogins than that they do not know how to go beyond the externals and practice tantra properly. Would it not be better if they had that knowledge?

At the time of the early spreading of Buddhist teachings in Tibet,

the ancient lineage, or *Nyingma* school, prospered.⁵⁰ Householder practitioners were esteemed as the white-robed class and renunciates as the
saffron-robed class. Both classes of practitioners were regarded with respect and confidence. Their relationship was seen as complementary and
mutually beneficial. There was no perception that the monastic community was dominant and that tantra was dependent on its teachings. Since
there was no obstacle to ordinary people practicing tantra and no resulting stigma in social status, many people did so. Since they contended for
excellence in their ongoing practice, tantra had a lofty reputation.

There are many reasons why it is no longer like that today. As an
example, beginning in the thirteenth century, at the time of the second
spreading of the Dharma in Tibet, the *Kagyü, Sakya, Jonang,* and *Gelug*
schools spread. As they increasingly flourished, the domination of monks,
little by little, became ever more powerful. Because monastics were celi-
bate, their social prestige increased; and so, as the monastic community
became ever more numerous, it also became ever more highly regarded.
Practitioners of tantra continued to exist, but almost all of the most important Dharma practitioners and masters were monastics. Except for those
who were independently wealthy, the tradition of tantrikas becoming
monks to support their practice spread ever more widely.

The greater the power of the monks became, the more numerous
were those who regarded individual liberation as the main point of the
teachings.⁵¹ *They continued to perform tantric liturgies, but increasingly in-*

---

50   During the reign of King Trisong Detsen (ca. 755-800), both monastic and tantric Buddhism were established. The mahāyāna monk Śhāntarakṣhita (725–788) came to Tibet to
establish Samye monastery, and ordain the first Tibetan monks. When obstacles threat-
ened to block the project, Śhāntarakṣhita brought in the tantrika Padmasaṃbhava
to subdue malevolent local deities. Then, after the monastery was completed,
Padmasaṃbhava went on to present many tantric teachings.

51   Although they displayed an external style or veneer of being bodhisattvas and tantrikas,
their real style of practice was that of individual liberation with all its strict rules of
conduct, practice of abandoning kleśhas by antidotes, and so forth.

terpreted their meaning through the lens of the monastic tradition of sūtra. The ideal of renunciation increasingly displaced the ideal of bringing or-dinary life to the path. In the end, the practice of tantra in the Land of Snow became effectively a subdivision of the sūtra tradition. Though the nice-sounding phrase "the path uniting sūtra and tantra" was applied to that approach, the sad reality was that, except for just a few individuals, tantrikas gradually became holders of a tradition where tantric practice was incapable of existing independently.[52]

From now on, if we are not concerned about tantric view and prac-tice being displaced by sūtra teachings and we do not reform that state of affairs, eventually, the world will be filled with tantrikas in name only. Most of them will cease to know the difference between authentic and inauthentic tantric practice. If they become increasingly unable to distin-guish what is correct and incorrect, eventually, as in the well-known story of revising the *Diamond Sūtra* in Bhutan,[53] may they not come to believe that what is incorrect is correct?[54]

---

52 This is not to say that there are no valid senses of "union of sūtra and tantra," as when Dolpopa says that the experience of Buddha nature is central to both. However, it is obvious from the words alone that no one can unite the sūtra practice of abandoning kleshas by antidotes with the tantric approach of making kleshas into aspects of the path.

53 According to that story, when publishers there were preparing a critical edition of the *Diamond Sūtra*, they looked at all the former editions and found that all but one had a different reading from the one they had chosen. They decided that the majority must be right. Only later was it discovered that they had rejected the only edition with the true reading. If that happens to tantra as well, no one will respect it at all. Their attitude will certainly be inappropriate for the genuine tantric teachings.

54 Just as when someone indiscriminately mixes fish and turnips, the rotting fish spoils everything, the tantric tradition would be rendered worthless.

4

Making Genuine Tibetan Tantric Teachings Available Outside of Tibet

Many Tibetans do not take the attempts of non-Tibetans to practice tantra seriously, pointing out that they know little of Tibetan culture, traditions, and monastic discipline.

It is true that Westerners, in general, face more obstacles in developing devotion to the teachings and teachers as they tend to focus too much on intellectual justification in a way that is overly skeptical. On the other hand, many of these students' genuine faith in the teachings leads them to study much harder than most lay Tibetans. As a result, their practice tends to be founded on genuine understanding, which makes up for their ignorance of Tibetan culture.

From that point of view, the paths of those outside of Tibet who enter into Tibetan Buddhist tantric teachings compare favorably to the paths of Tibetans. Even so, in terms of not knowing everything they need to know to practice the genuine tantra path, the Tibetans and foreigners are all too similar.

However, as I also saw many good qualities in these foreign would-be tantrikas, I wanted to write a book like this to allow them to go further.

I also have great hopes that non-Tibetans who have no faith at all in Tibetan tantra, and even those who see tantra as a total abomination, will consider this book. If they do, they may conclude that their negative assessment of Buddhist tantra has been inaccurate. Then, they may understand that this profound path, with its many special qualities, provides wonderful skillful means which can lead to ultimate benefit and happiness.

5

How Scandals Involving Lamas Indicate Problems in Tibetan Buddhism

Various scandalous situations that have occurred inside and outside of Tibet in recent years point to tantra having problems even worse than its being assimilated by the sūtra teachings.[55] The names of those involved included a few important Lamas in the Tibetan lineages. Some of them were famous Tibetan Lamas in the West whose altruistic activities were also some of the greatest.

I do not want to discuss individual cases because I have no way of judging the true mental state of the different people involved. That said, an internet search will quickly tell you what you need to know. Instead, I wish to point out shared features of these scandals that are relevant to the argument of this book, especially those regarding the alleged perpetrators' allegiance to the Buddhist teachings of sūtra or tantra.[56]

---

55 As Rinpoché concluded his original Tibetan manuscript early in 2022, he is obviously not referring to events that happened afterward.

56 (1) Some monastics get in trouble by accepting the ideal of renouncing the kleśhas as taught in the teachings of individual liberation. Then, when they are unable to eliminate their kleśhas, they stray into transgression. (2) As discussed in detail in Part Two

These accusations were suppressed by Tibetan media, but there was extensive coverage in important world news outlets and on the internet. The good name of Buddhists was severely damaged, not to mention the reputation of these Lamas' Tibetan Buddhst lineages. However, *once we understand that these actions were due to shortcomings of specific individuals, sometimes combined with misconceptions of the public, it is evident that no benefit of any kind will come from tarring all Buddhist tantrikas indiscriminately with the same brush.*

Though we cannot change the past, it is wise to prepare for the future. We must think deeply about what caused such disasters to occur, and what can be done to keep them from happening again. It is not enough to think, "This bad conduct happened because a few individuals went astray in the teachings." This implies that nothing needs to be done for the sake of the future.

If we reflect on the subject at length, many of the problems that caused these scandals occurred because the people involved had not been instructed in the proper practice of the holy Dharma in general and tantra

---

chapter 6, another category of tantric monastics correctly sees the vows of individual liberation as evolving upward into the tantric samayas so they can bring kleśhas to the path, practice the Path of Desire, and so forth, while still truthfully presenting themselves to the public as monastics. People who do not understand this sophisticated viewpoint may mistakenly accuse them of hypocrisy or corruption. (3) Other misunderstandings involve genuine tantric masters who specifically say they are trying to integrate tantric practice with modern daily life. Much of the information in Buddhist tradition about how to do this is out of date by about a thousand years, and little of it is presented publicly. After jumping from the lives of the mahāsiddhas to the teachings of thinkers like Gendün Chöphel, it would be easy for beginners to wrongly conclude, "If I am going to renounce everything, I must renounce renouncing as well; if I do not try to restrict my behavior, my actions will transcend concept. Is not that liberation?" Many of the scandalous stories on the internet suggest that all three of these approaches can lead to problems, to say the least. (4) Furthermore, as explained in chapter 9 below, very unfortunately, some teachers and their students fell into actual transgressions because of being literally-minded people with limited understanding of the tantric teachings; (5) others, maliciously, justified their transgressions while fraudulently saying that this was how tantra "must" be practiced.

in particular. To ensure that Buddhists might have the knowledge they need to prevent them from straying from the true path, I thought that a book like this had to be written.

6

The Need for Lay Practitioners of Tantra

The zeal for the Dharma of people in many regions of Tibet used to be such that, if a household had five sons, all but one would try to become monks. Because of that, compared to other countries, the population of Tibet was very small. Is such a way of doing things compatible with maintaining a functioning human society in Tibet?

As a sign that it is not and that Tibetans have historically put too high a value on monasticism, renunciates are becoming fewer and fewer, and those who abandon monasticism are becoming more and more numerous. Among those who remain monastics, the number of those who sneak out of their monasteries to engage in sexual activity seems to be increasing.[57] Within the monasteries, it is hard to determine how many are engaging in homosexual activities and pressing younger *Saṅgha* members to do the same.[58] Shared accounts and anec-

---

57 Here, Rinpoché is not referring to using desire as part of the path, but to ordinary saṃsāric desire. Because it is naturally so strong, it makes monastic life a challenge in our time.

58 Rinpoché does not criticize homosexuality as such (see Part Four chapter 2). However, generally speaking, any kind of sex is prohibited to monastics who are focusing upon the individual liberation path as their *main* path. The point is that some monastics, like incarcerated prisoners, whether they are homosexually oriented or not, engage in homosexual activities within the Saṅgha because monastic life is not natural for them.

dotal stories suggest that it is more than a few.

Concluding from people's involvement in scandalous situations that they cannot be realized or accomplished is unreliable.[59] In any case, whether the Buddha's tantric teachings should continue to be entrusted primarily to monastics as they have been increasingly in recent centuries, has become a very controversial topic. Doing this seems reasonable for sūtra teachings that espouse monastic life as the highest ideal. However, *why should tantric teachings intended for lay people not be entrusted to them as when tantra was first introduced?*

If tantrikas outside of the monastic discipline of individual liberation learn more about practicing the tantric path, they can take steps to preserve and restore it. However, if lay people do not assume responsibility for their tantric practice, in the future, there may be no more renunciates; or, those that exist may have become mere imitations of renunciates. They may still wear their saffron robes and perform the same liturgies, but genuine monastic discipline will have ceased to exist.[60] At that time, if we have failed to keep genuine tantra alive among ordinary people, there is a great danger that both Buddhist sūtra and tantra will vanish.

To that end, we must reinforce tantric practice from now on. If we do not, with deteriorating monastic conduct that merely apes the external forms of tantric liturgies and sūtra discipline, how will the precious essence of Buddhist practice not disappear? My hope is that the teachings will be preserved and fortified by giving instruction on how tantric practice can pervade every part of daily life.

Also, some young monastics participate due to coercion.

59   For example, the great siddhas Tilopa and Padmasaṃbhava were reviled for being the servant of a prostitute and living with a woman respectively.

60   See chapters 7 and 8 below.

7

How Overemphasis of Monasticism Defeats its Own Ultimate Purpose

Many Tibetan monks and nuns continue to practice diligently as they did in the past, and the practice of more than a few of them has resulted in good fruition in individual terms. Nevertheless, for reasons I will explain later, I predict that if past customs continue, no suitable accomplishment of the Great Vehicle goal of universal benefit will come to the Tibetan Saṅgha in the future.

According to what usually happens in Tibet, the children in each household with the best intelligence, ability, and character will become monastics. The ones left to propagate their family lineages will be those with the least intelligence, ability, and character. That the good qualities of later generations will increasingly deteriorate under these circumstances accords with the findings of both common sense and science.[61]

Since Tibetans have no means of avoiding that result, if their present

---

61 For example, if you want to create a breed of dogs with a certain characteristic, you breed animals in each generation who best exemplify that characteristic. This has been successful with many characteristics like intelligence, size, ferocity, and a pleasant disposition. It would also work with stupidity, incompetence, and bad character.

custom continues, will not their unthinking selection for stupidity and bad character be irreversible? If it is, since the ultimate goal of the ordained Saṅgha is to create universal benefit for the world, future monks and nuns will not be proper renunciates because they are unwittingly opposing that great goal. As their decaying family lineages continue to deteriorate, finally Tibetans, renunciates, and laypersons alike, will be only demented transgressors, with no good qualities at all. All the generations of monks and nuns who supported the Tibetan monastic system and all the lay people who did the same will bear the burden of responsibility for that.

Tibetans seem to ignore these conclusions. If I take myself as an example, by sending many of its sons to be monastics, my own family was without increase. Whether following this custom should continue to be regarded as an unqualified virtue is a big question. I am resolved that, from now on, Tibetans deliberating whether to depart from this long-standing custom will know at least, that they would not be acting alone.[62]

Recently the Chinese rulers of Tibet have removed large numbers of young monks from monasteries and put them into secular schools to compel them to live as laymen. Tibetans are very depressed about this; yet, in view of what has just been said, perhaps that dark cloud has a silver lining. If the energy that was used to maintain the monasteries is used

---

62 What if other countries, impressed by Tibetans, put as much emphasis on monasticism, as Tibetans historically have done? Presumably, almost all resources would go into building and maintaining monasteries. Little would be left to produce goods in factories, build a national infrastructure, promote social welfare, engage in business, or carry on all the other activities that modern countries engage in. Science would most likely be suppressed in the name of orthodoxy, as the Catholic Church did with Galileo. So would secular art. Population would plummet with the gross national product. Zealously authoritarian monastics who were sure that they were the wisest and best of beings would replace democratic institutions and suppress any diversity of opinion. Religious culture would flourish, but at the expense of ruining civilization as we know it. Would not a country of tantrikas who preserved and enhanced social diversity be far preferable? That is the description of Śhambhala in the *Kālachakra Tantra*.

instead to restore tantra, being forced to be laymen would not deprive these ex-monks of opportunities for serious Buddhist practice.

The Tibetan Buddhist lineages have two special teachings. These are the textual tradition of establishing valid knowledge through reasoning and the empowerments, transmissions, and practice instructions of tantra. If we say there are many Tibetans whose proficiency in valid reasoning is not bad at all, that should be sufficient. There are also many who, due to their tantric lineages being unbroken from their founders and so forth, are not bad at giving tantric empowerments, transmissions, and special instructions.

However, because of the prevalent custom of giving empowerments to lay people without adequate practice instructions, those who know how to practice tantra properly are becoming ever fewer. Since I had profound confidence that it would be beneficial for all, if I wrote to share with interested individuals how the actual practice of tantra should be performed, I saw that this book had to be written.

8

How Buddhist Prophecies Predict that the Future of the Teachings Depends on Tantra

The texts of the individual liberation vehicle prophesize that the teachings of Śhākyamuni will only endure for a certain number of periods of five hundred years. The *Minor Sayings of the Vinaya,*[63] in particular, and sūtras coordinated with it, teach that the remaining time of the individual liberation vehicle will not be long at all. In later Great Vehicle texts, the duration of the teachings is commonly presented as being somewhat longer than 2,500 or 5,000 years, excluding the final five hundred when only the verbal meanings of the teachings are grasped. Even in these later texts, is it not clear that the teachings were not prophesied to endure for an extremely long time? Even if you do not believe these scriptures, it would not be difficult to infer from the states of mind and activities observed in present followers of Dharma tradition that the monastic Saṅgha is in danger of disappearing.

To summarize these well-known prophecies found in Buddhist textual tradition, in a bad eon, which is said to be not far off, when correct

---

63 *'Dul ba phran tshegs kyi gzhi,* D0006 Kangyur, 'dul ba, tha.

sūtra Dharma is near to disappearing, most followers of traditional Dharma will have strong desire. As a result, people will have little inclination for monastic life, but the teachings of tantra will spread very widely and endure for a long time. If we seek a remedy for the precarious state of Buddhist teachings today, it seems there is no choice but to regard this prophecy as being very important.

In particular, the teachings of the glorious *Kālachakra Tantra* say not only that the duration of tantra on Earth will be very long, but also that these vast teachings will not deteriorate in the pure bodhisattva realm of Śhambhala. Moreover, they promise that before long, those teachings will spread from there and increase again in our world as we experience a second Golden Age. The cause of that second Golden Age as prophesied by the *Kālachakra*, is the widespread practice of tantra in this world. If we trust what the Buddha prophesied — that, through this cause, all people will have happiness even better than that of the gods — the tantric teachings, and especially those of the glorious *Kālachakra*, must be cultivated in people's minds.

Some people are unwilling to put complete trust in that scripture alone, but reasoning establishes that teaching tantric Dharma will be the cause of the happiness of which the Buddha spoke. We can establish that by valid cognition because that happiness is already being experienced by realized individuals as the fruition of their tantric practice. Some aspects of their fruition can be observed even by science. Therefore, it can be established from the power of the things themselves that teaching tantric practice more widely by which this happiness is realized will result in a proportionally widened fruition of this happiness itself.

In sum, if discerning individuals closely observe both the current difficulties faced by practitioners of the Buddhist teachings and the solution that the Buddha taught, they will be able to open the gates of their own and others' minds to that solution.

9

The Need for Clear Teaching on the Guru-Student Relationship

After Tibetan Buddhist tantric teachings spread throughout the world, many people misunderstood the special relationship of tantric students with the Gurus who are their spiritual masters. When they heard that a few tantric masters had engaged in sexual relationships with their students, some mistakenly concluded that this was a requirement for tantric practice.

Many others had preconceptions that made them infer that qualified masters who did this had made missteps due to serious moral miscalculations regarding the long-term consequences of their actions.[64] At the same time, unfortunately, some literally-minded teachers and students fell into actual transgressions by engaging in sexual union through a limited understanding of the tantric teachings.

Such misunderstandings clearly need to be rectified. As for one important example, in the West and elsewhere, many heard a little about

---

64 For example, some people who hold negative views about sexuality infer that any teacher who engages in any sexual activity with students must have committed serious moral transgressions.

the sexual nature of the Path of Desire and the higher empowerments of Highest Yoga Tantra. They mistakenly concluded that favorable conditions for tantric realization could be provided only through the Vajra Master engaging in sexual union with the student.

As almost all Tibetan Lamas followed a traditional approach, they avoided addressing sexual aspects of tantra with beginning students, but for that very reason, many of them also had problems with their hearers' preconceptions. By those Lamas avoiding the subject of sex, these students' wrong ideas were never properly addressed. As a result, some of them made the hostile judgment, "Those Lamas did not teach what they should have!"

At the same time, more than a few people outside of Tibet were indulging in immoral conduct, while claiming this was how tantra "must" be practiced. I am trying to draw clear borderlines between what is appropriate and inappropriate in such situations so that the same kind of hostility and bewilderment will not arise in the future.

There is another point opposed to that, where tantra is rejected due to ignorant, negative preconceptions. Often, many non-Buddhist Westerners have a bad opinion of Tibetan tantra because they read quotes from the Buddhist teachings taken out of context, like the following traditional saying about the relationship of tantric Gurus and students:

What Gurus say is the Dharma,
Where their fingers point is the east.

What Gurus do is Dharmic.
Since their deeds are skillful means,
Even if they do evil,
It is done with a holy purpose.

For someone who knows no more than this, on the surface it might seem that tantric students, against their will, must offer their Guru their bodies, and all the wealth and virtue they have accumulated in all their lives; if the Guru seems to commit bad deeds, the students must forcefully believe that it is only due to their own impure karma that they perceive their Guru doing such things. Such people mistakenly conclude that the relationship between Guru and student in the Tibetan Buddhist tantric teachings is one of arbitrary coercion with no relation at all to genuine human needs. Many people who think like that make a special effort to keep their own children, spouses, close relatives, and friends far away from Tibetan Buddhists.

For the benefit of such misinformed people, I see a clear and correct explanation of how things are in tantra as being very important. So that there may be auspicious, favorable conditions for facilitating an understanding that genuine tantra is something wonderful and marvelous, a book like this certainly had to be written to rectify the different kinds of ignorance and misconceptions of people who reject tantra.

10

How Buddhist Tantric Masters Are Not Giving Empowerment and Instruction in the Real Meaning and Practice of Tantra

When we consider those who practice the tantric path, let us not just idolize former great yogins who were genuine practitioners of tantra, and the biographies that teach how their realization was as stable as a rock mountain. Among all the Tibetan tantric teachings, which have chiefly been the responsibility of renunciates in recent centuries, Lamas have bestowed innumerable tantric empowerments. However, very few of these empowerments, in addition to being permissions to read and recite the relevant texts, were what tantrikas call "real empowerments" in the completion stage such as the ones accomplished masters like Drukpa Kunle[65] and Lelung Zhepe Dorjé[66] were known for giving. Aside from a few like those who were exponents of empowerments in their way of transmitting the

---

65 Also known as the mad yogī of Bhutan (1455–1529). His biography, translated by Keith Dowman, which presents him as a siddha who was preoccupied with sex, is very relevant to the subject of this book. Because of him, many buildings in Bhutan are decorated with penis murals to this day (see "Drukpa Kunley images.")

66 A well-known Gelug master, who was in his later years more inclined to the Nyingma school (1697-1740). His extraordinary sexual activities are described in Bailey, *A Feast of Scholars*, Chapter Two.

view of *Mahāmudrā, Dzogchen,* and *Madhyamaka,* actual empowerments of Highest Yoga Tantra have been absent for many centuries, at least in the knowledge of the public.[67]

When Lamas are asked why this is the case, most of them give canned traditional answers that are, at best, facile guesses. They say, for example, that merely symbolic empowerments to recite liturgical texts are given because "real" tantric empowerments and feasts can be performed only by great *siddhas* with miraculous powers. Some also said, "Such merely symbolic empowerments are intended as 'blessings,' so that the sun will proceed in its course, the land will be fertile with rain, the teachings will not be corrupted, and so forth." Nevertheless, just showing students symbolic cards with pictures while chanting a tantric liturgy is not an actual empowerment any more than giving a hungry person a picture of a sandwich provides them with an actual lunch.[68]

---

67   With regard to the four higher empowerments of Highest Yoga Tantra, giving a "real empowerment" means mentally transmitting the essence of these teachings while also following the specific requirements stated by the Buddha in the respective tantras being transmitted, as was done in ancient times. These higher empowerments are correlated with stages of mindful sexual congress, as described in Appendix II. That is done because sexual bliss, properly contemplated, is a very powerful experience available to ordinary people that can join practitioners directly to the blissful state of their true nature. The experience of empowerments is meant to be renewed for the rest of the student's lives through secret tantric feast practice, *tsok,* on auspicious days of each lunar cycle. Originally, these also involved sacramental sexual union between tantric students, without caste prejudice, and drinking and eating substances usually considered repugnant, in order to go beyond the concepts of relative reality. As you might expect, the tantrikas that participated in these real empowerments and tantric feasts experienced varied kinds of personal, social, and political difficulties. The pressure of these difficulties caused tantric empowerments and feasts to become increasingly symbolic over time. Tantric masters increasingly focused on symbolic instruction about where to encounter the essential experiences of bliss, such as symbolic cards depicting a consort and augmented less and less by oral instructions as time went on. Finally, the norm became empowerments with no instructions on the Path of Desire at all and became purely symbolic feasts that omitted any kind of sexual activity.

68   A literal return to these practices of ancient times is *not* being advocated here. Though some contemporary Lamas express a certain admiration for what Drukpa Kunle and

In recent centuries, virtually no Tibetan tantrika has admitted to giving, attaining, seeing, or even hearing about a real empowerment of Highest Yoga Tantra. Tantrikas and scholars began to doubt that real empowerments ever existed and that anyone practiced the fruition teachings allegedly empowered by them. In the end, they began to doubt that anyone ever believed in such things, saying, "We cannot even imagine what that would be like!" This does not mean that real empowerments never happened *at all*, but that we know so little about them is a sign of how diminished our tantra practice has become.

If I take my own students as an example, the empowerments they receive are symbolic, but not *merely* symbolic. They can be considered promissory notes to be redeemed by following my instructions for their personal practice.[69] There are no guarantees that following these practice instructions will bring all students to a particular level of realization.

Lelung Zhepe Dorjé did in the past, present Vajra Masters do not follow their example. Some of the practices described in the texts would be illegal in some countries today or would evoke strong moral condemnation in others. At present, Vajra Masters like the author perform symbolic empowerments thinking that actual ones would be more likely to drive prospective students away than to attract them to these profound teachings. Does that mean that the genuine tradition of Highest Yoga Tantra is dead? It does not. To see why, we need to look more closely at the essence of "actual empowerments." No special realization is required to put on a sex show, so what does it mean to say that only a realized master can perform an actual empowerment of Highest Yoga Tantra? It means that, as the Vajra Master and consort enter into non-duality beyond conception through the experience of the four joys, their non-dual experience pervades the minds of the students being empowered. Would accomplished masters powerful enough to do that necessarily need to be in sexual union with a human consort to transmit these experiences? They would not. Even if the Vajra Master does transmit the realized experience of tantra through union with a human consort, to regard this action as the point of the empowerment is putting the cart before the horse. Moreover, though merely symbolic empowerments that give no practice instructions use symbolic cards and objects, *not all symbolic empowerments are merely symbolic.* Fully prepared students may actually experience the four joys, and so forth, in such a case.

69   In this sense, part four of this book, especially the chapter about actual sex, can be interpreted as the "actual" higher empowerments; each practitioner can put them into practice according to their personal conditions.

However, it has happened many times in the past, when strong devotion, compassion, diligence, and so forth were present on the student's side. Those conditions are so important that if students are perfectly prepared, they may attain high realization even if the Vajra Master has not attained the highest level.

Unfortunately, all too many Tibetan Lamas today give even completion stage empowerments only as "blessings," which is a nice way of saying that they give no clear explanations and instructions at all about how to prepare for the empowerment and what to do during and after it. This approach lulls many students who have participated in such merely symbolic empowerment ceremonies into thinking that they need to do nothing more to progress on the path. This deceptive approach to teaching tantra should make us sad. In brief, it is not problematic at all for Lamas to bestow an empowerment using symbols like cards with pictures, but it is very much so when they do nothing else.

For spiritual progress to occur, when bestowing empowerments, it is also necessary to provide students with adequate explanations about the path they are going to practice, the tantric samayas or commitments they must keep, and practical instructions about what they should do. When that is done, some degree of genuine transmission from Vajra Master to a devoted student will certainly occur, sooner or later. When there is no clarity about these aspects, students are left bewildered in regard to many fundamental questions about tantra, like, "What is the real meaning of tantra?," and "What is this 'real empowerment' of which you speak?," or "What is genuine tantric practice?"

Another consideration is that many tantric texts that were traditionally secret and provided to tantric students only after bestowing them empowerments have been made publicly available in English for some time. Therefore, I have a choice between students hearing about them from me with these explanations, or reading about them through the lens of outsiders' misconceptions or without any explanations at all. If prospective tantra practitioners do not know the basics of treading their profound path, how can their practice not fail to stray into futility and disappointment? Then, their precious human bodies are sure to be sadly wasted. Since such students have no hope of success, until they understand more, I wanted to write this book, so that they could do so.

Verse Summary[70]

Indians say that tantra consists of malevolent mantras.
In other countries like China, tantra inspires horror.
The Snow Land's "tantra path" consists of sūtra practice.
Many will tell you, at present, that tantra is only sex.

By ignorance of the quintessence of the great tantrayāna,
Only the outer style of tantric Dharma is grasped.
Some spread the lie that improper sex is proper tantra.
Free from all limits of what is done and what is not,[71]
They need an antidote[72] for having destroyed their path.

Since the Earth is full of bad people, every day,
The news of the world is full of accounts of sexual scandals,
Committed by religious authorities everywhere.

I wrote this book so that people might have knowledge,
Of a path that can cure this destruction of tantra to its
     foundations,
The pure, true way of bringing desire to the path.

---

70 The verse passages at the end of this and subsequent chapters were all composed by Rinpoché.

71 When great siddhas like Saraha recommend such freedom, it is only in carefully prepared situations as described in the translator's preface.

72 They need an antidote for their mistakes that would allow them to enter the genuine path.

PART TWO

An Extended Explanation

Love for what is desired is passionate attachment;

So love for what is desired is also faith in that.

Fear of what is undesired is known as aversion;

So fear of the undesired is renunciation of that.

Gendün Chöpel

Treatise on Desire

1

The Meanings of "Tantra" and its Natural Secrecy

The Sanskrit terms, *tantra* and *guhyatantra* (secret tantra), do not have exactly the same meaning as their most common equivalents,[73] *sngags* (mantra) and *gsang sngags* (secret mantra), do in Tibetan.

In China, the best-known Mandarin word for tantra is 密宗, *mì zōng*. *Mì* means secret, and *zōng* means sect, tradition, or doctrine. This translation is not inaccurate, but it does not convey the inner meaning of secret mantra or tantra.

Another Chinese word for tantra, 密续, *mì xù* (secret continuum), has a meaning more like the primary meaning of the Tibetan for tantra, *rgyud* (continuity), referring to the continuity of the universal nature of things. These meanings are rather important, so the meaning of tantra is further explained below.

In the way of explaining the term *mantra* as found in Tibet, first, the Sanskrit *mantra*, translated into Tibetan as *sngags*[74] is defined by Tibetans

---

73 As explained in footnote 1, the Tibetan expression *gsang sngags* is the term most commonly used in Tibet to refer to Buddhist tantric teachings. Most Western translators prefer the literal translation "secret mantra," but Rinpoché prefers the non-literal "tantra."

74 Pronounced *ngag*.

as meaning "protecting the mind." Though the Sanskrit *tantra* is supposed to mean the same as *sngags* in Tibetan, the extraordinary understanding that the practitioner's mind is protected by the continuity of the natural state cannot be derived from the translation "protecting the mind."[75] However, if it is said that the mind is protected by special means that involve that continuity, that additional meaning can be deliberately "glued on," as it were, to the meaning of "mantra." Even then, the special understanding of protection by the continuity of the natural state cannot be naturally derived from the definition of "mantra" as "protecting the mind."

Translating the Sanskrit "tantra" by the Tibetan *rgyud* (continuity) is very good because tantra requires unbroken awareness that is continuous like a *chu rgyud* (river bank or coast) or a *mi rgyud* (family lineage.) This understanding of secret mantra, or tantra, as continuity, chiefly refers to the way tantra is practiced, which is different from, and higher than, sūtra practice.

In sūtra practice, a kleśha to be abandoned on the path and applying an antidote to abandon that kleśha are necessarily separate. These two cannot be in the continuum of one individual at the same time. Still less can they be the same thing at the same time. Therefore, *the path of sūtra consists of alternating stages that can never be continuous. However, on the tantric path, our kleśhas themselves constantly exist as skillful means that are part of the path.* The practice of tantra is necessarily continuous like a river.

Genuine tantric practitioners have no need to switch between what is abandoned and antidotes for abandoning it. The kleśhas are encountered in the tantra path as both what is to be abandoned and its antidote. For example, the Path of Desire does not abandon desire but puts it to work in various ways. The kleśhas abandoned in sūtra practice are continuously joined to the tantric path, and any path in which that continuous joining occurs is a tantric path. Any path that alternates between

---

75   The definition of mantra as "protecting the mind" also exists in the sūtra teachings.

consciousness of something to be abandoned and of its antidote is a sūtric path. Whatever is part of a tantric path must continuously be in the continuum of those who practice that path. Does not *rgyud,* "continuity," clearly capture that meaning?

In Tibet, "secret mantra" is the most common expression referring to tantra. Here, "secret," *gsang,* is an ordinary word that everyone understands. However, we should clarify the logic of secrecy. When certain knowledge is kept secret, there must be:

1. The secret knowledge itself.
2. Individuals who know that secret knowledge.
3. A commitment by those individuals to keep that secret knowledge from others.
4. Other individuals who do not know the secret knowledge.

To sum up these criteria in another way: to be secret, knowledge must be kept from *someone,* but what is kept from *everyone* is not knowledge.

To say that tantra should be kept secret means that tantrikas know that there are good reasons for not telling everyone everything they know about it. Because tantra is very profound, many people cannot understand it at all; many who can, need a gradual approach by understanding other teachings first. Otherwise, they may find tantra shocking, or they may be attracted to the distorted idea that merely not restraining their negative emotions will bring them closer to enlightenment. Tantrikas need to keep their tantric practice secret from those who would be harmed by its knowledge so as to protect them both.[76]

Unfortunately, people easily fall into extreme views about secrecy. Some think that there is an absolute command that everything should be

---

76   The other person's negative reaction could easily harm the tantrika; for example, if the person is trusted, highly regarded, and so on like close family members and friends.

secret in tantra so that they cannot show any non-tantrikas tantric images or allow them to hear *sādhanas* being chanted. Such blind secrecy is far from skillful and wise. The secrecy of tantra has specific reasons, similar to the reasons people have for keeping small children away from a fire.

The other extreme is for people to show everyone everything related to tantric practice because they do not understand the harm that may result. If tantrikas are not extremely insightful about who would and would not benefit from being shown certain aspects of tantra, damaging misconceptions may be established in many people's minds.

Now that tantra is being spread around the world, it is important to develop an approach to secrecy that is free from extremes. Therefore, if you ask me, "Can we then show our Kālachakra *yab yum* statue to visitors to our temple?" I would answer, "Of course, unless you cannot explain briefly and comprehensibly why Tibetan Buddhists venerate such representations." Nowadays, tantric images are everywhere on the internet, so they cannot be hidden completely. It is best to give a simple explanation that questioners can relate to as good and honorable. Then you offer them a chance to connect with the more profound meanings of such representations later on.

The situation is more complex with higher practices of the completion stage. Nowadays even very high pith instructions are translated into books available to the Western public. You may have to deal skilfully with questions about these as you do with tantric images. On the other hand, do not take this as permission to share or publish secret teachings of tantra with no restraint at all. Has the number of accomplished practitioners increased by doing this? The sad truth is that it has not. If something has an extremely precious inner meaning for you, you usually do not flaunt it with everyone you meet. This only encourages a casual attitude that is incompatible with successful spiritual practice.

We could also say that the teachings of tantra are "naturally" secret until their meaning is personally experienced. That is the meaning of the common saying, "When the student is ready, the Guru appears." Even then, many higher aspects of tantra will remain naturally hidden until they are unveiled by further spiritual progress.

A good quality for people is a good quality for them whether it has actually arisen in them or not. For example, patience is a virtue even if no one is actually patient at a certain time. In the same way, all people are capable of manifesting the good quality of understanding and practicing tantra, whether or not they do so at present, or have even heard of it because their true nature is Buddha nature. If they accumulate sufficient merit, their natural development will cause the Guru to appear. Then further secrets will be naturally revealed as they progress through tantric practice.

Some say that tantrayāna can be the path of only
The greatest siddhas who have the fruition of the Great Vehicle;[77]
But if the true criteria of that path are revealed,
This path can exist for anyone who has the kleśhas.
Tantra exists when all those kleśhas are brought to the path.

People say of high Lamas with many reincarnations,
Even when their compassion and wisdom are minimal,
'All the deeds they do are truly excellent.'
For those of low rank, expressing the kleśhas is denigrated.[78]
What intelligent person has respect for bias like that?[79]

---

77   In this sense, all Buddhist teachings are included either in the individual liberation vehicle, or the Great Vehicle, which here means both the bodhisattva and tantra vehicles.

78   Because of Tibetans' reverence for teachers with high status, people believe that everything they do is excellent and praise their actions even if they do something that would usually be considered immoral. However, if low ranking monastics do the same thing, people say that they are bad people and failed monastics. They never consider whether they may be trying to make their kleśhas into the path. This proves that they are not following tantric principles.

79   This kind of biased judgment cannot be respected by the intelligent.

2

Distorted Views that People in Tibet and Other Countries Have of Tantra

It is said that the source of secret mantra, or tantra, was not India alone,[80] but everyone is sure that India is the source of the words "mantra" and "tantra." Paradoxically, in present-day India, few people say publicly that they practice tantra. However, as previously mentioned, many religious practices on the subcontinent have many characteristics of tantra, and, in that sense, tantrikas have not disappeared at all in India.

Many contemporary Indians think that tantra involves black magic and wrathful rituals involving malevolent mantras.[81] They also think that tantra involves "tana gaṇa," "union and liberation," in the grossest sense of sexual exploitation and sacrificial murder.[82] Unfortunately, people who

---

80 For example, some tantras are said to have come from what is now Pakistan and Afghanistan, and the source of the *Kālachakra* is said to be Śhambhala.

81 Padoux Op. Cit., pp 153-154 has a section, "Tantra: Pervasive but not (or hardly) Perceived as Such."

82 As for degraded "liberation," or "tana," a cult known as the "Thugs" horrified the British in India by robbing and strangling travelers as sacrifices to Kālī. Traumatic memories of what they did inspired the evil Indian cult portrayed in the film *Indiana Jones and the Temple of Doom.* (Lucasfilm Ltd, 1984). Novelist M. P. Taylor says in *Confessions of a Thug,* p. 6 that 3263 thugs were arraigned between 1831 and 1837. According to W. H. Sleeman, head

claimed to be tantrikas have really performed such actions, and they bear much of the responsibility for the bad name tantra now has in India.[83]

Not surprisingly, given these facts, Indians see tantra as frightening and dangerous. Another way Indians look at tantra is that its ancient practices are outmoded. Contemporary people tend to see such practices as belonging to an approach to life opposed to their own. Many reasons have been put forward for that state of affairs, but one that could arguably be the real one is that when the British Raj brought India under its power, tantra was so far from British culture that it was viewed as an unmitigated evil and forbidden. After that, it had to be kept secret, and thus, apparently, it became intellectually and emotionally incomprehensible to most Indians.[84] Generally, if some religious tradition is kept secret by its practitioners because everyone else sees it as unwholesome, that tradition is likely to contract or vanish.

Before the Dharma spread in Tibet, there was a vigorous spreading of sūtra Dharma in China, starting in the third century. However, Buddhist tantra was never widely accepted because it was too far from Chi-

---

of the British Thug Department, "From the time of the conquest of Mysore in 1799 [until] 1808... hundreds of persons were annually destroyed." (*Op. cit.*, p. 37.) Degraded "union," or "gaṇa," in the form of tantric temple prostitutes known as devadasis, though now illegal, remains an underground Indian institution. Long ago these women had a legitimate religious function related to the Path of Desire, and they were educated and skilled in the arts like Japanese geishas and the hetaerae of classical Greece. Now they are usually lower class women who can make more as prostitutes than in other jobs available to them. (Battersby, Matilda, for the *Independent* [digital news] Monday 20 September, 2010 00:00:.)

83   These lamentable activities are opposed to proper interpretation of "union and liberation" as blissful and wrathful bodhisattva activities. The blissful activity is synonymous with the Path of Desire. Proper practice of "liberation" consists of wrathful bodhisattva activity to help sentient beings, undertaken only when peaceful activities prove ineffective and when the result for all beings concerned is better than if the activity was not performed. See the extended explanation at the end of Appendix II.

84   Tantra was also excluded by the rationalized and expurgated version of Hinduism Indians had to produce to withstand Colonial indoctrination, according to scholar Ravi S. Kudesia in an April 10, 2023 message.

nese culture. Only teachings of lower tantra classes, whose viewpoint was similar to that of the Great Vehicle, were assimilated in China. Even now, most Chinese have a very negative view of tantra. Most of the few who view it favorably have heard teachings from Tibetan Lamas.

As noted above, Indians worship deities with devotional offering *pūjās* whose external form is very similar to that of tantric sādhanas in Tibet but do so without calling it tantra. Classes in yoga systems with tantric roots can be found everywhere, and, just from the people involved not keeping their activities secret, it is clear that what they are doing is not secret tantra in the fullest sense.

In the traditional Indian approach to tantra, it is commonly said that, if a prospective student does not act as a servant for three years without a single word of Dharma being spoken, no explanation of Dharma will ever be received.[85] If you think that such things happened only in the distant past, stories of incredible devotion, like those in the biographies of Tilopa, Nāropā, Marpa, and Milarepa are said to occur in India even today although the details are not known to the general public. Might not an understanding of Indian tantra develop with the thought, "Was not Indian tantra even more profound than present Tibetan tantra?[86]"

A key difference between Indian and Tibetan tantras is that the former is not focused on the altruistic ideal of attaining enlightenment for the benefit of all sentient beings. In Tibetan tantra, such a "mind of enlightenment," or *bodhichitta*, is the motivation for tantric practice. Nevertheless, Tibetans and Indians are the same in that a profound, genuine understanding of tantra is almost non-existent in the community at large.

---

85 To offer a modern example, Dzongsar Khyentse Rinpoché publicly mentioned how he could not learn Indian tantra because of this prerequisite. The author Khentrul Rinpoché referred to that from memory of a public talk he attended.

86 Although the stories mentioned chronicle the beginnings of the Tibetan Kagyü lineage, the stories of the first three figures are mostly concerned with tantric practice in eleventh century India.

Contemporary Tibetans' views are increasingly becoming like those of non-Buddhist Indians. For example, when the Path of Desire is discussed, they both think that only great siddhas can experience it.

Though the present Indian and Chinese populations are alike in holding a negative opinion of tantra, most Indians practice tantra without calling it "tantra," while people in China avoid tantra like poison. In that respect, the two are polar opposites. Most people in other Eastern countries are like the Chinese in having little liking for tantra and even less understanding of it. Thus, worldwide, those who misunderstand and disapprove tantra are very many and those who have joyful faith in it are extremely few.

The viewpoint of tantra held by most Westerners is almost the reverse of that of Easterners. There is little fascination with wrathful activity, which they regard as a controversial and dangerous teaching. They focus instead on sexual union alone. Thus, when you search "tantra" on the internet, most of the numerous results that appear are concerned with sexual techniques often presented with a Hindu flavor. Many people think that these are good skills to know. Though Asians historically produced classics on sex like the *Kāma Sūtra*, most people in Asia today are reluctant to talk about sex at all, so they tend to know less than Westerners. Even adult material is harder to find in Asian countries. I usually consider Westerners to be quite liberated on the subject. However, they mostly think that "tantra" does not go beyond special skills in sexual techniques.

During the early spread of Tibetan Buddhism in the West, when Westerners who believed that tantra was mostly about sex heard how most Tibetan Lamas were explaining Tibetan tantra, many did not want to call those Tibetan teachings "tantra" because they were not clearly concerned with sex. They preferred to call what those Lamas taught "vajrayāna." The word vajrayāna is actually a synonym of tantra or tantrayāna, which focuses on the indestructible ("vajra") nature of ultimate reality. However, some Dharma groups distorted what was before their eyes through the lenses of their preconceptions. They called themselves "vajrayāna" groups, thinking that the teachings they had received could not be tantra because they were not about sex.[87]

There are definitely practices using sexuality as skillful means in Tibetan tantric tradition, but traditionally, when Lamas are explaining the basics, such topics are not included. When Westerners asked these Lamas about sex in Tibetan tantra, they did not answer clearly. That made these Westerners suspicious. Some even got angry, thinking that the Lamas were deliberately deceiving them. Tibetan teachers were very surprised by these reactions.

Do lay Tibetans understand tantra? Not really. Saying that they think tantra is a good thing covers their viewpoint pretty well. For example, when Tibetans see paintings and statues of deities in sexual union, the obvious association of sexual intercourse is not their predominant response, but rather, devoted faith in their tradition as a whole. They have a vague sense that tantra is something good, but very few ordinary people who generate such faith know the symbolic significance of these depictions.

Tibetan monastics and scholars who study and contemplate tantric texts are mostly concerned with the superficial verbal meaning and the verbal referents of symbols. They may explain the history of the Path of Desire, but when asked how it should be practiced, they are just dancing on books. How they might come to know and apply the direct instructions on actual practice is difficult to imagine.

In present Tibetan tantra, there are chiefly superficial practices of

---

87 Others did the same because they feared that if they said they practiced "tantra," many people interested primarily in sex would want to join their group. They said things like, "Do not call us a 'tantra group!' We are a righteous Buddhist center!" Some journals that published papers on Buddhism had instructions that those writing about tantra need not apply.

sādhanas and pūjās, merely symbolic empowerments, healing and blessing rituals, formal group practice sessions with occasional extended ones,
and elaborate costumed ceremonies like dances. Except for training in
sacred outlook, most of what goes on is a mere show of practicing tantra. In brief, critical observation lets us know very clearly that most contemporary Tibetans are not fundamentally better off in regard to tantra
than their Western counterparts because they have fallen into extreme
approaches of their own.

> In the source of tantra, India, at the present time,
> Many yogins practice secret tantra that is not secret.[88]
> That people unknowingly practice tantra is very strange;
> Real tantra is still powerful, but secret and hard to find.

> China is a desert, like the southern and eastern countries;
> They all have Buddhist teachings, but tantrayāna is rare.
> On the whole, discordant viewpoints bewilder everyone,
> Westerners too have various conflicting understandings.

---

88 The physical yoga they practice arose, in the past, in conjunction with secret tantric
practice; now people are usually unaware of this connection, and they have no idea
of keeping certain yoga practices secret. The same could be said of some liturgies they
practice.

3

Problems of Present Tibetan Tantra

Only the Tibetan Buddhist tantric teachings unite sūtra and tantra, and it goes without saying that the teachings on the side of tantra are the more profound and powerful ones. However, when foreigners think about Tibetan Buddhism, aside from seeing that its tantric teachings are predominant, they do not take sufficient account of the influence of other Buddhist approaches. If we look at the real situation, *most followers of the Tibetan Buddhist teachings are wearing an outer costume of tantra, but their actual practice has the approach of the sūtra teachings.*

For example, if we observe the adherence to monastic discipline in the Tibetan Buddhist lineages and compare it to the monasticism of other traditions, the allegedly tantric Tibetans' observance of minute details is no less than that of others. In fact, they cannot get enough of it. When they practice tantra, they eliminate anything that contradicts the vinaya. If it is said that the present Tibetan Buddhist lineages are practicing a mere imitation of tantra because they treat tantra as a division of sūtra practice, not much is missing. Moreover, even within sūtra practice, the Tibetan lineages say that they practice the bodhisattva vehicle of compassion, but the truth is that they chiefly practice the conduct and viewpoint of the individual liberation path.

Pure perception is the ground and root of the tantric viewpoint. Thus, to disparage pure perception, not only of tantrikas, but that of any Buddhists, and even outsiders, is not proper tantric conduct. However, most Tibetan Buddhists think they are supposed to be like lawyers who defend and praise their own traditions while attacking and criticizing the traditions of others.

Some Tibetans think that outsiders not only have false and harmful doctrines but have deep propensities to being possessed by unseen evil beings as well. They criticize the *Kālachakra* teachings of the Jonang Tradition because originally it borrowed terms from *Sāṅkhya* so that it would be more accessible to Vedic yogins in Śhambhala. Some absurdly claim that the Jonang view that Buddha nature truly exists as eternal, permanent, and so forth was corrupted by Hindu extremist views so that it is no longer a Buddhist view at all.

They want to prove that everything said by non-Buddhists is false. How can that be done except by postulating propositions that entail the desired conclusion, such as "All non-Buddhist views are conceptual, they fall into extremes and are refutable." Indian outsiders' view of Buddhists was historically no better, and no room was left in the minds of either party for any word to the contrary. Then how could the views on either side be regarded as attempts to determine the truth? That both held prejudiced, wrong views can be known from history, and there has been no great change since.

Many religious people in the world, including Buddhists, think they are supposed to be compassionate only to people who believe as they do. In the path of individual liberation, associating with non-Buddhists is forbidden for monastics. The sixth tantric branch vow teaches that it is wrong to stay among practitioners of individual liberation for more than seven days if their prejudice against the bodhisattva or tantra vehicles would be a bad influence. While these precepts are not taught to generate prejudice toward others, some Buddhists wrongly condemn outsiders as bad without qualification. They do not understand that such religious precepts on proper conduct are *temporary* skillful means to help beginners stabilize their practice.

In general, the Highest Yoga Tantra view does not sanction such strong bias. The *Kālachakra* teachings in particular actively oppose it. However, people who espouse prejudice have no true perspective on the matter. The views and doctrines of individual liberation of the monastics entrusted with the Tibetan Buddhist lineages, including those of tantra, typically have such faults. However, *since they all agree that absolute truth transcends words and expression, they should view all doctrinal viewpoints as incidental statements intended to lead students on a good path.* In that case, we cannot say that one doctrine is absolutely right and another absolutely wrong.[89] We can only distinguish whether the path they teach leads to a beneficial outcome or not. Within Buddhism itself, some teachings are said to be merely provisional and not absolutely true. Provisional teachings are said to be good or bad, depending on whether they lead followers who cannot understand the whole truth to a good outcome.[90]

If we consider contemporary Tibetan tantric meditation, the chief supports of meditation are external. There are representations of male and female wrathful deities of Highest Yoga Tantra, *yidam* deities joined in a sexual embrace, and so forth. There are also paintings and statues of gold, clay, and so forth that belong to the monastic community. Usually, people's minds are full of such images when they do tantric meditation. The true meaning of these symbolic representations is the continuity of the ground that abides in our own minds. That is *Sugatagarbha*, Buddha nature, as our inherently existing characteristic. The best practitioners know how to meditate on non-conceptual experience of this ultimate, and

---

89 Rinpoché wrote a book providing an abridged presentation of many religious traditions called *Ocean of Diversity*.

90 Even if their current spiritual path is not a complete path teaching how to achieve full enlightenment, they can connect with a higher path in the future, or in future rebirths, when inner conditions for deeper understanding have been gathered.

they need nothing else. However, if you ask what percentage of Tibetans are accomplished in such meditation, very clearly it is minuscule. Most of them can only meditate conceptually, and so they always need symbolic supports for their practice such as the above images of deities.

Moreover, going back to meditating on deities in an external manner, whether individuals who do this in the Highest Yoga Tantra traditions are going beyond the merely verbal approach of the explanatory tantras is hard to say. The best really apprehend that their kleśhas are pure aspects of wisdom that are the essence of the tantric deities.[91] Intermediate ones meditate while thinking that the kleśhas are like that. The ones of inferior capacity make a habit of thinking this way when they study Dharma. That only a tiny percentage of Tibetans actually do any of this is clearly known by them all.

In any case, those who enter into the genuine practice of Highest Yoga Tantra, those who merely want to do so, and even those who falsely claim that they want to do so, are extremely few. Other Tibetans follow a sūtra path of struggle in a war between what is abandoned and antidotes. That is obvious to anyone who has even a little familiarity with the Tibetan Saṅgha. If the tantra approach of using kleśhas as part of the path is recommended, only a few exceptional Tibetans who understand it properly agree. The others are afraid of that approach because it does not fit with what they know. If advocates of this sūtra approach say, "Everyone should minimize passion and aversion," almost all Tibetans, whether they can do that or not, will understand that familiar sūtric approach of suppressing the kleśhas.

If the path of abandoning by antidotes is explained with the honest qualification that it is an endless struggle that is extremely difficult, those

---

91   As explained in *Kālachakra*: Amoghasiddhi: Great jealousy, Ratnasambhava: Great pride, Amitābha: Great attachment/desire, Vairochana: Great ignorance, Akṣhobhya: Great aversion, Vajrasattva: Great anger. *Kālachakra's* wisdoms of these six Buddha families are the enlightened "versions" of these six poisons.

who hear that in tantra there is no need to struggle like that may well prefer it, but, as most Tibetans do not think about such things at all, those who prefer the tantric approach are few. As they have only the vaguest, abstract idea of how to enter into the tantric path, they cannot do so, even partially. Thus, while Tibetans theorize all the time about how tantra should be practiced, the teachings that they actually practice are those of sūtra with an outer veneer of tantra. Even among high-ranking Dharma practitioners, people with real proficiency in transmuting the kleśhas are rare.

If we think about conduct, according to all that was previously explained, the activities of practice genuinely seem to be part of the everyday life of ordinary people in Tibet. They receive the devoted faith and respect of the community. The actual conduct that most Tibetans revere, however, is that of the sūtra approach, the struggle between abandoning and antidotes. Almost none think favorably of transcending that war, by bringing the kleśhas to the path.

For example, consider what happens if tantric practitioners show anger. Most Tibetans simply conclude that they are bad people. No one wonders whether, since they are tantrikas, they may be trying to bring their kleśhas to the path.[92] It is very clear that genuine tantra is no more than a mere logical possibility for such people.

Among people in the Tibetan community, high and low alike, those most likely to be regarded with genuine faith and respect that comes from the heart are yogins who are free from worldly activities. They have no need for non-essential worldly goals like wealth and fame. They seek profound Dharmic wealth that is not like worldly wealth. Even so, some people have faith in these yogins, but some do not. Some are even hostile to them as useless people. Moreover, among famous scholars who are proud

---

92 Similarly, in other parts of the world, such as many European countries, even small displays of anger or other strong emotions result in a denigrating social judgment. See Part Three chapter 1.

of their learning, no matter how many books they have read or how many excellent monastic or secular schools they attended, those who integrate the practice instructions of the genuine tantra path with their conduct are mostly non-existent as is clear to everyone.

If you wonder what the signs of this may be, most great and high learned ones in the Tibetan community have little confidence in tantra. Ordinary people may have blind faith in it, but educated Lamas and other leaders who are the quintessence of the community think that no genuine tantrikas exist anymore. There is not even a social custom of pretending that they do. They do not think about tantra at all really because they believe that it has no relevance today. They think they are very sophisticated, but their so-called learning is a superficial rationalization that misses the point of human life.[93]

Superficially, the Tibetan Buddhist tantric lineages may seem to be benevolent, excellent, and sublime. There are numerous depictions of tantric imagery — such things as outer divine palaces of great splendor, the inner *maṇḍala* with its many male and female peaceful and wrathful deities, good and capable *ḍākas* and *ḍākinīs*, offering goddesses with their beautiful faces, "father" and "mother" deities joined in a sexual embrace, symbolizing the union of bliss and emptiness. This wondrous iconography leads to sincere faith, and, for those who see it for the first time, its wealth is difficult to contain in the conceptual mind. Nevertheless, when most people high in the sphere of Dharma are asked how to bring kleśhas to the path, they respond with black looks and deflect the question with a curt reply. That is the end of it. For example, when such people are asked if there is any truth in former tales of practitioners who knew how to bring anger to the path, aside from admitting the mere possibility, they say, "Not much is taught openly about that," and by never saying more,

---

93   That is like some modern Christians or Jews who say, "There may have been miracles long ago in biblical times, but educated people know that such things do not happen anymore."

they make their own statement true.

In sum, compared with the splendid and extensive external displays of tantra that are found everywhere, the scanty presence of its worthy and suitable inner wealth is a hundred thousand times less. When prominent people say that bringing kleśhas to the path is a recipe for trouble, that we should deemphasize and forget about it, is not that clearly wrong? When others say nothing in that approach is worthy of debating, are they not being disingenuous?

> Though "Buddhists" say that *Bön* is bad, they steal its liturgies.
> Then augmenting their style, they call them "tantrayāna."
> Proud of just counting mantras in the generation stage,[94]
> They cheat on the vow they made to practice the stage of
>   completion.[95]

> Their empowerments are Lamas merely chanting liturgies.[96]
> Their explanations are *Khenpos*[97] merely parroting books.
> Their instructions try to satisfy with only a dance on books.[98]

---

94 In mantra practice, many Tibetan Buddhists do not bother to learn the generation stage visualizations properly in order to experience divine purity. They just say mantras and are arrogant about how many they have done, mistakenly thinking that that alone will give them spiritual attainment.

95 Like people who cheat on their taxes if they can, they do not keep their samaya of properly practicing the completion stage which brings tantric practice to the fruition. They regard doing so as a burden, and they grudgingly do as little as they can.

96 Rinpoché means that often when some Lamas say they are giving empowerments, they merely chant the liturgy and go through the associated ritual, giving no explanations or practice instructions.

97 Monastics with learning and practice experience who receive a higher status as professors.

98 Instead of genuine practice instructions of how to bring kleśhas to the path, they offer useless verbal sophistries, like saying we do not need to worry about kleśhas because they are empty of true existence. They are skilled at constructing logical arguments by

Even their Anuttara views[99] sex as an enemy.

Their shell of secret tantra has many tantric deities;
Inside, they spend their time on the three objects of vinaya.[100]
Their bodhichitta is empty words devoid of practice.
Tibetans are very devoted — to their customary ways.

---

quoting texts and so forth, but misuse that skill to argue falsely that the practices of sūtra and tantra are identical.

99 Anuttarayoga-tantra, or Highest Yoga Tantra.

100 They employ a lot of external tantric imagery, but inside, they are just doing individual liberation practice.

4

How Tantra is a Natural Path and Anyone Can Learn It

Usually, people think that the higher a teaching is, the more difficult it is to understand. Because of that, they also think that practicing a higher teaching will also be more difficult than practicing a lower one. The actuality is more likely to be the reverse. For example, the foundational path, individual liberation, where we must constantly struggle in the war between abandoning and antidotes, is actually the hardest path to practice.

In this path, we need to abandon everything that is naturally present in our continuum. In that approach, the arising of desire, aversion, and other kleśhas that naturally exist in all people must be made non-existent. Eliminating the arising and existence of some of these phenomena is possible, but if none of them must ever arise, how exhausting it will be to suppress all of them all the time! Though sometimes we think we can do it, one day they will be back, and then they will manifest even more powerfully than before. We will be worse off than if we never tried to suppress them at all. That is because, in trying to suppress them, we are opposing human nature.[101]

---

101 Here *rang byung chos nyid* does not refer to the absolute nature of phenomena, but rela-

How many people in the world have really made the kleśhas for-ever non-existent? If we weigh the kleśhas against the understanding of ordinary individuals and the meditative experience of higher ones with whom we are familiar, is not it clear that kleśhas continue to manifest in spite of all they do to stop them? Then, is not the path of the bodhisattvas more suitable and pleasant to practice? Why? The bodhisattva path pre-sented in the Buddha's third turning of the wheel of Dharma teaches that the nature of enlightenment exists in each individual's continuum as the true nature of all phenomena. If we realize that true nature of phenom-ena, we no longer have to struggle in a war between what is abandoned and antidotes.

For example, desire does not have to be abandoned because power-ful desires can simply be transmuted into the ultimate nature of phenom-ena which is also the ultimate nature of human beings. Thus, compared to the path of individual liberation, whose views and practices are very difficult to work with, it is much easier just to contemplate the way things are. The bodhisattva path eliminates having to think intensely about every phenomenon, one by one, in order to suppress it. The laborious mechanisms of the path of individual liberation become superfluous. The advantages of the bodhisattva path need to be thoroughly re-examined by those who say they practice it but actually cling to the approach of individual liberation.

The tantric path is incomparably more exalted than even the bod-hisattva path. The innate natural state is known to be the true nature of all persons and all phenomena of relative truth as in the bodhisattva path, but genuine tantric practitioners also know how to enjoy these phenom-ena properly, just as they are. That this makes tantra a wondrous, pro-found path is undeniable.

The reason is very clear. Whether we have excellent, inferior, or

---

tive human nature, in which the kleśhas naturally exist.

middling capacities in this life, the basis of ultimate enjoyment is innately within us. Except for kleśhas like attachment and anger being more or less powerful in different individuals, they arise in all of us, whenever supportive conditions are met with. Furthermore, as we were all born in the desire realm, not even one person is without the passion of desire. Why so? Without it, there is no way to be born in the desire realm.

To eradicate the kleśhas that naturally exist in human minds is extremely difficult, but when we know the essence of these kleśhas, we know the pure and true way they really are. The better we know that, the better we are at putting the kleśhas to use. This is a very brief summary of the tantric path.

In the path of individual liberation, the kleśha of desire is understood only as something to be abandoned. The eleven virtuous mental factors and their intentions are understood as something to be accepted. In actual practice, when a particular desire is abandoned in a particular situation, the two features essential to that situation are (1) the desire to be abandoned and (2) the antidote by which it is abandoned. Only these two phenomena need to be determined, and they are easy to know.

However, of these two, the desire must be forever eliminated. Moreover, the intention to do that using a certain antidote must be multiplied to deal with limitless instances. Is there a more difficult activity than this in the world? Therefore, what individual, wise or unwise, might not think, "If I learned how to use desire instead of eliminating it, would not that be much easier?"

The essence of the tantric path is that none of the kleśhas of the five or three poisons need to be abandoned when we know how to use them on this excellent path. For example, if powerful mechanisms that generate illusion exist within us, there is no need to say, "These are dangerous, so we need to get rid of them right away." Once we know how these can be well-employed for our ends, it is actually better for us if these mechanisms of illusion exist, than if they do not. Similarly, *when the kleśhas are seen to be pure as they are, there is no need to abandon them;* we can put them to work as our friends. That is the unsurpassable path of tantra.

For all these reasons, *if people understand the tantric path, everyone can put it into practice. Whether they have excellent, inferior, or middling abilities, it will produce extensive happiness.* However, up to the present, almost all Tibetans, let alone others, have had no idea how to practice tantra properly. Not only that, they tell each other that it is a very dangerous topic that they want nothing to do with. We may wonder, "Why do they keep repeating these thoughts?"

Directing the powerful mental mechanisms employed in tantra is like handling the controls of an airplane. People who do not know how to fly airplanes are afraid to do so even though they are aware that they are wonderful means of transportation. While they are ignorant of a pilot's skills, it will always be dangerous for them to try and fly one but should they learn, they may well find piloting an airplane easier than riding a bicycle.

Even the most common actions in the world are a little dangerous. For example, some people choke and die while eating a meal. Clothing often contains traces of toxic chemicals that were used to process it. It can get caught in machines or impede movement so that we fall and are injured. An excellent medicine may be poisonous for some people. Even being in crowded cities and traveling on roads have obvious dangers. Travel and tantra are similar in that regard. Although the bad consequences in the worst possible situation are serious, to say that none of these things should be done at all is like the babbling of a fool.

Every day in the American city of Atlanta, approximately 3,000 airplanes take off from the airport. Every flight involves some danger. Some people overreact and say, "Since airplanes are so dangerous, I will never go on one," or "Being miles up in the air is just too dangerous." They make excuses like, "My baggage is too heavy to travel by airplane." All this is just foolishness.

Some people think, "Since the tantric path is very high, it cannot be completely known. If we try to practice it, there will be great danger; it is best if we keep away!" That too is no better than the exaggerated fears of a fool. Not listening to such blind and narrow talk, everyone who can should enter the tantric path of great bliss. This path is very high, but that does not mean it is very dangerous. On the contrary, since it is high, it is excellent. People mistakenly think that, since tantra directly realizes ultimate reality, it must be difficult. Actually, seeing its goal directly makes it an easier path to navigate. There is no need to herd ourselves into the pens of small-minded fools who are afraid of themselves and their abilities. We simply should not let ourselves stray into such wretched and miserable territory.

We may wonder, "How does the path of individual liberation benefit its practitioners?" Most of those who practice the path of individual liberation, as discussed above, rather than experiencing phenomena associated with happiness, must constantly confront unpleasant qualities like craving and hatred. These qualities can lead individual liberation practitioners into an expanse of suffering. Strong faith and ceaseless exertion serve in that path as antidotes that produce victory over the kleśhas. In order to deploy these antidotes, we have to battle ceaselessly with the enemies of desire and so forth.

In the tantric path, nothing that is naturally present in our mind needs to be eliminated. Instead, we learn means for making mental phenomena work for us. Then we know how to use everything in our mind, including our negative emotions, in a beneficial way. When all these phenomena are subjugated by the brilliance of pure and true reality, they become our friends.

Passionate men and women of the desire realm,
Apart from these means that bring desire to the path,
Lack the excellent qualities of the natural state.
Alas! They can never reach the essence of the path.

"Profound tantrayāna cannot be practiced," they caution us;
Instead we ought to practice the inferior vehicles,
Of individual liberation and bodhisattvas.[102]
Though we may never reach the genuine heart within us,
We can turn all obstacles into nothingness.

Our ultimate nature is self-arising and self-fulfilling;
It is the path to the kingdom of the eternal deities;
Its valor brings great benefits for oneself and others;
Who would not aspire to be that itself?

---

102 The tantric practitioner must also be a follower of the bodhisattva path, but not all who
follow that path are also tantrikas. The individual liberation and bodhisattva paths are
beneficial, but the tantric approach is undoubtedly higher.

5

Human Nature in Relation to the Individual Liberation, Bodhisattva, and Tantra Paths

The Individual Liberation Path

Human nature is such that, except for being more or less powerful in certain individuals, desire, aversion, anger, pride, jealousy and greed, and likewise, fright, concerned preoccupation, deceit, shamelessness, and all the other kleśhas naturally exist within us all. Likewise, virtues such as faith, diligence, mindfulness, *samādhi*, loving-kindness, and compassion, except for being more or less powerful in certain individuals, are also naturally present. In particular, the passion of desire, is naturally within us all since it is a prerequisite for being born here in the desire realm. This is very clear, and no one can deny it.

Liberation seldom arises on a path that views desire as an enemy. Such a path requires that all the kleśhas that naturally exist in everyone must be forever eliminated. To be motivated to undertake that practice, you must have confidence that you can accomplish this. However, only paragons who are unrivaled, perfect renunciates can do this. Ordinary people can suppress desire and other kleśhas only temporarily. Once we reject the position that desires temporarily subsiding is liberation, attaining liberation by completely abandoning desire in the course of one human life is a very challenging undertaking indeed.

Someone who must constantly employ such strenuous means is unlikely to enjoy even ordinary happiness in life. If I explain it like that, though some people may not let it into their ears, those who do listen will be realistic about their dim prospects of liberation through renunciation. From then on, they will be able to understand the actual way of things. If some want to spend their lives rejecting what they are, far be it from me to say, "Do not do that!" As they try to reach their goal of perfect denial, they must murder all their loves and desires, one by one, even the desire to attain the wisdom of realization.[103]

To practice the path of individual liberation successfully, our outer conduct and inner attitudes must correspond. If they do, our lives are likely to be fruitful and significant. If our inner aspirations conflict with our outer actions, attaining our inner goals is impossible. Therefore, investigation of whether such a path is suitable for beings like us has consequences that are quite profound. Tibetans have no tradition of investigating such things, so they seldom think very hard about them. Is not it clear that they should? Should not renunciates, in particular, consider very carefully the consequences of renouncing their own nature?

Renunciation is a commitment to homelessness. Homelessness means not only giving up living in a house but also the self-oriented attitudes of those who live in them so that one abides only in virtuous, selfless states of mind. The Tibetan term for a fully ordained monk or nun is *dge slong(ma)*. The meaning is a person who maintains renunciate virtue, *dge ba*, by begging for food, *slong ba*. Being a novice monk, who practices the way of such virtue, *dge tshul*, is preparation for being such a fully ordained monastic. Renunciates being people who train in virtue, *dge sbyong*, should

---

103 Their practice will be the mental equivalent of the Chinese torture called "the death of a thousand cuts," without even the grace of death to ease their pain at the end.

be understood similarly. Nowadays, no monastics actually beg in Tibet, although donations to the ordained Saṅgha are commonly solicited.

If even collecting food to be eaten tomorrow is not allowed for a homeless renunciate, so much the more should householders' property and enjoyments be abandoned. Relationships with relatives must be cut off. Companions, lovers, and sex must be forever abandoned. In brief, the society of ordinary people must be given up.

In brief, monastic renunciation deprives the individual of all that our human nature longs for. *When monks and nuns expel themselves from society, that "exile" must result in something sufficiently beneficial to compensate for their loss.* If renunciates deny this, how is their protestation better than the groundless insistence of a fool?

After the Buddha proclaimed that monastics should be homeless, their response was not in the spirit of his proclamation at all. Monks and nuns wore nice robes. They were increasingly concerned with communal wealth, political influence, and so forth. In the end, they were not much different from householders. Exile from the ranks of the worldly served only to push them back into worldly concerns.

These monastics certainly had an approach in which outer and inner were in contradiction. Was not their calculated hypocrisy something that even animals would not engage in?[104] If Tibetan monastics purified their path of hypocritical inconsistencies, they would no longer have to live a life of inner contradictions that guarantee failure. Would not that be a good thing?

In the Buddha's time, monks and nuns were wandering beggars most of the year. They came together only for special occasions like the summer rains retreat in temporary facilities provided by generous patrons. There

---

104 Animals instinctively employ deceptive camouflage and lures to capture prey, just as humans scheme how they can entice fish to bite a hook. However, these monastics' behavior entirely defeats their own goals. It is as futile as a spider ignoring flies and trying to catch rocks.

was nothing like the huge, luxurious, and expensive monasteries of today, whose accommodations look like those of normal saṃsāric homes. Being attached to such housing defeats the purpose of homelessness. A few monks do not even pretend to be homeless. Some Tibetan lineages allow "village monks" to stay in their homes, sometimes even with wives and children. This is "justified" by their conducting offerings and other rituals for their villages. There are also ordained monks who keep their vows and wear robes, but who stay at home and do small jobs for their families rather than living in monasteries.

Monastics typically succeed in abandoning houses and sex externally, but they are forced to the conclusion that renouncing all internal aspects of sex such as mental fantasies and desires is prohibitively difficult. Psychologists have come to a similar conclusion. People who can actually do this are very rare.

In sum, when monastics enter into the path of individual liberation, if their karma is so good that outer and inner are in consonance like the equal purity of the flower and covering of a lotus bud, everything is wonderful. However, we can see that most people who enter the path of individual liberation spend their lives with a dissonance of outer and inner. When the present dilemmas that torment monastics are observed in the world and so many serious scandals are reported in the news media, those who still have the confidence to enter such a path are becoming increasingly few. No one seems to want to discuss this issue in its totality, but since the need is obvious, I am doing so anyway.

In the Tibetan community, when people become aware of something bad, they avert their eyes. As an example, when there are disturbing scandals among the ordained Saṅgha, they keep them hidden. There is little inclination to examine and improve the situation, which is rather alarming, in the same way as doing nothing to prevent serious epidemics is alarming.

If Tibetans habitually conceal such things, is that any better than deliberately deceiving people, so that they fall heedlessly into calamity? If what they do not want to think about keeps happening, has not their loving-kindness collapsed into indifference? Those who are kind and compassionate must speak straightforwardly even when others will not so that these situations become part of our shared experience. If we analyze even a little, we can easily know why these problems exist. The whole list of sexual and other transgressions that these supposed renunciates have committed is due to disparity between outer and inner.

This is not a problem for Buddhist renunciates alone. It is estimated that over the past seventy years, priests and other individuals connected to the Catholic Church molested about 333,000 children in France alone.[105] After an overwhelming number of cases of this kind were brought to light in the media, now, when religion is mentioned, it is an object of fear and revulsion in the minds of many people. This is true even though many sincere believers continue to practice in an exemplary fashion.

Although to a lesser extent, Tibetan Lamas, monks, and nuns living outside of Tibet have a similar history, but, since many Tibetans are short-sighted, these incidents were carefully concealed like national secrets, though they were well-known to the public at large. Nevertheless, anxious concern about such things was quietly becoming endemic in the Tibetan community. Is that not a clear sign that Tibetans will have to deal with these concerns eventually?

While we are worrying about whether these scandals about renunciates and spiritual teachers will give Tibetan Buddhism a bad name, it is actually more important that we understand their causes. Heaping abuse on individuals is a poor substitute for insight. It will be difficult to produce a good result by righteous anger alone.

---

105 Reported by the BBC on October 5th 2021 and other international media channels. One of the intentions of this quote is to show how some other religions in other parts of the world are setting a good example by allowing a careful investigation of their structural issues regarding celibacy, rather than concealing them.

If we take renunciates in the Tibetan community as an example, most of them become renunciates in their childhood, when their bodies and minds had yet to mature. As they decided to be ordained when they were extremely young, they had no idea what they were committing themselves to. Many did not even decide for themselves at all, their parents decided for them. Their deep-seated, natural desire would manifest only later. When it did, realization of the disparity between their chosen path and their own nature came much too late. When their sexuality manifested and they became unhappy with their lives, it was easy for them to violate their vows because they never had a genuine commitment to monasticism to start with. Their renunciation was merely a convenient pretense made to gain their livelihood, and so they lost their self-control as soon as they were tempted. The prevalence of scandals tells us that many renunciates of varied traditions are in the same situation. The parents of young Tibetan monastics never gave serious thought to what would happen after their children were ordained. Had they done so with due diligence, many would not now carry such a burden of remorse for the unsavory results.

The different rates of returning to lay life of monastics in Tibet, India, and other foreign countries seem to have been due to differing amounts of social pressure in those environments. Tibet had the highest retention rate because social pressure to continue as a renunciate was strongest. More monastics who fled from Tibet to India returned to lay life because social pressure there was less, but among those who went to Western countries with minimal social pressure, most disrobed, according to my personal observation.

You might think that it was difficult for monastics in foreign countries to continue their way of life as no suitable facilities for them existed there. Actually, it was easier to be a monastic in India than in Tibet because everything was taken care of. In Tibet, monastics are usually sponsored by families, and so they have responsibilities toward them. If they

really want to, monks and nuns can follow their inner discipline of renunciation almost anywhere and live by taking a simple job. So, in my honest view, most monastics returning to lay life was primarily due to their
own desires, facilitated by decreased social pressure to remain ordained
in their new environment.

To summarize, the motivation to enter the path of individual liberation comes from the view that, due to desire and aversion, this world has
the nature of suffering. The meditation consists of struggling constantly
in the war between abandoning and antidotes. The conduct is such that
practitioners try to eliminate kleśhas that are innate in human life because they are the cause of suffering. For engaging in this path to make
sense, practitioners must be confident that they can accomplish its goal.
If, later on, they fail to do so, it is hard for them to know whether practicing that path was ever a worthy pursuit. Individuals like me who explain
Buddhist teachings cannot resolve that doubt for them. That is because
these individuals must re-evaluate carefully not only the teachings they
have received, but their own capabilities of practicing them.

The Bodhisattva Path

In the bodhisattva path, the view is one in which the wishes of all sentient
beings are regarded as being of equal value. As no one does not desire to
attain ultimate happiness and joy, this approach aims at attaining them
for all sentient beings without distinction.[106] *There is no way to reject it as
biased toward particular beings as its focus is universal.*

The meditation is like the view. The meditators can only fulfill their
heroically difficult goals by making themselves into vajra heroes and

---

106 It is true that some individuals *temporarily* do not know what the true meanings of love
and compassion are; but this does not mean they do not have them innately or that they
are unable to unveil through stages of practice; they all are in this or subsequent lives.

heroines that no obstacle can destroy.[107] The conduct is similarly demanding. All their practice is included in accomplishing the six perfections, four means of gathering disciples, and so forth.

Meditative practice aims at experiencing the true, pure nature of things that is empty of all conceptualized characteristics. All enlightened conduct and the fulfillment of the fruition are possible only through experiencing this non-dual purity of how things are. According to the Buddha's third and final turning of the wheel of Dharma, that true state is empty of all impermanent, painful phenomena of the relative but not of the innumerable phenomena of the natural state that truly exists as aspects of ultimate Sugatagarbha.

Since seeing the nature of things accomplishes all, the view, meditation, and conduct of the bodhisattva path are much more easily accomplished than those of individual liberation. For these reasons, this path is an admirable one. Not only that, this precious path pervades the universe. Since the view, meditation, and conduct are faultless and universally applicable, they can be understood by ordinary people in the world. No one does not want to be loved, and everyone needs and enjoys the kindness of others.[108]

Bodhisattvas aspire to temporal and ultimate happiness for all sentient beings. Since what they desire to establish is the same for everyone, it is not of primary importance to them whether they themselves attain

---

107 A Zen version of the bodhisattva vow exemplifies this heroic approach clearly, "Sentient beings are numberless. We vow to save them all. / Delusions are endless. We vow to cut through them all. / The teachings are infinite. We vow to learn them all. / The Buddha Way is inconceivable. We vow to attain it." https://www.emptygatezen.com/blog/the-four-great-vows-in-zen-practice.

108 Though in particular places, times, and occasions, in the minds of particular people, there may be some who do not love at all and do not want to be objects of love, generally speaking, no one on this earth does not appreciate and value love even if only for a short time or without being aware of it. Perfect beings who do not need loving-kindness are conceivable, but almost non-existent.

Buddhahood quickly or not. They focus only on benefiting all sentient beings with the happiness of the natural state. After that goal has been attained, there is no other. For that reason, if bodhisattvas themselves do not attain enlightenment quickly, there is no problem at all for them as long as they can continue to benefit others.

Unlike practitioners of the path of individual liberation, bodhisattvas have no desire to attain their own liberation from *saṃsāra* as quickly as possible, by struggling to eliminate what is to be abandoned. They are able to transmute their saṃsāric view of delusive, dualistic phenomena of the kleśhas into a realized view of beneficial, absolute phenomena perceived by non-dual, non-conceptual wisdom. Thus, theirs is a path where practitioners do not have to struggle in the war between what is to be abandoned and antidotes. However, bodhisattva practitioners lack most of the skillful means of putting kleśhas to work on the path possessed by tantrikas.

If a good result for all beings is certain, the seven actions of body and speech from the ten non-virtues need not always be avoided by bodhisattvas. These seven actions consist of the three non-virtuous actions of body — killing, stealing, and sexual misconduct — plus the four non-virtuous actions of speech — lying, divisive talk, harsh speech, and idle chatter. Only the three non-virtues of mind are never allowed. These are greed, malice, and wrong views — like denying emptiness in the absolute or karmic cause and effect in the relative.

The essence of the bodhisattva's approach is that benefitting beings is more important than abstract rules.[109] According to the vehicle of individual

---

109 For example, during the Second World War, if a Nazi asked you where a group of Jews or Romani was hiding, because he wanted to exterminate them, and you could save them only by lying, as a bodhisattva you would do that. Such actions should be performed if the overall result will be certainly good. Therefore, such altruistic "wrong" behavior is best performed by realized beings who know what the long-term consequences of their actions will be. Thus, in this example, if you saved a few people from the Nazis by lying, but that made them so angry that they destroyed a whole region, the overall result would be bad.

liberation, these seven actions of body and speech are absolute transgressions involving configurations of absolute dharmas, while the illusory selfhood of sentient beings is not a value. Therefore, these seven non-virtuous actions are never allowed, however bad the result may be. That this feature of the path of individual liberation is counterintuitive is easy to know.

The Tantra Path

The tantra path is exponentially more profound and skillful in means than the bodhisattva path. It surpasses the paths of individual liberation and bodhisattvas, as the brilliant light of the sun overcomes the light of the moon and the host of stars. Though these lesser paths are overcome by the brilliance of tantra, all their aspects are still present within it by their essence being included in tantric manifestations.

As the bodhisattva path and its cultivation of relative bodhichitta have many practices of different depths, the same is true of tantra. Highest Yoga Tantra is the most profound of all because it is a path of skillful means that rapidly pierce to ultimate reality. Practitioners are happy to enter it because it produces true happiness.

The traditional tantric path is divided into two stages of generation and completion. The generation stage involves visualizing or perceiving, insofar as possible, the absolute purity of tantric deities and their environment. Most people grasp such visualizations too tightly or too loosely,[110] yet, if there is gratitude and devotion to the Guru and lineage, a strong generation of bodhichitta, and so forth, generation practice can increase or become more elaborate by these blessings. Especially if those quali-

---

110 In the first case, they try to control every aspect of their visualization because they have little trust that the generation stage will develop naturally. In the second case, they have so much trust that the visualization will develop spontaneously that they make no effort to control the prescribed qualities or be mindful of them. Their minds then stray into preoccupation with all kinds of irrelevant phenomena.

ties are strong and manifest purely, fathoming the profound completion stage[111] afterward will become a relatively quick and direct process, with enhancement of realized experience by primordial wisdom naturally occurring.

Today, many tantrikas do not know that they should emphasize these qualities because they do not know the essence of tantrayāna at all. Due to such deficiencies, most practitioners of tantra never reach profound experiences of the natural state. In that case, they tend to grasp and emphasize subsidiary aspects that they can understand and experience, but that are extraneous to the main point. By that, they deny themselves the good fortune of realization, and that is a great loss. Instead, they need to recognize phenomena of their ordinary lives as aspects of their innate nature, and hence, of the fruition path that leads to it. This happens when we regard desire, aversion, and other kleśhas as interconnected aspects of our innate nature.

In particular, in tantric practice, the passion of desire that innately exists within everyone is not regarded as an enemy that requires us to "mobilize for war" and do battle. *Desires can be excellent companions in establishing our desired goals and reliable defenders against all dangers.* The same is true of anger and other kleśhas.

Therefore, compared to the approach of individual liberation, and even the bodhisattva path, the tantric path is relatively easy and convenient. If all people knew how good it is to practice this path, it would be impossible for them to not want to enter into it and feel joy about the prospect.

Through tantra, all the lesser good and bad mental states existing within us can become like perfect jewels. What informed person would not want to enter this rich supporting environment that enhances the good qualities of everyone and everything? *By being in accord with hu-*

---

111   In Khentrul Rinpoché's Jonang school of Tibetan Buddhism, the completion stage consists of non-conceptual practices of the Six Vajra Yogas of *Kālachakra, sbyor ba drug.*

man nature, tantra is in accord with everything. Its supreme skillful means bring all phenomena to the path. All of you should enter into it with joy and delight.

> How to be armed with weapons to fight the enemy, kleśhas,
> How sometimes enemy kleśhas may be transmuted to friends,
> And how they may always be friends; these three kinds of
>   knowledge,
> Characterize the practice found within the three vehicles,
> Of personal liberation, bodhisattvas, and tantra.

> By knowing the distinctions of abandoning, transforming,
> And making all the kleśhas essential parts of the path,
> What is higher and lower and better and worse is known.
> More and more easily, we go higher and higher;
> The higher we go, the easier is the path we go on.

> When we know it is like that, we realize that the three vehicles
> Are a related series, joined by the natural state;
> Knowing that, we know that they are not contradictory,
> We need not see them as yak horns that veer to the left and
>   right.[112]

---

112 "Yak horns…" exemplify something separate and incompatible. Jonangpas say that, if we understand how the three vehicles deal with the kleśhas, we understand that they are a series of successively higher and better applications of the same principles. For example, selfish, attached desire and anger are always renounced, due to realization of something better. What is realized evolves from simple lack of suffering, to the blissful nature, and then to kleśhas that are aspects of that nature being used as part of the path.

6

How the Essence of the Lower Vows Exists within the Higher Ones

Knowledgeable people who evaluate the Tibetan Buddhist lineages agree that they are very extensive. Very few Tibetans understand all the different teachings of Tibetan Buddhism, with their many subdivisions such as the ordinary and extraordinary vehicles. Still less can they explain the reasoning by which the lower and higher paths are said to support each other without contradiction.

The sign of one path being higher than another is its being more closely associated with the unconditioned true nature of things. The sign of one path being lower than another is its being more closely associated with relative causal means outside of that true nature.

In particular, someone who wants to practice the higher teachings of Tibetan Buddhism correctly must know how they include and build upon all the lower Buddhist practices that precede them. Therefore, we should review these different stages from that perspective.

The Individual Liberation Path

The first of these is the path or vehicle of individual liberation, also called the "Lesser Vehicle," and "Foundational Vehicle." It is primarily practiced in five central and eastern Asian countries, Thailand, Myanmar, Śhrī Laṅka, Laos, and Cambodia. At one time, this vehicle was divided into eighteen schools, one of which was the *Sthavira* school. One of its branches, the *Theravāda*, is the only descendant of the eighteen schools to survive today.

The vehicle of individual liberation is called that because the individuals who practice it to liberate themselves from saṃsāric suffering do not want the burden of liberating other sentient beings as well. When we talk about the vehicle or path of individual liberation, we are talking about all aspects of its practice as a path to focus on. The vow of individual liberation is only one aspect of that path; it is taken by male and female renunciates and all householder devotees as well.

Lay practitioners take up to five pratimokṣha or individual liberation vows,[113] while for monks and nuns, the list of vows is much longer. The number of vows also increases with their level of ordination. With the exception of the four defeats, the vinaya specifies strict rules for restoring these vows if they are broken. In general, they cannot be so easily amended as the bodhisattva pledges and tantric samayas.[114]

It is also important to understand that there are other styles of ordination besides that of individual liberation. You can be ordained in individual liberation, bodhisattva, or tantric style. Tibetan and Chinese mo-

---

113 Against killing, stealing, sexual misconduct, lying, and taking intoxicants.

114 Bodhisattva pledges, and tantric samayas, totalling three types of "vows," along with the individual liberation vows. "Pledge" for the bodhisattva vows, and "samaya" for the tantric vows, are Rinpoché's preference, as the sense of "vow" is not the same in these three vehicles. All these types of vows are described by Rinpoché in detail in his book series *Unveiling Your Sacred Truth*.

nastics take the individual liberation vow with bodhisattva motivation. The Tibetans also take tantric samayas. Frequently though, in practice, Tibetan monastics regard their individual liberation approach as predominant. Then they are actually monastics of individual liberation, whatever qualities of the other two vehicles they say they possess.

If the practitioner wants to focus on the path of individual liberation, it is important to know their vows and the processes of amending violations very well as these processes can be quite difficult. Unfortunately, some monastics who focus on this path follow cultural customs rather than the main points of the vows and the process of amending violations prescribed in the vinaya, so it is easy to know that no good fruition on this path will be attained by them. On the other hand, *for those keeping individual liberation vows, but focusing on higher vehicles as their main path, the sense in which these vows are kept changes*; this is because their essence is regarded as being included within their higher vows if they are properly kept as described in the next section.

Bodhisattva and Tantra Paths

The Buddhist teachings that spread in China, Japan, Vietnam, and Korea are those of the Great Vehicle sūtras. *Adherents of these teachings accept the liberation of all sentient beings as their responsibility.*

The bodhichitta pledge of the Great Vehicle is also fundamental in the Tibetan Buddhist lineages. In the New Translation schools other than the Nyingma, it is enhanced by four classes of tantra, Kriyā, Charya, Yoga, and Anuttarayoga (Highest Yoga Tantra.) The Nyingma, or old translation school, instead of Anuttarayoga, has Mahāyoga, Anuyoga, and Atiyoga or Dzogchen, six tantric vehicles in all. These tantric teachings are mainly practiced in Tibet, Bhutan, India, Nepal, Mongolia, Japan,[115] other places

---

115 Shingon Buddhism (真言宗, Shingon-shū), though most Japanese Buddhists belong to

in the Himalayas like Ladakh, and ethnically Tibetan parts of China.

This last kind of Buddhism first spread to Tibet from India and other countries, including some located where Pakistan and Afghanistan are today. It then spread from Tibet to the countries listed above. In addition to taking the *refuges* of the individual liberation vehicle and generating the bodhichitta of the Great Vehicle, adherents must learn how to practice many paths of tantra without contradiction.

In countries like China, where the Great Vehicle is well-known, only certain aspects of tantra have spread. Since most of these powerful teachings are absent there, when we say that these countries practice the "Great Vehicle," we mean that the Great Vehicle sūtra teachings are found there and hardly any of the tantric ones.

Not surprisingly, the correct way of entering into the Tibetan Buddhist teachings that include tantra is different from the approach in China. There is one tradition of taking the individual liberation vows using actual liturgies of individual liberation. Though Tibetans take these vows, their motivation for doing so accords with the Great Vehicle approach that all sentient beings should be liberated from saṃsāra. However, if you wonder whether everyone in the Tibetan Buddhist lineages is required to take vows of individual liberation using the corresponding liturgies, particular individuals do what is necessary and suitable for them.

It is traditional for all Tibetan Buddhists to take the vow of individual liberation, but individuals with sufficient ability are usually allowed to enter into tantra practice right away. If you wonder whether they are allowed to omit the sūtra path of the Great Vehicle as well, it is indeed the same. Qualified individuals need not receive the bodhisattva pledges formally through liturgies of the Great Vehicle before they enter into tantra.

There are two ways for Tibetans to enter directly into tantra. In the usual way, the vows of the individual liberation and bodhisattva vehicles

---

Great Vehicle branches like Zen and Nichiren.

occur in an abbreviated form in the liturgy of their tantric empowerment. In that case, they enter the three vehicles successively, like the steps of a staircase, with the empowerments of tantra attained at the top. This gradual approach with three steps is the way most Tibetans enter into tantra.

In the extraordinary way, when the tantric samayas are received, the lower individual liberation vows and bodhisattva pledges are regarded as being implicitly received as well, because their essence is included within the higher samayas or secret tantric commitments.

To offer a metaphor of how the essence of lower teachings is included within higher ones, individuals with very high mental capacity sometimes skip elementary school and go directly to middle school.[116] Similarly, individuals of sufficiently sharp mental capacity can master the individual liberation vehicle, which is comparable to elementary school without explicitly practicing it because its essence is included in the bodhisattva vehicle, which is comparable to middle school.[117]

A few geniuses can learn almost anything on their own, so they begin their formal studies in high school or even at university. Similarly, the sharpest students enter the path of tantra directly. Excellent tantric practitioners do not need to study the lower vehicles explicitly because

---

116 There, for example, they are able to solve problems of algebra, write essays about history based on books they have read, and so forth because they have learned the basic skills of reading, writing, and arithmetic on their own, without needing to attend elementary school. Then, they go on to learn the higher levels of those skills in middle school.

117 For example, the individual liberation vehicle teaches that there is no personal self, so being attached to kleśhas of the three poisons which motivate actions for its benefit is delusive. The teachings of the second turning of the wheel of Dharma of the bodhisattva vehicle teach that there is neither a personal self nor a selfhood of phenomena. Therefore, there is no personal self who has the kleśhas, no kleśhas, no actions inspired by them, and no phenomena that are objects of those actions. Being attached to *any* of these is delusive. People who have mastered the view of the bodhisattva vehicle do not need to study the view of the vehicle of individual liberation separately because the view of the bodhisattva vehicle includes it and much more.

the essence of both the individual liberation and bodhisattva vehicles exist within tantra. For such persons, the vows of the first two vehicles need not be explicitly taken, and the study and practice of them need not be explicitly engaged in. They know all they need to know to understand the goal of all Buddhist studies — wisdom that knows the ultimate meaning of life and how to enjoy great happiness.[118] Still, if they study elementary knowledge anyway, no harm is done.

"If going directly to the main point in such a way is possible, why does anyone need to receive the individual liberation vows and bodhisattva pledges explicitly at all?" Most people are incapable of learning middle-level Buddhist knowledge like correct philosophical reasoning without explicit study of elementary knowledge. Without that, they have no hope of achieving the ultimate goal of their studies. Nothing can be achieved by pretending otherwise. Students with sufficient intelligence to follow the step-by-step approach can still achieve that ultimate goal, but they must explicitly take the first two types of vows and engage in the corresponding studies and practices. Those who cannot follow even the path of individual liberation cannot succeed in the Buddha-Dharma in their present life.

"When the vows of individual liberation, the bodhisattva pledges, and the tantric samayas have all been received, either separately or implicitly in a tantric empowerment liturgy, do those who have received these three types of vows have to keep them all?" They do, but the sense in which they have to be kept may differ.

If people received the vows of individual liberation and bodhisattva pledges when they were quite young, and later they enter into tantra

---

118 To offer further examples, in ordinary life, some people have never attended any formal studies at all, but are very skilled in their projects and attain great success both in their professional and private lives. Others who cannot even read — and, therefore, are incapable of understanding any reasonings from philosophical views — are still able to discover profound meanings of life and attain happiness and success, which are the main reasons for the formal studies they did not need.

and keep the tantric samayas, the literal words of their former individual liberation vows and bodhisattva pledges seem to contradict their new tantric samayas. However, their three vows are not actually in conflict because the essence of the individual liberation vows and bodhisattva pledges are included within the tantric samayas, and the first two may be kept non-literally. Even if neither is kept in an external manner, their essence is kept, and so they are not regarded as violated.

In brief, *if only the tantric samayas are perfectly kept, that is enough. Whether the individual liberation vows and bodhisattva pledges need to be literally kept depends on whether the next higher one is kept.* For example, if people cannot properly keep their tantric samayas but can keep their bodhisattva pledges, then the essence of the individual liberation vows will be included within their bodhisattva pledges. In this case, the bodhisattva pledges must be kept literally, and if they are kept, even if the individual liberation vows are not kept literally, that practitioner's continuum will not be defiled by transgressions.

If they cannot correctly keep either their tantric samayas or their bodhisattva pledges, then they must keep their individual liberation vows literally. By keeping their individual liberation vows as pure as possible, as they progress, they will be able to keep their bodhisattva pledges and their tantric samayas as well, even if they cannot relate to those in their present situation.[119]

As said, the *tantric samayas are like sunlight, bodhisattva pledges are like moonlight, and individual liberation vows are like dim starlight.* When you have sunlight, you do not need moonlight; but you do need it at night

---

119 In both cases, where keeping the tantric samayas and bodhisattva pledges is not possible, these limitations can be remedied by regular purification practice. In the Tibetan tradition, a powerful way of purification is the Vajrasattva practice, with visualization and mantra recitation based on the four powers of support, regret, confession, and resolve. Rinpoché explains this in detail in his previous books *Hidden Treasure of the Profound Path* and *Unveiling Your Sacred Truth — Book 2.*

when the sun is not shining. On moonless nights, you can see very little by starlight, but you still need it because it is better than nothing at all.

Nevertheless, in special situations there may be a benefit in keeping the individual liberation vows literally, even when doing this is not necessary for oneself; for example, when doing so generates faith in the minds of others.[120] The analogous statement is true for the bodhisattva pledges.

According to the principle of the higher vows including the essence of the lower ones, monastics who properly keep their tantric samayas can truthfully say that they practice tantra without breaking their monastic vows in essence.[121] However, if monastics who do not keep their samayas try to use tantra as an excuse for breaking their individual liberation vows, they will break all their vows, with dire consequences. In general, practitioners who are unsure of their own capacity to practice the higher paths as their focus — for example, if they are not sure they are keeping the samayas, and are not sure whether they are practicing even the bodhisattva path correctly — are wise to follow the rules of the individual liberation vehicle literally. This "safe" approach is sure to keep their practice moving toward liberation.

In brief, *whether those who have achieved all the main points of the individual liberation, bodhisattva, and tantra paths are keeping their three vows cannot be evaluated by their external conduct alone.* Apparent faults and virtues may arise, but cannot resolve the question of whether they are keeping their vows. Making judgments on that basis alone is always

---

120 A common example is when a nun or monk who is a genuine tantrika—and as such does not have to keep their individual liberation vows literally— still do keep their lower vows literally, in special situations, for the sake of others.

121 Monastic vows are included in the category of pratimokṣa or individual liberation vows. Thus, as explained above, if monastics keep their tantric samayas exemplarily, with incredible pure perception, devotion, appreciation, and so forth, they are allowed to practice all aspects of tantra, including the Path of Desire, without losing their status as monastics.

inappropriate.[122] It is also a source of many misunderstandings in the relationship between Guru and student, and in evaluating the conduct of any accomplished spiritual teacher.

All who keep the Great Vehicle bodhisattva vows,
Keep the vows of Lesser Vehicle pratimokṣha.
If the tantric vows are followed properly,
So are those of pratimokṣha and bodhichitta.
If a lower vow is kept, keeping higher ones is uncertain,
But all who keep a higher vow keep the lower ones.

Prātimokṣha, bodhisattva, and tantric vows,
Exist as upward-evolving qualities,
In the sense that those that are higher include the ones that are lower.
Though higher vows do not rely on lower ones,
Nevertheless, they include the lower ones' qualities.

---

122 One common example of this is when Lamas who are also monastics behave like a perfect monastic when giving public teachings; then, when going out in the world to perform diverse altruistic activities and connect with different sentient beings, they can manifest according to their bodhisattva conduct and not strictly according to the individual liberation conduct that would prevent them from performing such activities; moreover, when it is necessary to train their close disciples, they can display unconventional behavior as tantrikas who are not afraid of the naked truth of reality. Outsiders who do not understand that they are acting to fulfill the needs of different beings may mistakenly judge them to be hypocrites. However, Rinpoché is not saying that all persons acting in these ways are necessarily perfect in their conduct of keeping their three vows, but that we should not judge them by their external behavior alone. It is helpful to remember that even in everyday life, we are constantly changing our behavior and style according to our roles. The same person can be a mother, a doctor, a university professor, a sister, a driver, a volunteer, a lover, and so forth all at the same time and without contradiction.

Thus, growing up occurs depending on children's growth,
And there is that dependence, as long as they are growing;
But after that, vanished youth no longer supports maturity,
Though maturity is the completion of youthful qualities.[123]

---

123 Tibetans say, "Maturity does not rely on youth." Nevertheless, youth evolves into maturity.

PART THREE

Bringing Kleśhas to the Path

As *desire and lack of desire are intrinsic mental phenomena,*
They can be transformed, but can never be abandoned.
For that reason, making the kleśhas into a path,
When we analyze in detail, is the way of all the vehicles.
Gendün Chöpel,
Treatise on Desire

Introduction

The crown ornament of all the learned ones, Gendün Chöpel, sounded a warning bell[124] to alert the modern age to coming problems when he wrote,

89. As desire and lack of desire are intrinsic mental phenomena,
     They can be transformed, but can never be abandoned.
     For that reason, ma king the kleśhas into a path,
     When we analyze in detail, is the way of all the vehicles.[125]

The deep meaning of what is taught there is unfathomable by literalistic scholars. The solar rays of these changeless, diamond words shine their revelation on us all from the lofty space of the sky, and so now I should write at length about them in these next chapters.

---

124 Monasteries often have large bells to alert and summon the monastics. Similarly, monastics are often woken from sleep in the morning by the blowing of a horn made from a conch, and so a visionary person is called "morning conch" because they try to wake Tibetans from ignorance.

125 If we analyze carefully, the lower vehicles do not destroy passion as they claim. Monastics of the path of individual liberation who see desire as an enemy to be abandoned actually bring saṃsāric desire to the path by changing its object so that they desire to renounce saṃsāra and practice the path to nirvāṇa. Bodhisattvas transmute ordinary desire into a pure desire to experience the empty way things are that is free from kleśhas. Tantrikas use desire in skillful ways to progress quicker on the path.

The kleśhas are described in many different ways in the Buddhist textual tradition. In the *Abhidharma*, among the fifty-one mental factors are the six root kleśhas and the twenty subsidiary ones. In tantra, kleśhas consisting of eighty kinds of conceptualized emotional states are well-known. There is no need to discuss every one of them since their essence is the five poisons or the six root kleśhas.[126]

In tantra, in "making the kleśhas into a path," for example, the natural anger within all people need not be abandoned. Bringing anger to the path is accomplished by knowing how to employ phenomena of anger to facilitate benefit and happiness.

To offer an analogy, if we know how to use nuclear power for the sake of others, that inconceivable power can establish unsurpassable benefit. If we do not know how to control that power but try to use it anyway, the danger of disaster is extremely great. That danger is not a defect of nuclear power but is due to our own ignorance. Similarly, our kleśhas are not something with an unavoidably bad nature that can only be abandoned. *Our kleśhas are a problem only because we do not know how to use them.* Here too, our ignorance is our actual problem.

In bringing kleśhas to the path, it does not mean indulging in them without any boundaries at all. That is the path to the lower realms, not the path to enlightenment. Nor does it mean that we relax and release attachment to all the kleśhas in your continuum. If that were possible, whenever any typical desire or anger arose, even people who had never trained on the path could simply stop being attached to them whenever they liked, but that ordinary people cannot do this is quite clear. Everyone knows that human nature is not like that.

What is human nature like? An explanation can be given by pointing out the ultimate nature of things that is common to the paths of sūtra and tantra. For example, if we can practice through resting in the experience of

---

126 All these lists are in the glossary.

the ultimate nature of the kleśhas as Sugatagarbha, we will never be overwhelmed by the flames of the kleśhas any more than we would be by jumping into a lotus pond.[127] In this case, these poisons will become medicine. If the level of our experience is sufficiently high, a proliferation of the kleśhas will spontaneously cease; if the level is intermediate, non-proliferation will occur just by remembering the real nature of the kleśhas.

In doing this, the main focus of practice is the experience of Sugatagarbha, the nature and ground of all phenomena. In addition, we should *be mindful of any ordinary kleśhas in our minds as aspects of that ground.* If we do that, we will gradually enter into very high levels of practice as if we were ascending the stairs of a staircase. Then, we will no longer have to be worried about the kleśhas within us. Those *kleśhas do not have to be abandoned because if we persist we will no longer be controlled by them; they will be controlled by us.*[128]

---

127 This is how that common nature is explained by the author's Jonang school. Some other schools explain it in terms of emptiness of self-nature, as taught in the second turning of the wheel of Dharma. This statement is reminiscent of those in the *Lotus Sūtra*, especially one in Chapter 25, "Suppose that vicious ones push you into a fiery pit. / Abide in [Avalokiteśhvara] and the fiery pit / Will turn into a delightful [lotus] pond."

128 Though sometimes our practice may focus on the kleśhas' empty appearance, following a sūtric approach, we need to keep in mind that sūtra and tantra have no ultimate contradiction.

1

Bringing Anger to the Path

If the reasons presented above are exemplified by anger, anger is not something that must always be abandoned. If anger is made serviceable, it can bring great benefit. In training on the tantric path, *we do not need to change the intrinsic nature of anger; instead, we change the reason for anger, its object, our attitude toward it, and so forth.*

When educated people who want to be tantric practitioners ask their teachers questions like, "How do we bring anger to the path?" a common answer is, "Recognize that your anger does not truly exist. Its essence is emptiness. In absolute truth, your anger is Vajrasattva, who represents the vajra-like primordial wisdom." Such answers are true from the viewpoint of doctrine. However, as guides for practice, they are mostly empty words that should be disregarded because they are unaccompanied by instructions on how to apply them.

Even when correct understanding can be acquired from such an answer, it is usually very hard to connect that understanding to any particular action that we might perform. Only a few exceptional individuals can follow high-level instructions like, "Stop focusing on your relative attachment to anger and look at the absolute essence of anger. That one ability will liberate all." Traversing the whole path in a single leap like that is generally only within the sphere of beings with the highest ability who are experiencing the fruition of good karma resulting from extensive practice in former lives.

Ordinary people, more than likely, will receive only a dry, abstract understanding from such answers. We can be pretty sure from former experience that no true benefit will come to them. Practitioners on all levels should not pretend to be satisfied by answers that make no sense to them. They need an answer that tells them how to practice properly according to their own capabilities. Such an answer for beginners might be as follows.

In general, "bringing the kleśhas to the path" does not mean that the kleśhas should be left unchecked so that we act on their impulses, whatever they may be, without holding back. The meaning is that anger and so forth can be put to use as part of the tantric path rather than having to be repressed or abandoned. Nevertheless, many tantrikas may not have developed the skills required to bring powerful kleśhas to the path. Then their only choice is to temporarily abandon them, as they would on the sūtra path.

When typical anger arises in the mind of those who have never trained on the path, they usually lose control of themselves like a car that loses its brakes. This helpless state is not bringing anger to the path. It is not part of the path to happiness and benefit at all. The anger in these beginners' minds is powerful, yet that power, in its present form, cannot be used to perform good actions in the name of love and compassion. Being helpless in the face of pain makes that power manifest irresistibly as saṃsāric anger, malice, hatred, and so forth. Lacking the necessary knowledge, such people cannot make their anger controllable. They do not know how to recognize that their anger, from the time it arises, is a clear and luminous aspect of the absolute nature of things.

In general, when anger first arises in you, your mind experiences discontent. The anger controls you so that you have very little autonomy. You may very well need to abandon your anger in such a situation. However, do not just despondently wallow in your defeat. That anger in your mind can supply you with energy. If you can gain the ability to control it, that energy can be used however you like. If you can do that, your anger need not necessarily be abandoned. Consider how much good will result from using your anger, and how much good will result from abandoning it. Choose whatever course has the best result. The main point is that your anger need not be abandoned just because it is a kleśha.[129]

Recall that anger commonly motivates cruelty to others. Observe whether your anger has such an attitude of cruelty. Even if it does, you do not need to abandon it if you can change its object and direction. The powerful nature of anger may be left as it is as long as your anger and malice are redirected to something appropriate. Then, if you see that the action of your anger will no longer be harmful and that its result will be beneficial, you should not abandon it.

For example, when an ordinary person who has not trained on the path is angry with others, a cruel attitude arises toward them, and there is a desire for them to suffer. When you are making anger into the path, the direction of that cruelty must be changed. Otherwise, your proliferating thoughts may become so strongly fixated that later you will be unable to change them.[130]

In such a case, at first, you may think something like, "The object of my anger is that person who did such and such harmful actions to me or to my close friends and relatives. Therefore, I want to take revenge by

---

129 Paraphrasing Dr. Adrian Hekel in an April 2023 message: often anger manifests too quickly for us to be able to think about how we might change the object of anger and so forth. One way to get around this is to use a journal to reflect on specific angry interactions with others, identify how our ego responses got in the way of a beneficial response, and then write down things that we could say or do more skillfully in future situations. Typical angry reactions often arise in response to a feeling of powerlessness; recognizing this relationship helps us not be overwhelmed by our own anger.

130 Not paying attention to this could, for example, allow strong feelings of grudge, spite, rancor, resentment, and so forth to take root in your mind.

doing such and such harm to this person." Such a thought may be clear and conscious, but it may also arise unconsciously, deep beneath the surface, and be shown just by angry looks, a pained expression, and so forth.

To bring this anger to the path, some aspects of its focus must be changed. To do this, with an undisturbed mind, think the following, "This person did this harm to me. If her bad actions are not stopped, she will harm others with similar bad actions. Even if those others are not successfully harmed, habitual propensities to commit similar bad actions will be established in her mind. If she does not recognize the danger of this familiarity with such malignant ways, she will continue to do such things. And if such feelings and actions cannot be quickly stopped, she will be severely harmed by her bad karma. Therefore, I must try to stop these feelings and actions. If peaceful means are not sufficient, I should try to stop them by wrathful means."

By thinking in this way, you do not abandon your anger and malice, you just change the object of their focus. You are no longer angry with the person who harmed you but with anger itself, its causes, and the resulting harm. You want to defeat them because of the harm they cause. Due to that change of focus, your anger is no longer something that should be abandoned.

If you have sufficient confidence to adopt this means, making the kleśhas into the path actually begins. Otherwise, even if your understanding above is correct, if there is not enough confidence, you will need to hold back your anger temporarily, using whatever suitable antidote you are familiar with. In this case, though an observer may see no overt anger manifesting in you, it is just being suppressed until more confidence is gained. In any case, as the focus should be what is of benefit to others, even if confidence in your wrathful performance is high, when the object of your anger does not benefit much from it, you may need to let aside your wrathful approach and investigate other skillful ways for overcoming the situation.

People often fall into extremes regarding anger. Some get furious at the slightest provocation or over simple misunderstandings in day-to-day life. The people around them avoid speaking plainly to them out of trepidation concerning their reaction. Others are so fragile that they cannot deal with angry reactions at all. People around them become afraid to show anger externally and so pretend to always be calm and unaffected. Fearing conflicts, people avoid talking about issues that need to be addressed. This creates even more confused conflict later on.

In general, many people in highly educated Western countries think that anger is always bad. Though anger arises in everyone, they pretend it is not there. Rather than benefiting from this concealment, these people experience severe harm. Trying to suppress and ignore anger[131] is like taking a pain-killing medicine to eliminate the pain of a disease and ignoring the disease itself. For a time, the disease seems to be overcome by doing that. Deep down though, karmic propensities of disease are being constantly accumulated. Eventually, you will get even more painfully sick than ever.

Similarly, rather than trying to suppress your anger, know how to use your anger by changing the object of your anger to something appropriate. If anger arises internally, let it manifest externally. People may perceive this as inappropriate, but at least there is no danger of greater harm occurring later. If you do not do that, as your anger continues to gather internally, one day it will be impossible to resist. Then, it will certainly release itself in the form of seriously bad actions in spite of all you do to resist it.

---

131 Rinpoché is referring here to people who always repress their anger because of the moral condemnation they will suffer and so forth. As explained above, he is *not* teaching that anger should never be held back.

How Beginners Should Train

If a practitioner with only a little experience is wondering how to proceed, it is done like this. If anger arises within you, *first, consider whether this anger will produce a good result.* If you are confident that there will be a good fruition, you need not abandon that anger. *You must also ascertain whether your anger will benefit the object of your anger.* If it will not, consider how, by changing the object of your anger, you can change its effect on your original object to one of benefit.

If you are *not* confident that the conduct motivated by your anger will have a good result, think like this, "The individual who is the object of my anger could not help doing their bad behavior. My anger arose from external causes that hinder my freedom of action as well. That person who, like me, has little autonomy, has given me an auspicious occasion of recognizing my own limitations." Then, pleasant feelings of compassion or kindness toward the object of your anger will naturally begin to arise. If that does not eliminate your anger, try again and again to find a viewpoint from which that typical anger will not arise.

If you want to go deeper, think in this way, "Anger is a delusion that results from not knowing how things are. Just as when I am drunk, when I get angry, I do not recognize the way things are. Not only do factual errors accumulate, saṃsāric anger temporarily conceals both its relative harm and its absolute nature. Anger results in harm only when we fail to recognize these two. When that failure occurs, angry individuals are controlled by their anger."

If the real essence of anger is recognized, relative[132] anger toward a person who has harmed you dissolves. It then becomes great, absolute anger against the hosts of *māras*, and that is a virtue that should not be abandoned. Remember that the ultimate nature of anger is Vajrasattva,

---

132 Referring to relative truth.

and let that thought create a gap in your obscuring anger, filled by a flash of the ultimate, divine nature. On one level, the relative drama of anger continues, but on another, you are a dispassionate watcher in a bubble of non-attachment. From there, you can consider the possible results of your anger objectively and redirect its object to the one that will produce the best result.

Know whether incidental thoughts of cruelty to others exist in your angry mind. Remember that the karmic appearances of two separate persons, one who has anger and one who is the object of that anger are delusive phenomena. If the two of you were truly separate, you could have no causal relationships that would allow you to perceive each other's actions and react to them with feelings like anger. As you recall again and again that your apparent anger consists of delusive appearances, your mind will gradually evolve until your anger becomes workable.[133] You need not do this with every angry thought. By being thoroughly mindful of even one such thought within a situation of anger, your anger will eventually have a different result.

Now you are not abandoning anger. You are making anger into the path because learning how to see your anger as it is, allows you to experience the nature of phenomena. Being mindful of even a little experience of ultimate reality pacifies cruel thoughts of saṃsāric anger. Losing self-control, so that you are unable to change or re-direct them, will then be impossible.

How to Train With More Skilful Means

Once a practitioner has dealt with the kleśhas long enough to have developed more skillful means, the procedure is done like this. Think, "When

---

133 If there is no identification with the feeling of saṃsāric anger, then even when it arises strongly, anger will be workable.

I act against an individual who is the object of my anger, I am lost in the deluded phenomena of being angry. My actions, as well as her actions, are the result of being deceived by deluded appearances. Acting in this way only strengthens my habitual propensities for experiencing these deluded phenomena again. However, *in reality, all of these phenomena are the natural state — great, all-pervading, and encompassing Dharmadhātu.*"

Contemplate the natural state where anger, the person who is angry, and the object of anger are one and non-dual. Let your one-pointed mind be that *true Selfhood.* If conceptualized thoughts and apprehensions of anything else arise, loudly shouting PHAṬ,[134] go into groundless, rootless, bright clarity. When shouting PHAṬ is not appropriate, you can do so only in your mind.

Training for Those Who Have Prepared for Higher Practice and Conclusion

For those who have developed proficiency by training for some time in applying these instructions, the path gradually transforms the phenomena of the kleśhas so that they become forever workable. To increase that proficiency, when you are alone, practice with an imagined object of anger,

1. Generate one such object in your mind to make anger arise.[135]
2. Then, pacify or control that anger.
3. Make it useful with any of the various means explained above.
4. Then, make anger arise again as before.
5. When you have made such efforts again and again, finally, you can

---

134 A "mystical" Sanskrit syllable, used as an exclamation and incantation, often appearing at the end of wrathful mantras, in order to dispel external, internal, and hidden obstacles.

135 The object does not necessarily have to be another being, it can be a specific situation, one's own limitations, etc.

make anger arise any time you like. When you no longer want to work with it, you will be able to let it easily vanish.

When you have attained real autonomy in that way, you will be victorious over anger from then on. Then, why can you not say that, to that extent, you are a Victorious One?

Regarding the differences between unworkable anger that should be abandoned and workable anger that can be brought to the tantric path because its essence is realized as the true essence of phenomena: (1) the focal object and the motivation are different; (2) the level of confidence is different; (3) the amount of benefit achieved by the fruition is different. All the other qualities are similar.

For example, (1) the motivation of typical, unworkable anger is a selfish wish. Sometimes it appears to be for the sake of others, but its root is self-cherishing. *When anger is seen to have the essence of the path, its temporal focal object is the benefit for both oneself and others, but the ultimate focal object should always be the benefit for others.* (2) Confidence in a favorable fruition for ordinary anger is extremely low, but for anger brought to the path, it is high. (3) For ordinary anger, good fruition with great benefit is almost impossible; but for anger brought to the path, it is likely.

Through repeated practice, autonomy in regard to becoming angry is eventually reached. Being able to create that kind of usable anger is very important because it has the nature of the tantric path. Still, someone might wonder, "The sūtra vehicles make all phenomena that are not kleśhas aspects of the causal path. Why does tantra say without qualification that kleśhas are what must be made into aspects of the path?"

This characterization of tantra is misleading. All phenomena are brought to the path in tantra. Saying that kleśhas should be brought to the path does not exclude other phenomena being brought to the path as well as they are in the sūtra vehicles. Moreover, in the tantric approach, whatever kleśhas arise are brought to the path. Yet, the point is not that we must always be generating phenomena of anger, desire, and so forth so that we can bring kleśhas to the path.

The kleśhas cause the suffering of saṃsāra. Making only non-kleśhas aspects of the path can never be a sufficient cause for liberation from suffering because the kleśhas will continue to cause suffering. Since kleśhas are not made part of sūtra paths, those paths can reach enlightenment only through eliminating kleśhas with antidotes that are not kleśhas. Success at doing that is rare. When kleśhas are brought to the tantric path, freedom from suffering caused by the kleśhas is attained without having to abandon them. That approach is more in accord with human nature than the sūtra approach, so the chances of success are much higher.

If we do not know how to bring kleśhas to the path at all, we do not know how to practice tantra. Then, the only available paths are sūtra paths that abandon kleśhas. We may still tell ourselves that what we are doing is part of a tantric path, but it is *not*. However, if we think that abandoning kleśhas is *always* wrong in tantra, not only is that incorrect, negative results are possible if we fail to use them skillfully. Temporarily abandoning or holding back kleśhas in complex cases can be a part of a tantric path that ultimately leads to bringing them to the path.

To realize that the kleśhas are merely empty delusions as is done in some presentations of the second turning of the wheel of Dharma is not sufficient for tantric practice.[136] To give an example, when the generation stage practice of visualizing the pure phenomena of the father and mother deities in union is discussed, these days, the phenomena of the deities are often said to be empty of essence, as taught in the second turning, in the sense that they do not truly exist. If such an explanation is taken liter-

---

136 We cannot work with the kleśhas if they have been emptied into nothingness. The kleśhas' relative qualities are seen to be empty in that way, but those qualities are also re-evaluated in tantric practice as aspects of absolute Sugatagarbha that are also qualities of the ultimate kāyas of Buddhahood and the wisdoms of the absolute deities. That allows the kleśhas to be worked with as part of the path.

ally, it is useless for tantra. Tantric practice requires us to experience the limitless pure qualities of the deities and their environment as they are and then employ skillful means of working with them.

Saying that anger arises from aversion is true in terms of relative causation. However, to understand tantra, we must also understand how aversion, anger, and related phenomena are aspects of the developing energy of the absolute mind. How can aspects of the fundamentally virtuous ultimate mind be bad qualities? If anger was a fault from the viewpoint that sees the ultimate, then the absolute aspects of the five poisons, the five wisdoms, would also be viewed as faults, but that is impossible.

"How can malice, wanting to harm others, be classified as a good quality?" Malicious anger arises due to ignorant grasping and cherishing of a relative self that wants to harm those who are seen as hindering the wishes of that self; however, that does not entail that anger and malice are faults in all situations. Is the exemplary courage of great heroines and heroes a fault? Their courage is the great strength of mind by which they are capable of fighting evil enemies. When righteous malice toward such enemies exists in their minds, how can that heroic resolve be classified as a fault?

If that malice invalidates these heroes' and heroines' courage, are they cowards? Surely not. Cowards are incapable of fighting enemies. However powerful enemies may be, heroes and heroines will fearlessly stand up to them. The ultimate heroes and heroines are bodhisattvas because a heroic attitude that resolves, "I will establish all beings on the level of perfect Buddhahood," abides deeply within their hearts. The true scope of their transcendent, heroic qualities is only perceivable by pure perception.[137]

---

137 As explained in the glorious *Kālachakra Tantra*, the ultimate bodhisattva warriors are the Kalkī Kings and Queens of Śhambhala. They will lead us in overcoming obstacles to the coming of a second Golden Age on our Earth. According to Rinpoché, the time has come for all of us who are compassionate to prepare to join with them. If we follow the example of these tantric heroes and heroines in compassionately overcoming the self-centered approach of opponents of the Golden Age, we will know how to bring anger to the path.

2

Bringing Pride to the Path

The preceding chapter about anger is more elaborate than the subsequent ones because we constantly face anger in our daily lives. We can see with our own eyes the bad results that arise from dealing with it poorly. It is clear that most of us do not know how to use anger properly, so I thought it would be beneficial to write about it in detail. Nonetheless, the following kleśhas, presented here more briefly, are also powerful means for us to embrace in our practice. Once we read how to bring anger to the path, we can apply similar principles we applied to anger to other kleśhas like pride, and the former explanations of these principles do not need to be repeated one by one.

Many people say that pride is being pleased with yourself or being indignantly irritated, when you are crossed. Actually, pride is a kind of arrogance. When someone thinks, "I am better than others," or looks down upon them, that is arrogant, saṃsāric pride.

Is pride always a kleśha and a fault? No. *Realistic pride is a good quality; without pride in what is worthy and appropriate, we could not recognize virtue at all.* The same is not true for anger. Some anger, like heroic anger at injustice, is virtuous; but anger is not required to recognize virtue.

On the other hand, unrealistic, inappropriate pride is always a fault. As an example, if a person has one hundred good qualities, but with mistaken pride claims he has two hundred, his pride is inappropriate. Since, in this case, the truth is clearly evident, the example need not be explained at length.

Worthy and appropriate pride is necessary because people need it to recognize the good qualities within them. Without that recognition, there is no bigger loss in the world. For example, if a poor man has 500 gold pieces but does not realize their value, he is no better off than if he threw them away as garbage. Similarly, *the virtues within us must first be recognized so that we can know how to use them.* That recognition is a kind of pride.

Worthy and suitable pride is also called "strength of mind" and "confidence." No action that needs to be accomplished would ever be undertaken without it. For example, practitioners of Highest Yoga Tantra desire quick attainment of Buddhahood. To be able to perform the practice by which Buddhahood is attained, they must have strong confidence that Buddha nature intrinsically exists within them. Pride in having the good qualities that are important to advance on the path is absolutely necessary for all practice.

Additionally, at the time of practicing the Highest Yoga Tantra path, transcendent pride that your true nature is the same as that of the yidam deity whose realization is the same as that of the Buddha is called divine pride or the pride of the yidam deity. Without having that pure perception as the ground and root of your practice, there is no way for you to practice the stages of generation and completion on a high level. All other aspects of practice within the Highest Yoga Tantra path similarly presuppose pure perception.

3

Bringing Jealousy to the Path[138]

When there is the kleśha of typical jealousy or envy, the apprehension of others' excellent qualities or attainments is so intolerable that we can hardly bear to perceive them. It is as if feelings of jealousy were solid objects, and our shoulders (*phrag*) were too narrow (*dog*) to carry them; and so, in Tibetan, jealousy is called *phrag dog*.

Because becoming overwhelmed by such comparisons is avoidable, we can say that jealousy is less realistic than anger, which usually arises from aversion to something in our environment that may harm us and has to be dealt with in some way.

Since jealousy, like anger, must be brought to the path in tantra, we can use our unbearable distress about others' good qualities and belongings to create an aspiration that even better qualities may arise in ourselves.[139] Then we will not have to be jealous anymore.

The principal focus must be changed from resenting the apparently superior qualities and possessions of others to trying to increase our own virtues. This feeling of "competition" energizes you. While you do not wish them to fail, still, others' success motivates your determination and

---

138 How to bring jealousy to the path will be addressed again in Part Five 5 chapter 1.

139 This is similar to what some people call "good envy."

discipline to progress on the path even quicker than they do, so that you can help them. As a consequence, your self-centered, narrow view will expand into benevolence.

The usual antidote to overcoming jealousy is to rejoice in other people's success and good qualities. By doing this, others' success becomes a cause of your own happiness, and additionally, you accumulate merit in your mind stream. Yet here you are not only rejoicing in what others have done or have, but you are also becoming much more diligent in attaining similar goals.

In particular, when our good qualities reach a higher level than before, we must never think "this is enough" until we reach complete enlightenment. Before that occurs, dissatisfaction must always motivate further effort so that we can swiftly accomplish the path.[140]

---

140 If you want to go deeper, for connecting with the ultimate aspect of jealousy, you can meditate on it as the Buddha Amoghasiddhi (Infallible Accomplishment) who embodies the all-accomplishing wisdom. You can refer to the advice in the chapter on anger regarding meditation on the ultimate aspect of anger as Vajrasattva.

4

Bringing Miserliness to the Path

Miserliness is excessive self-cherishing which is a direct sign of excessive attachment to possessions and enjoyments. The kleśha of typical miserliness, avarice, or greed is not one of the root or main poisons, but one of the twenty subsidiary afflictions. Nevertheless, I wanted to write about it here briefly because it commonly causes harm in human life and because it becomes very useful when brought to the path.

The kleśha of avarice and the virtue of thriftiness have a similar essence, but the cause and conditions from which they arise are dissimilar and they also have different foci and actions. The avarice that becomes part of the path views situations with far-seeing eyes, contemplating large-scale plans to produce wealth for all, and so forth. It involves care for small details and extensive effort to ensure that possessions are well-managed. The focus is avoiding waste and the wrong use of wealth. The fruition resembles generosity in establishing extensive enjoyment and benefits. *The ultimate focus must be on creating favorable conditions for establishing these goals for all beings.*

If we try to fulfill these requirements without due examination, they may appear difficult; but as we consider them diligently until no relevant aspect is unknown, the required methods become easier. With sufficient familiarity, finally, thriftiness becomes autonomous. Knowing how to act so that our thrift does not fall into the two extremes of too much and too little is the beginning of being able to bring avarice to the path.

5

Bringing Ignorance to the Path

It is harder to understand how ignorance can be brought to the path, but it is well worth trying because no affliction is more basic and pervasive than ignorance, and complete victory over ignorance is synonymous with enlightenment.

From the viewpoint that sees absolute truth, the relative truth of the path is non-existent. People with typical, deluded ignorance of absolute truth cannot see the way things really are, but they can see the incidental relative,[141] including how the path to absolute knowledge should be practiced. On the other hand, being ignorant of such things as why anyone would want to resort to cruel deceit and murder for personal gain is a good thing.[142]

If we think about the absolute way things are, in the glorious *Kālachakra Tantra*, among three qualities taken from Sāṅkhya — energy, darkness or inertia, and spiritual power[143] — darkness is identified with ignorance. From that viewpoint, none of the delusive phenomena of saṃsāra

---

141 Referring to relative truth.

142 For example, it would have saved the protagonist of the traditional murder ballad *Down in the Willow Garden* from a dreadful fate. Bill Monroe and the Bluegrass Boys, *Willow Garden*, https://www.youtube.com/watch? v=5xgwiFg-kzw.

143 Or heat, darkness, and light.

appear. As in the example above, that can be regarded as a favorable condition.[144]

For an ignorant mind that does not realize the way things are, the absolute does not appear, but that a mind does not realize the absolute natural state now does not entail that it cannot follow a path leading to that realization later. Those of us on the relative path are ignorant about the ultimate natural state by definition, but we still have a path to realizing it. If that were not true, it would absurdly follow that there are no paths to enlightenment, and therefore, that no one ever attained it. Ignorance of a certain phenomenon does not entail ignorance of all phenomena. Therefore, it does not rule out a path to knowledge of that phenomenon. If it did, we could not even look up information on the internet.

Moreover, saṃsāric beings who are ignorant of their ultimate enlightened essence may unknowingly manifest virtuous aspects of that essence. Even though we may be ignorant of enlightenment itself, we can manifest its good qualities on the path to enlightenment and eventually realize it. That potential is Buddha nature. Since ignorant people can cease to be ignorant by attaining enlightenment, how could their ignorance of enlightenment be absolute and unchangeable like a diamond? That ignorance is necessarily relative and incidental, and therefore, changeable. The only arguments that some people are forever incapable of attaining enlightenment are based on literalistic, verbal inferences with little real meaning.[145]

There are different possibilities for working with ignorance on the path. When we practice the altruistic motivation of relative bodhichitta, we want to attain full enlightenment in order to be able to lead all innumerable sentient beings to enlightenment. This powerful and virtuous

---

144 If we are ignorant of them, none of them can corrupt us.

145 Even if a certain being cannot attain enlightenment in the current lifetime, that being will eventually attain full enlightenment in future rebirths because all sentient beings innately have Buddha nature.

motivation will be the cause for us eventually attaining full enlightenment even if, from the point of view of ultimate reality, there are no truly existent sentient beings to save.

One-pointed meditative concentration is ignorant of everything but its focal object. Devoted Guru Yoga focuses on the Guru alone, virtually "ignoring" everything else. Such strong devotion to one's own root Guru, lineage, and Saṅgha, not knowing anything about other teachers and traditions, is a kind of ignorance that can allow practitioners to deepen their practice quickly by having a clear focus.[146] In Tibet, for example, incredible spiritual benefit comes from devotion toward Padmasaṃbhava even though some historians say his existence is questionable.

---

146 In a famous traditional story, a man who went on a pilgrimage promised to bring his grandmother one of the Buddha's teeth. In reality, he gave her a tooth he pulled from a dog's skull near her cottage. Because she was ignorant of this, the grandmother had limitless faith and devotion toward the supposed relic. As a result, it exhibited all the miraculous signs of the real thing, and the old woman gained enlightenment.

6

Bringing Doubt to the Path

There are three kinds of doubt, (1) doubt inclined to truth, (2) doubt inclined to falsity, and (3) neutral doubt. If you doubt whether sound is impermanent, in the first case, you are inclined to think that that statement is true; in the second case, that it is false, and in the third case, you incline to neither.

In Abhidharma, doubt is classified as one of six root kleśhas. In learning about unknown objects, any of these three kinds of doubt may be present until knowledge eliminates them. They may motivate a search for that knowledge, but we cannot classify doubt as good quality just because of that. That doubt is classified as a root kleśha suggests that it involves more bad qualities than good ones, but that these bad qualities are removed by attaining knowledge about what was formerly doubted.

In addition, need I mention that at the time of practicing Highest Yoga Tantra, doubt is the last thing we need? Practicing the Highest Yoga Tantra path depends on Sugatagarbha, Buddha nature naturally existing within us. Yet, until we actually realize Sugatagarbha in our own experience, if we do not have faith and confidence that it is there, we are unlikely to have the motivation to practice that path. Even when we begin to glimpse Sugatagarbha, we have no motivation to practice the fruition path without faith and confidence that our present fleeting glimpses of pure perception can expand into the universal fruition.

If you are a beginner in this tantra path, having confidence and faith in the Vajra Master, who first gave you the empowerment that ripens your mind and entered you into the fruition path that liberates, is essential. Even in everyday life, if we doubt whether someone is a good person with a good heart, we may be missing an opportunity to establish a precious relationship.

If doubt were one of our essential characteristics, we could not eliminate it by any means. Then we could not progress on the path. Doubt, however, is not necessarily bad. Whether doubt will lead to bad or good results depends on the object of doubt. If you doubt the good path to enlightenment, you are deprived of its good qualities. If you doubt that you can profit in the long run from evil deeds, your doubt is advantageous. For example, consider the situation of a person who is convinced that it is good to kill, steal, and so forth because she does not believe in karmic cause and effect. Her wrong conviction will surely send her to the lower realms. If a doubt arises for her, like, "If I did not continue doing these things, maybe my life would be better," she may decide to stop such actions and instead connect with virtue.

If you cannot perceive the natural state but desire to find it, your thoughts on that subject may involve some doubt. Doubt about what the qualities of Sugatagarbha are like can motivate you to "taste" it through diligent practice of the completion stage. As your path continues, you replace relative phenomena of doubt with ultimate phenomena of pristine wisdom. Finally, you will have the opposite of doubt, true knowledge of the natural state.

Conclusion

If we take once again the work with anger as an analogy, exploring in detail how to be skillful with your anger can provide you the grounding of how to make other kleśhas into friends as well. The same can be said of desire which is the main topic of the following chapters. As further advice, you can observe your mind carefully and discover which kleśhas are strongly manifesting in your own current life. Some may have special personal significance or important consequences for your life and for those around you. Why not investigate them further and explore how to work with them on the path?[147]

---

147 Paraphrasing a message sent by Dr. Adrian Hekel in April 2023: nowadays, for example, many people struggle with feelings of loneliness and depression. Although they may be hard on themselves, this opens their hearts to become more compassionate toward the suffering and limitations of others. Honestly embracing this "dark side" sets an inspiring example for others as far as saṃsāric depression which is based on self-cherishing can be recognized and overcome. Likewise, fear and anxiety can help people be cautious and careful in dealing with others. Fear motivates prudence to quickly run away from unworkable situations and to find skillful solutions on how to replace them with workable ones. In that way, fear can be brought to the path as courage and appropriate pride in overcoming challenges.

Verse Summary

From the excellent viewpoint of our self-existing nature,
"Making kleśhas the path" is knowing how to use them.
Do not waste this body with the freedoms and favors
Disputing verbal points, such as what is really a kleśha.

In bringing kleśhas of the three poisons to the path,
Though every step is set out within the highest tantras,
I shall not present each one of these at length;
Here I shall deal with only the essential points.

By the wrathful anger of a warrior's courage,
The proud and jealous troops, arrayed in the great war[148]
Let fall a rain of weapons on the poisonous kleśhas,
Conquering all that is incidental, not their nature.[149]

Hold that all-pervading embodiment of Buddhahood,
The completely pure nature, pure of incidental defilements,
Having two kāyas, with two purities and two wisdoms,[150]
Of a single ground, a single path and single fruition.[151]

---

148 Here the kleśhas have been redirected into a war against their own harmful aspects.

149 When the "bad" relative aspects of the kleśhas have been eliminated, they are revealed as manifestations of their absolute nature, Sugatagarbha.

150 The two kāyas are Dharmakāya and Rūpakāya. The two purities are those of the absolute nature and the incidental relative. The two wisdoms are those of the nature and extent of phenomena.

151 All three are aspects of the single ultimate nature, Sugatagarbha.

PART FOUR

The Path of Desire

By ascetic restraint that is unbearable,

There may be practice, but will be no accomplishment.

Relying on all the qualities of desire,

Is the way that siddhi can be attained.

Guhyasamāja Tantra

Thus, in bliss there is the essence of bliss.

By that, the highest bliss may be established.

Chakrasaṃvara Tantra

1

How Desire Pervades Our Human Life

Introduction

Generally speaking, the Path of Desire occurs within the tantra path. As this path must deal with all phenomena, it cannot be traversed by working with desire alone. Since that is so, the Tibetan teachings of tantra consist more than of the Path of Desire. Nonetheless, *the Path of Desire is the quintessence, pith, and root of all the paths of Highest Yoga Tantra.* Especially for us as beings of the desire realm, there should be no doubt in the importance of skillfully bringing the passion of desire to our path.

Identifying the Essence of Desire and Its Different Manifestations

When we say "desire," the meaning many people are accustomed to is "sexual desire." Though they may be used to that sense of the word, there are many other kinds of desire. We all experience how desire saturates our experience as oil pervades sesame seeds. If we say that every action of our lives is driven by desire, that sums it up. It is true that sex is the principal subject of the Path of Desire, but as we all live in the desire realm, in which all aspects of life are governed by corresponding desires, we cannot be satisfied by sexual desire alone. It would therefore be appropriate to discuss desire in general first and then look into sexual desire as its most powerful manifestation.

Usually, Dharma texts define desire as it is understood in the individual liberation vehicle where the kleśha of desire should always be abandoned as an enemy,[152] "When a defiled object is focused on, we are delusively attached to it as pleasant, and so we want and seek it." In tantra, while there are also undefiled, non-delusive phenomena of enlightenment and non-delusive desires for them, these are not the only focus. Desire in tantra can be defined as *wanting to get either what is defiled or what is undefiled because both are seen as pleasant and attractive.*

Why is that so? For tantrikas, all desires, defiled or not, are sources of energy that can be used to progress on the path. *Perceiving any desired object as pleasant, or sometimes inconceivably blissful, is the most significant characteristic of the tantric path that uses bliss as the principal means of achieving realization.* Thus, any kind of desire, and, in particular, sexual desire, are brought to the heart of the path *by pure perception of their undefiled essence.* By doing this, tantrikas are no longer ordinary individuals who are controlled by the passion of their desires.[153]

Ordinary saṃsāric individuals are controlled by defiled, dualistic desire that is separate from the path. Genuine tantrikas control their desire by making it part of the path. "Going with the flow," just relaxing and doing as you like, is *not* enough to properly bring desire to the path. That requires following special instructions that will be presented below.

---

152 In this sense, all desires are kleśhas that should be abandoned, and all objects of desire are defiled saṃsāric delusions that entice us to suffering. In this environment, abandoning kleśhas like the passion of desire is the only good alternative, and *arhats* who succeed in doing so are praised for their passionlessness.

153 To the extent that they do this, practitioners are individuals who put their powerful desires to work on the path. Vajra holders who have perfected this ability are said to have realized the great ultimate desire beyond the delusive existence of ordinary attached desire and the emptiness of abandoned desire.

There are multiple kinds of desires for many things, as everyone knows. If the different objects of desire of ordinary life are distinguished, there are power, wealth, attainment, rank, recognition, enjoyment, comfort, and so forth. Virtually everyone in this world must deal with the passion of various desires in some way. Ordinary individuals are enslaved by their desires and that slavery produces the suffering of saṃsāra. That is why sūtra practitioners perceive desire as an enemy. They believe that if it can be abandoned, they can eliminate the painful bondage of *saṃsāra* and attain *nirvāṇa* as its absence. However, those who are victorious over the kleśhas as enemies by practicing such a path are extremely few. That is so because abandoning kleśhas is not the most suitable path for human beings, whose nature constantly produces kleśhas. That is especially true in this present dark age when the kleśhas are running rampant. Paṇḍita Dönyö Dorje says in *Oral Instructions on Entering into the Yoga of Suchness through Passionate Union,*[154]

In this approach, those who have the kleśhas,
Have kleśhas of abandoning the kleśhas.
Yet, as with hunger, there is desire for food,
And with thirst, water leads to craving,
And, for example, as fuel to feed a fire,
If it is not at hand, must be sought and gathered,
And if the fire is not kept bright, it dies;
Like that, the causal mind[155] of sentient beings,
By abandoning desire, will cease to function.
This mind compelled by extreme desires for objects
Will be snuffed out when desire is renounced.

---

154 D 1745 Tengyur, rgyud, sha, f113b.

155 Relative saṃsāric mind is governed by interdependent, causal origination. Changeless enlightened mind is beyond cause and effect.

By inferior means that cannot destroy this mind,
There is only increase of the kleśhas.[156]

Then people whose bondage is utterly extreme,
Letting their passion reside in external objects,
Make their thoughts addicted to them forever.
The more their bodies and minds go straight to hell,
The more their desperate minds will strive for heaven.
As they continue to fail in achieving that,
Conceptual thoughts, increasing ever more,
Never abide within the natural state.

The *Tantra of Establishing Pristine Wisdom* points out that the liberation produced by all paths consists of the experience by pristine wisdom of the nature of phenomena,[157]

The ocean of what was taught by the Teacher, the Buddha,
Is embodied, making its heart essence manifest.
This is the great, true secret. Without its appearance,
There can be no experience of liberation.

What is taught there and in other places, briefly summarized, is that a path to liberation relying on an endless alternation of relative opposites, such as the kleśhas and their antidotes, is not the best kind of path. If you can properly practice the path of Highest Yoga Tantra, you are not under the power of passion, so you need not abandon desire. Desire still exists

---

156 Antidotes that cannot fully eliminate the kleśhas only make them stronger as taking an insufficient dose of antibiotics eliminates only the weakest bacteria, making the others stronger than before.

157 *Ye shes grub pa'i rgyud.* The bibliographical reference of this text was not found by the translator.

within you, but it is under your control. However, you do not need to control it with hostility as with an enemy. You can make it your friend.

You may wonder how this can be done. You may have many desires for things that you want for yourself such as wealth and enjoyment, comfort, recognition, praise, and even wanting success with hypocritical pretenses and false humility. Thus, if any of these are attained, you think, "What is wrong with that?" and you naturally have no wish to abandon what you formerly wanted to gain. In the path of abandoning, you must renounce everything *because* you do not want them. In the Path of Desire, you may leave all these desires as they are, and you do not need to abandon any of them. That is because you ride them, they do not ride you anymore. You make your desires your friends, by changing their focal object and direction.

Usually, when people are greedy for wealth, pleasure, and enjoyment, their long-term goal is merely pleasing themselves. They wish only that they can enjoy and brag about a luxurious lifestyle, persevering in it in spite of the rivalry of others and so forth. If you are practicing Highest Yoga Tantra, the direction of these desires evolves. Because you have a pure intention, your desires transform into favorable conditions for benefiting others. Your greedy, short-sighted craving for wealth becomes a far-seeing vision of wealth as generosity for all. Your small-minded, shallow, self-centered aspirations naturally evolve into vast, deep, universal ones. These changes are the beginning of the special style of Highest Yoga Tantra practice.

With this change of perspective, none of the desires that naturally exist in your continuum need to be abandoned as enemies. By releasing their self-existing, ultimate nature, they all become your allies on the pure and true tantric path.

Life in this world is a life based only on desire;
The passion of desire is established as human nature.
Action with your established nature is very easy;
Action against your established nature is very hard.

Therefore, as all the glory and mastery of desire,
Are what establish the level of the Omniscient King,[158]
Do not reject your heart's desire like deadly poison;
Not viewing it as an enemy, embrace it as your friend.

---

158 A poetic metaphor for a fully enlightened being.

2

The Great Power of Desire

Regarding the ubiquitous desire for sex, the *Guhyasamāja Tantra*[159] says,

> By ascetic restraint that is unbearable,
> There may be practice, but will be no accomplishment.
> Relying on all the qualities of desire,
> Is the way that siddhi can be attained.

Also, Gendün Chöpel says in his *Kāma Śhāstra,*

88. Love for what is desired is passionate attachment;
     So love for what is desired is also faith in that.
     Fear of what is undesired is known as aversion;
     So fear of the undesired is renunciation of that.[160]

---

159 We found individual lines from this stanza in a number of texts, but not all of them together.

160 This verse explains the previous one. If we analyze carefully, the lower vehicles do not "destroy" passion as they claim. They bring it to the path as passion for renunciation. Therefore, all the Buddhist vehicles bring the kleśhas to the path, but tantra does it much more skillfully.

What is taught there as the real way things are is extremely profound, and it is necessary to have an equally profound understanding of it.

In this world of the desire realm, where all people have immense cravings to attain what they want, among all the objects we desire and strive for, one is paramount, and it cannot be eradicated. It is not beauty and youth, wealth and property, success and status, reputation and fame, or personal comfort as most ordinary people might assume. If the greatest form of desire is named, though many would say that it is faith or aspiration, another candidate is even more essential, sex.

Why? Without sex, there could be no sentient beings at all and without them, no phenomena of this desire realm could exist. These phenomena are established through sex. This is true of no other relative knowable. Since human beings are created through the sexual union of women and men, it is easy to know that all enjoyments related to human sexual activity are extremely valuable.

Sex never excludes the rich or the poor, those more or less highly regarded by society. High and low alike, all are equally able to enjoy it. Moreover, having sex does not depend on many conditions established by laborious effort. The conditions of enjoying it are just the meeting of a man and a woman, or in a larger sense, the meeting of the masculine and feminine principles. Sex alone includes its own favorable conditions.

Also, the mutual necessity of feminine and masculine exists not only in the case of sex but in all areas of human activity. Though there are a few people with non-binary sex organs or atypical chromosomes, their actions are still motivated by interactions of masculine and feminine principles. This is true independently of sexual orientation. That this interaction exists in some form in all people is undeniable, so there is no need to say much. Again the lord of learned ones Gendün Chöpel says,

90.   One's personal benefit, the benefit of the country,
       The king's dominion, and the beggar's means of life,
       And any actions, great or small, that are performed,
       Whose absence would be lamented, are indispensable women.

The Tibetan word for women, *bud med,* literally means "indispensable."
This passage says that all indispensable actions are like women in the
sense that they embody *prajñā,* the feminine principle. Generally speaking, we could say that for all men, some kind of feminine principle is necessary to motivate action, and the analogous statement applies to women
as well.

Moreover, men and women being attracted to someone of the same
sex should not be condemned as necessarily unnatural. The reason, as
explained above, is that in males not only the masculine nature exists,
and in females, not only the feminine nature. For example, some people
look like men externally, but inside the feminine nature is more powerful,
and so they may be attracted to other men. Some people look like women
externally, but inside the masculine nature is stronger, and so they are
attracted to other women.[161] Subtle degrees of these combinations are innumerable, depending on the specific karma of each individual.

These various forms and degrees of attraction manifest themselves
through different human interactions that may or may not include sex. If
we think that same-sex attractions are perverted and unnatural, it is important to know that such a belief is not aligned either with the way of the
modern world or the essence of the Dharma. Women and the feminine
principle have the sacred nature of prajñā; thus, to label as "perverted"
men blessed with more than what may be usual of this feminine nature

---

161 Or such a woman may be attracted to a man whose inner character is feminine in nature and vice-versa etc.

does not accord with the tantric view.[162]

In general, if we think about the value of sex, desire for amenities like wealth, enjoyment, food, clothing, homes, and bedding simply cannot compare with sexual desire. That its intensity is unrivaled is undeniable. However, in this world, sexual desire is contaminated by cultural overlays of shame, pretenses of being above desire, and so forth. Almost everyone is an imposter wearing a disguise of propriety, claiming that what actually exists does not. That keeps the mutual desire that is expressed in sexual union from manifesting as it should. Moreover, Easterners have more of a disguise than Westerners, and as for Tibetans, in my observation, no hypocrisy is more powerfully fixated than this.

Sex is a very strong and powerful virtue that must be part of the path to liberation in some sense. *That path of non-dual union must possess the good qualities of love,* and so, coarse compulsion and non-consensual sexual exploitation can never have a place within such a path. Such actions and the associated feelings negate all the virtues of the Path of Desire. If we manifest the good qualities of love and express them with unconditional confidence, our path will be very powerful. We will naturally know how to enjoy the excellence of these innate good qualities of wondrous power.

Though this is necessarily so, those who think that they must pretend that they have no desire to enjoy such things are continually damaging themselves. Those who fixate upon such unnatural approaches lose the value of human life and their lives are literally rendered pointless. The unhelpful clerical vice squad who proclaims that abstinence is necessary to avoid the torments of hell only wounds us with their needless intimidation. Needless obstacles created by their hypocritical deceptions are all too many.

---

162 The analogous statement applies to women regarding the masculine nature of compassion as skillful means.

The opposite of hypocritical concealment, inconsiderate assertiveness, is also troublesome. Generally speaking, this attitude is the opposite of shyness. Although assertiveness can be either good or bad, it is always bad to force sex on others. Those who make a brazenly presumptuous habit of self-centered and inconsiderate greed in their lust, with no realization at all of the holy nature of what they exploit and the profound secrets they defile, had better take care. Their compulsion to rut like unreflective animals is condemning them to waste their lives in twisted misconduct. Alternatively, by embracing shared desire, they should find the essence of enlightenment hidden within their hearts. As the second Buddha of Uḍḍiyana, Padmasaṃbhava, said in the *Path of Means, the Essence of Great Bliss*,[163]

In tantrayāna that produces the path of bliss,
As defilements are washed away by defilements,
Conceptions are purified by conceptions themselves,
Saṃsāra is abandoned by saṃsāra itself.

Just as fire may be kindled from a fire,
It can also be extinguished by a fire;
So, what is kindled by the fire of desire,
Can be extinguished by the fire of desire.

---

163 The exact bibliographical reference of this text by Padmasaṃbhava was not found by the translator.

3

How Sexual Desire is Natural in Human Life and the Faults of Fighting Against It

Monastics of individual liberation continue to see sex as being like an enemy and poison, and therefore they continue to tout their discipline of celibacy. This unnaturalness is the source of their pride and self-respect, the rock that is their bulwark.

As its external fashion statement, monastics wear three saffron-colored Dharma robes. In Tibet, the virtue of monks is codified in the two hundred and fifty-three precepts of the vinaya, excluding just the vows of the *four defeats* and *thirteen offenses with remainder*. Weaker practitioners of this tradition never strive for liberation from their hearts, they waste their lives following cultural customs. If one analyzes this topic carefully, it becomes clear that they experience very little meaning or fulfillment in human life.

When this tradition is practiced diligently and responsibly, those who improve themselves are many. *If you are a monastic focusing on individual liberation who truly believes that desires are poisons, and you have complete certainty of having abandoned them, then we must respect you tremendously and rejoice in your accomplishments.* Nevertheless, those with inferior dedication do not have the slightest interest in seeking the fulfillment of life in liberation. Wilfully ignorant of such things, they only avoid what they fear, like rabbits frightened by a splashing sound.

For those whose moral obsessions[164] are especially powerful, putting a woman in front of them is like shaking a red cloth in front of a yak.[165] Even if their discipline is intact, the *eight worldly concerns* attend them like a retinue in the six periods of each day and night.[166] Though they abandon the home provided by their loving parents, nothing is gained by that because they cling to a monastery as their second home.[167] Jealous of superiors, competitive with peers, and contemptuous of inferiors, these monks are dedicated only as servants of the 84,000 kleśhas.[168]

If they have to associate with women, they obsess about them at all times and occasions, summer and winter, all year around, even in their dreams. Since they do not reverse even a corner of saṃsāra, their craving is more intense than if they had acted out their lurid fantasies. If they do not realize this crucial point, the consequences will be severe. Over a full human life, from the obsessive desire for hundreds of women, multiplied in intensity a thousand times by frustration, immense bad karma of profound craving will accumulate within their minds, yet all the time they

---

164 These monastics put immense effort into renouncing all the desires of ordinary people. Although they can do this externally, most of them cannot eliminate desire internally. However, they do not want others to know that, and they cannot even admit it to themselves. Therefore, they spend much of their time proclaiming to anyone who will listen how disgusting such desires are.

165 They respond like a bull in a bullfight to the matador's red cape.

166 Generally speaking, certain practices are supposed to be performed regularly in the three divisions of every day and night, *dus drug*. This poetic expression means that for these unfortunate practitioners, the arising of the eight worldly concerns is just as regular.

167 The problem here is not living in a monastery, but clinging to one's own monastery as if it were a home or nest. Some monastics are so attached to their particular conditions that they do not even go to other nearby monasteries to learn or exchange with other practice lineages.

168 A way of saying that there are almost limitless subtly different kinds of kleśhas.

are establishing these deep habitual propensities. Most of these Tibetan monks of individual liberation and renunciates like them all around the world — who externally seem to be pure devotees of celibacy — were never suited for such a path of denial. Is not it clear that they can never achieve even a little of its intended goal?

It is difficult to evaluate the minds of others, and so it is wrong to judge others' ultimate worth. However, as individuals' minds are not hidden from those individuals themselves, be objective. If you look into your own mind and reflect carefully, you will know whether you belong to the family just described. If you conclude that there is nothing within you but a hypocritical pretense of renunciation, why reject your innate desire as an enemy? Accept these desires that are closer to you than your own family as friends. Employ means of making them allies on your path. Is not that a better choice?

The wise investigate what path is appropriate for them because they believe in karmic cause and effect. According to all Buddhist traditions, karma is accumulated in the mind. If even a little negative karma is not pacified, it constantly corrupts us. Then all activities of the body must be guarded as a government guards its country. By the time discipline has to be mobilized against a horde of violators like a police force, is not it already broken beyond repair? In such cases, examining whether you have lost the essence of your goal is essential. Is not it doubtful whether the discipline of celibacy is being kept anymore? Considering that this discipline undoubtedly has its benefits, we need to analyze what is happening carefully. If the essence of that discipline is being rejected, the associated benefits will no longer be attained.

In describing the lineages of the Tibetan Buddhist teachings, it is usually considered sufficient to say that in its external style, the Tibetan monastic community has lived according to the Buddha's teachings of the vinaya from its foundation up to the present day. If we add that many Dharma practitioners guard the vinaya precepts of the holy Dharma as carefully as their eyes, why is that not enough? Well, for example, let us consider the conditions of restoring the vows for monks who have committed the thirteen offenses with remainder that are taught by the Buddha in the *Vinaya Piṭaka*. The vinaya makes it clear that the Buddha's idea of good monastics was not just the infinitesimal percentage who never broke any of the hundreds of rules. His ideal included scrupulously honest, humble practitioners who willingly confessed lapses so that their vows could be restored. The Buddha teaches three steps of restoration from a downfall that must be carried out by the Saṅgha, after the offending monks voluntarily confess before them, ideally before their faults have been discovered. The three steps are,

1. Removing the good standing of a monk who has committed the fault.
2. Making the Saṅgha rejoice by penitential service, usually for a number of days specified by the Saṅgha.
3. Bestowing, once again, the status of a respectable monk, with a special ceremony.

Thus, such fallen monks formally renew their vows. If disputes exist about these requirements, I do not know about them. Though the principal texts of the vinaya scriptures teach that these steps are necessary to amend these specific violations, do Tibetan monks who practice them presently exist? To my knowledge, they do not. Without these three means of amending, if one of the thirteen faults with remainder occurs, the offender's monastic discipline is ruined forever. No other means of restoring it is found in the vinaya root texts and commentaries, and it is clear to anyone who knows the vinaya that no other way of doing that exists.

These violations include sexual offenses. If we take the internet scandals involving Tibetan monastics as a guide, their occurrence is not at all infrequent, and those who offend are likely to do so repeatedly. As these violations occur again and again, over an entire human life, by the time of death, the heap of violations will be a burden taller than a mountain and deeper than an ocean. Rather than carrying that mountain of transgressions to their deaths, if these failed monastics were to make close friends and relatives of their desires, how could that be bad? It would surely be better than making relentless enemies of them in this and subsequent lives.

Moreover, we should recall that the sūtras teach that monastics enjoying offerings to the Saṅgha while pure discipline being absent creates a debt to the Buddha. The *Hundred Actions Sūtra* says that when you are very close to achieving liberation, you may enjoy the enjoyments of the whole universe as if they were your own. If you are still on the path, using something that is given to you as a monastic is without fault only if your ethical discipline is intact. Anyone else creates a karmic debt that will eventually be collected. Thus, are not hypocrites with impure discipline in a terrible situation? Glorious Shépé Dorjé's *Clear Points of the Path of Means* says,[169]

These days, most of us practice what is not the Dharma.
Sūtra followers denigrate the tantric life.
The 'educated' leave tantric conduct for later lives.
Disciples of charlatans indulge in wanton living,
Thinking sūtra and tantra are opposites, like hot and cold.
Not accepting any distinctions of dos and don'ts,
We see them fling themselves into distorted paths.
Therefore, these weighty points are explained, as a word to the
    wise.[170]

If we analyze by reasoning, who can deny that "not viewing desire as an enemy, grasping desire as a friend," is a path of excellent skillful means?

---

169 *Vol. 60, pp. 17–138.* BDRC, purl.bdrc.io/resource/MW3PD982_D6A2D5, f60a.1. 60a.3.

170 As is said, "a word to the wise is sufficient counsel."

We may be more skillful at making friends with some kleśhas than others. When our practice does not go very well, we may create relatively "bad" friendships where our kleśhas still harm us to some degree; but we are usually much better off with these bad friends than with the enemies they originally were. As in ordinary life, we may have some relatively "bad" friends who are sometimes jealous of us, say unnecessary harsh words, and so forth; still, they help us in emergency situations. It is much better to learn how to work with these challenging friendships than to let our emotions be our sworn enemies.[171]

Depending on the scriptures alone, other ways of thinking are permissible, but if we think according to correct reasoning, there are certainly means of transforming enemies into friends and vice versa. Having even one enemy in the world is too many, and however many friends we have, more would be better. Since this path of tantra changes all our enemies into friends, does a better word for the wise exist in this world than saying we should do that?

Those who know the textual tradition of Highest Yoga Tantra know that of all the kleśhas, the passion of desire is our best potential friend because it can provide the highest and quickest path to realization. That is verified for those who realize the inner meaning of the four higher em-

---

171 For example, we discussed before how anger and assertive ambition can be brought to the path by being turned into heroic courage that laudably serves virtue. We might have various percentages of success and failure at doing this. If our percentage of failure is fairly small, our "friend" is a little bit unreliable at times but mostly serves and protects us for overcoming obstacles. So Kṛiṣhṇa urges Arjuna in the *Bhagavad Gītā* 11.34 to fight his human enemies by vanquishing his spiritual ones. "Do not be dejected. Fight and you will conquer the enemies of your mind because God wants you to succeed. Your effort will be instrumental, while God will fashion your victory by his grace," https:// www.holy-bhagavad-gita.org/chapter/11/verse/34. If the percentage of failure is quite large, our anger is not a reliable friend at all, and we have failed to bring it to the path. If we are not mindful enough, our great heroism may be overcome by a tragic flaw of courageous but selfish ambition. Then, as in Shakespeare's *Macbeth* when MacBeth kills his king, we might murder for personal gain those we are sworn to protect. In the end, Macbeth's flawed courage led him only to madness and disgraceful death.

powerments of Highest Yoga Tantra, and it also exists as something to be learned from tantric texts.[172]

> We live by the disguise of the world's external manner,
> And so, each day, we lose control of our natural feelings.
> Our bag of gathered years and months of futility,
> Wears out one day and is seen to be completely pointless.[173]
>
> Therefore, the self-arising of the natural state,
> That manifests in all true passion of desire,
> As realization of human beings' ground and root,
> Being supported by the great sexual passion[174] is the point.

---

172 See chapter 7 below and the relevant quotations from the *Kālachakra Tantra* in Appendix II.

173 People try to abandon emotions like desire or anger, but they cannot, because they always arise naturally. Trying to suppress them, as if they were hiding them in a bag, leads to suffering. Since they do this constantly, they are increasingly stressed. Finally, the bag falls apart, and they realize their effort was futile. Instead of that, they should see emotions as a natural manifestation and try to use it for good purposes, as is done in genuine tantra.

174 The "great" sexual desire goes beyond literal sex to all its deeper implications of union and great bliss, ultimately embodied in the realization of how things are, Sugatagarbha.

4

How All Individuals Can Start with the Capabilities They Have

When the Victorious One's intention regarding this profound subject of desire is understood, it accords with the following words of glorious Shépé Dorjé's *Eliminating the Torment of People's Sexual Desire*:[175]

I know what is forbidden and why it is forbidden,[176]
And a thing or two about the essence and application.[177]
I have also received experience into my hand.[178]

These days those trained in this are excessively reserved;
Others who claim they know them well ignore the guidelines.[179]

---

175 *Rgyo 'dod skye bu'i gdung sel*, f15b.1. 15b.6.

176 Shépé Dorjé says he knows what ethical conduct and practice instructions allow and do not allow and the many reasons why.

177 He also knows the deeper essence behind these rules and therefore, how their application might change in different situations.

178 Moreover, he knows these things very well not just in theory but from personal practice experience.

179 Most of those trained in the theory and practice of tantra fall into extremes. Some are

Those who have the right balance, who do notcontradict the
   tantras,
And enjoy desirable qualities are as rare as stars in daytime.[180]
Some, though they know the practice, are unable to do it properly.
Leaving this life behind them, they put their hopes on the next.[181]

Since I have neither hopes nor fears,[182] whatever I do,
My experience is better than that of others who still have them.
Though we all must relate to sex, the way I do so is different.[183]
My followers who have interest in sexual union,
Referring to the instructions I have composed on sex,
May understand how to proceed, by learning them properly.

---

too "reserved" because they put too much emphasis on the rules of external conduct.
They tend to suppress their true feelings and meditational experiences to conform to
the expectation of others. Some overemphasize outwardly expressing their experiences
but disregard most rules of ethical conduct. We have seen that neither of these two
extremes leads to great fruition.

180 People who perfectly follow the tantric approach taught in the scriptures, and whose
conduct is controlled neither too rigidly nor too loosely so that their enjoyment becomes
a perfect means of realization are almost never seen, like stars in the daytime.

181 Some know well the verbal teachings and technical instructions such as the subtle yogas
of the winds and drops and so forth, but they do not know how to apply them properly,
and therefore, their practice is unsuccessful. Others often fail by being preoccupied with
hopes and fears about their own capacities, and postpone actual practice for their next
lives.

182 In the sense of being free from fixed expectations and doubts.

183 Central to the Path of Desire is understanding sexuality. Everyone must relate to sexuality in some way, but knowledgeable yogins like Shépé Dorjé know how to relate to it as a
path to enlightenment. Even if the sexual activity of different people looks similar externally, internally they are not the same; his sexual activity, in particular, is not saṃsāric.
That, of course, is the subject of this book.

All appearances that are viewed are of the nature of sex.[184]
Suspended in open space, amidst these enchanting dynamics,[185]
Blazing with natural bliss, the whole body builds to a climax.[186]
Let desire's sweet fragrance permeate everywhere.[187]

The purified goal of generation and completion
Thus is liberated as a body of light.[188]
In the fields of a wondrous, marvelous display,[189]
As the dominion of irreversible vajra teachings,
May there be establishment of the ultimate kāyas,[190]
For the great awareness holders of sexual union.

These are just a few of the many things said there. Generally speaking, *tantric practice, including sexual practice, should be enhanced to the full measure of our ability to benefit both ourselves and our society.* However,

---

184 This is also explained by Gendün Chöpel in Appendix I. In short, he means here that after understanding properly the sacred sexual union, the blissful interaction of the feminine and masculine principles, and so forth, all appearances, even when "out of bed," are perceived by practitioners as having the same nature as sacred sex in being blissful, delighting, inspiring, and so forth.

185 The interplay of masculine and feminine principles pulls us out of our normal selves so that we are suspended in the limitless space of mind between thoughts. A deep appreciation for phenomena manifests.

186 The whole body spontaneously blazes forth with bliss that goes everywhere. It builds toward a climactic moment that stops the flow of inner karmic winds like the moment preceding a sneeze or an orgasm.

187 The inner nature of desire as the bliss of Sugatagarbha begins to manifest.

188 Thus, the goals of the generation and completion stages are achieved and eventually the practitioner becomes a Buddha with a body of light, a rainbow body, even though externally the body appears as an ordinary saṃsāric body.

189 At this point the environment becomes a wondrous and delightful display of Buddha fields, tantric deities, and so forth.

190 This is like attaining the ultimate, changeless level of Buddhahood, spontaneously manifesting the kāyas and pristine wisdoms.

until problematic hindrances to doing this are eliminated, the Path of Desire's promises of happiness for all cannot be actualized. To ennoble this path of sexual activity by abandoning corruption and accepting the pure, true essence of reality, it certainly needs to be cleansed of adulterating impurities. Among these are three fundamental misunderstandings about the tantric Path of Desire,

1. For the most part, Indians, Chinese, and other Easterners persistently maintain old beliefs holding that paths involving sexual activity are not only immoral but deadly like poison.
2. Many Westerners, on the other hand, think that tantra involves only sexual skills, with no deeper implications.[191]
3. Most contemporary Tibetans, regardless of their education or status, think that the genuine Path of Desire that includes sexual activity can only be practiced by great yogins who have advanced to inconceivably high levels, and that no others can successfully follow their example.

When people are not free from these kinds of deluded slumber that result from misapprehensions, whatever the texts may say about the Path of Desire being valuable, even those with understanding and meditative experience can make no progress in this area. For those bound by the preconceptions of their textual tradition, it is very hard to do anything about it. Even those who claim to be scholars who have grasped the highest view or to be yogins who have mastered the highest yogic proficiency, will never have sufficient means of joining themselves to the true way things are until these hindrances are eliminated.

---

191 It is essential to distinguish the sexual literalism of "internet tantra" from the multi-layered depth of genuine tantric sexuality. Sexual technique in the former is an end in itself. The latter seeks the essence of enlightenment at the heart of sexual union.

Direct Advice to Put into Practice as Much as You Can

The third point from the above list of misunderstandings is a very important one, so if we do not discuss it a little first, there will be no way to enter this path.

Learning about the worldly and world-transcending qualities and paths[192] that you wish to know and practice must be done by first facing in the right direction, so obviously, starting with small points, you have to turn in that direction and practice as much as you can, regardless of whether you can do it perfectly or not.[193] Begin with whatever you know about making the kleśhas into a path. Until you reach the ultimate level of yogic union, bring kleśhas to the path as well as you can in the environment of the genuine view.

How could you do that by pretending that the sūtra path is the tantric path? You cannot. There is no way that just repeating over and over that sūtra is tantra as if you were reciting a mantra, and then performing no tantric practice other than accumulating mantras alone could do the job of the authentic tantra path. If you wait because you fear that you do not know enough to make progress, you will never be ready to begin tantra. Your foolish belief that you cannot begin the tantric path until you master the sūtra paths is justified by neither scripture nor reasoning.

Each individual who practices tantra must begin with the basics. When children are learning to read and write, first, no matter how many

---

192 The worldly corresponds to the relative and the world-transcending to the absolute. Therefore, worldly paths are those whose activities are causal means for supporting realization. A world-transcending path is one that uses the absolute fruition as a path as previously discussed.

193 Rinpoché is pointing out that we should go step by step and be clear about the direction we are going on the Path of Desire, following the instructions he is giving in this book. He is emphasizing the importance of focusing on the right direction and never giving up rather than being frustrated if we cannot understand the principles perfectly or if we cannot immediately succeed when engaging in actual practice.

mistakes they make, they must learn how to recognize each letter. Then, one by one, they must join the letters they have learned into words whose meanings they already know. Only then, no matter how many mistakes they make, can they begin to read word by word; no one can read right from the start. Similarly, when you enter into the tantra path, *no matter how many errors and failures you make, you must try to bring the kleśhas to the path, step by step, without abandoning them.*

Look again and again to see what you have to do. *Even if you fail at first, based on that very experience of defeat, learn how to improve yourself.* How could it be right to hold that, from the first, error and defeat are impossible? As in learning how to ride a bicycle, mistakes are inevitable. Thinking that error cannot occur is the ultimate error. What you can and cannot do should not be a mere untested view. If you just remain miserable about your prospects that one day you will suddenly attain power, success is impossible. Do not be put off by temporary setbacks. That well-accomplished actions will eventually reward those who keep trying is the nature of things.

Although this may all seem obvious, contemporary Tibetans who are arrogant about their learning turn the admittedly elusive textual tradition that says this can and should be done into its opposite. Many of them fixate on their own conceptual view or a specific type of moral conduct as being the most important and forget the main point. Moreover, they think that if they are not highly advanced in the sūtra paths, they lack the prerequisites for practicing tantra, still less the Path of Desire. This misconception has been repeated again and again over the centuries until now, remaining as a generally accepted dogma.

If you are building a castle out of heavy, solid stones, you must build it from a foundation that is equally hard and solid. If you pile heavy stones on a foundation that is insubstantial like paper, your castle will collapse. The difficulties facing those who prepare for tantra by training extensively in a merely intellectual version of the sūtra path of the second turning of the wheel of Dharma are comparable. That approach is as "easy to handle" as paper because in dealing with the kleśhas and obscurations, their main focus is to prove their intrinsic emptiness. When later they try to train in the many "weighty" and substantial tantric practices for bringing kleśhas to the path, they will be completely unprepared to work with their actual emotions. The result will be as catastrophic as if they had piled heavy stones on cotton wool.

The main difference encountered in advancing from sūtra to tantra is that *bringing* kleśhas to the path must replace *abandoning* them by antidotes. If, for your whole life, you have practiced a sūtra path that views desire as an enemy, you may claim that you also capably practice tantra.[194] However, more than likely, your untrained attempts to navigate tantra will be like suddenly forcing soldiers who have been fighting enemies their whole lives to make friends with them. You may succeed in compelling a senile nanny to take care of a young, unruly child or arrogant lords and ladies to act as servants, but they will probably fail. Most present Tibetan tantrikas who rely on the sūtra approach of abandoning and antidotes are like that. The methods they employed simply cannot support genuine tantric practice.

If you are entering into tantra, you must train from the first in its special teachings, beginning with a few simple ones. If someone with only familiarity with the sūtra path must suddenly function as a tantrika in a single day's time, it is simply human nature that they will not be able to do so correctly. Therefore, if you want to enter into not only the tantra path but also the Path of Desire and its principal manifestation — the path of sexual union — you must train properly in stages from the moment you begin. Moreover, you must do this with an appropriate long-term plan for the eventual manifestation of the vast and profound reality behind it all. Otherwise, with only empty words in an empty mouth, you will be

---

194 Rinpoché advocates an earlier tantric education so that practitioners can have a better chance of accomplishment.

engaging in a mere pretense of training. When some who present themselves as great Lamas of revered monasteries say that they are teaching the tantric path but never give any practical instructions at all, we can be sure that their teachings are not complete.

> The kind of desire that is the highest of all desires,
> Is that of the path of wisdom, the union of heroes and heroines.
> Who would prefer a lesser path that rejects our nature,
> And so reject the highest path of innate great bliss?

> The family of the innermost pith of tantra practice
> Is the great, ultimate secret that is utterly profound.
> It is the supreme quintessence fulfilling the glory of students.
> If you want to be it, you had better be in it;
> Mere words and dreams will never reach the goal, the essence.

5

The Sacred Nature of Sex
and Preliminary Perceptions

The first and most important point of the Path of Desire is that not only do all the different kinds of sentient beings in this world have both masculine and feminine qualities to some degree; all of their actions and interactions as well as the goals they want to achieve also need both of these qualities. If one of those two natures is absent, or if they do not cooperate well with each other, nothing will be properly accomplished.

When talking about masculine and feminine qualities, I am not referring only to coarse physical aspects of men and women that you can distinguish with your eyes. These qualities include subtle aspects like the red and white essences of our body that lead to differences on many subtle levels. All that is undesirable and chaotic comes from not balancing and coordinating the masculine and feminine qualities. All aspects of perfect virtue and happiness arise from balancing and coordinating these two.[195]

As the masculine and feminine aspects have both gross and subtle manifestations, understanding that the entire Path of Desire is concerned

---

195 Rinpoché means that, before starting the actual practice of the Path of Desire, it is crucial to develop a proper attitude gained from understanding the interaction between these two principles.

only with sexual activity is completely off the mark. Understanding the practice of the Path of Desire as consisting only of practice with a physical consort, the Karma Mudrā, is also wrong. As explained later in the book, just in terms of *mudrās* or *consorts*, the Path of Desire is not practiced only with the human Karma Mudrā, but with mental Wisdom, Dharma, and Samaya Mudrās as well. The fruition is self-existing ultimate love and bliss of the great consort of empty-form, Mahāmudrā.

Initial Advice on How to Establish Sacred Sexual Union

If you do practice with a Karma Mudrā, it is not proper to engage in sexual union right away.

1. First, enjoy the pleasure of just looking at each other.
2. Then savor the pleasure of smiling and laughing.
3. After that, if you know how to enhance your mutual pleasure by touching parts of the consort's body little by little, you will begin to progress on this excellent path.

Whether or not you can correctly link all these stages in succession, as advice regarding the desired goal of sexual union,

4. If you are female, perceive the special qualities that are mostly non-existent in a female, but exist predominantly in a male, as better than gold. If you are male, see all the special qualities that predominantly exist in a female as priceless. Establishing this perception is necessary but not enough. Both partners need to feel that relating to the special qualities of the consort's body and mind is really a great blessing, and they need to know that this is a very touchy and sensitive sacred practice that can easily go wrong.

5. As much as you can, be open to the pure perception that your part-ner's body and mind contain the innumerable maṇḍalas of the ocean of Victorious Ones.[196]

6. As you increasingly perceive your consort's body, speech, and mind as the infinite maṇḍalas of the inexhaustible circles of ornament of enlightened body, speech, and mind,[197] appreciate the great auspi-ciousness of your good fortune to participate in such a realization.

In brief, as you enjoy the experience of union with the perception that this is an extremely great, holy, and precious blessing, think, not just verbally but from your heart, "What is happening now is not just sex. This is the actual empowerment of the Path of Desire that ripens the mind so that it can connect with absolute phenomena." *Do not doubt that these are the excellent, special instructions on how to practice the Path of Desire that liberates.* You can in fact be sure that in order to experience such a bless-ing, you and your consort have incredibly good karma and must have

---

196 If you are starting out in the Path of Desire and these ideas are hard to relate to, work instead with the other prerequisites outlined here and below. In short, appreciate your partner as "divine" as much as you can, and have great admiration and gratitude for this precious occasion of practice. Try to feel this appreciation as much as you can, not just as a thought. For a detailed explanation, read the next footnote.

197 *sku gsung thugs mi zad pa rgyan gyi 'khor rab byams kyi dkyil 'khor*: As part of the frui-tion of tantric practices like the Path of Desire, all phenomena of body, speech and mind are perceived as empty-form sound, and so forth that are aspects of the blissful absolute nature of things. All phenomena are apprehended from the ultimate viewpoint as not going beyond being aspects of the truly existing nature of things, Sugatagarbha. Beyond the physical body, you may perceive limitless Buddha realms and within the body centers of energy that are capable of manifesting as the environment and inhabitants of infinite maṇḍalas of tantric deities with all their pure qualities and enlightened activities. This is the perception of the highest form realm, Akaniṣhṭa. Beginners on tantra train by rec-ollecting this underlying purity until they can experience glimpses of it and eventually attain it. See "pure perception"and "maṇḍala" in the glossary. (As said in the previous footnote, if you just are starting out, focus instead on other prerequisites that you can relate to.)

accumulated merit over many lifetimes. That you are individuals with excellent discernment is certain. How could people with small minds and small accumulations of merit experience such a high practice? It would be extremely unlikely.

More surprisingly excellent even than finding pure gold in ordinary sand, or a pure lotus growing from filth, is tasting the enlightened wisdom of absolute great bliss at the heart of sexual activity. People with a saṃsāric attitude cannot experience that. They think that sex is like eating tasty food or drinking good drinks as they do every day. They have no idea that its essence is so high and holy. They cannot even imagine such a possibility, let alone know why it is a topic of such exalted praise. Their enjoyment of sex is short-sighted and self-centered like animals, so why even speak of their regarding it as holy worship? Depending on their degraded viewpoint, that much disgusting, inappropriate, and exploitative conduct has been, and continues to be indulged in, is as well-known to everyone as the wind.

Some enjoy sex with enthusiasm whenever they can, but they outwardly present themselves as pillars of "righteousness" if others do the same; they regard them as base and low, accusing them of immorality, and so forth. As they hypocritically engage in various kinds of deceptive concealment, their outer words clash with their internal reality. Those with this frame of mind are legion and can be found everywhere in the world. Eastern countries like Tibet are probably the worst in that regard.

Nevertheless, some of you may still be contemplating the possibility of correct practice of the sexual activity of the Path of Desire, and so I shall offer further advice on how to establish a sacred sexual union.

Further Advice on How to Establish a Sacred Sexual Union

1. To begin with, as much as you can, *abandon the fixated dualistic perceptions of that which is considered pure and that which is considered*

defiled that usually exist as reference points in peoples' minds. In doing so, do not regard any outer or inner parts of the body as being either pure or defiled.[198] Even these minimal conditions conflict with the local culture in some countries, while in others, tantric instructions like these are simply incomprehensible.

2. While you are engaged in this sacred activity, *any worries and shifting thoughts about the quality or standard of your engagement should be cast aside.* Hopes that you can perform well, fears that you are doing it badly, and so forth are *completely out of place* in the Path of Desire. In brief, whenever you are turning a mental wheel that mass produces distracting thoughts of expectation or doubt, you are not bringing your feelings and actions to the path. Such thoughts are great obstacles to tantric practice.

3. Many practitioners fail in attaining liberation due to being sidetracked by thoughts, so they are a hindrance to be reckoned with. Therefore, when you are having sacred sex, as much as you can, *relax one-pointedly in what is immediately taking place.* Let your mind be satisfied in freedom from mental proliferations.

In brief, while your view should be expansive, your mind needs to focus on what you are doing but without expectations, doubts, or fears. If you cannot do that, whatever good qualities you may have, and however good your practice may be in other respects, you are *not* practicing the tantra path.[199] You are just having ordinary worldly sex, with its usual dualistic

---

198 At the very least, until your sexual activity is over, do not fixate on anything as clean or dirty.

199 Being aware of yourself, your partner and the quality of interaction between the two of you is important. The problem is when the practitioner gets stuck by generating conflicting doubts, expectations, and so forth regarding one's own capacity or performance because it prevents the practitioner from entering deeper levels of experience.

concepts and feelings.[200]

Many people in Tibet say that before practitioners enjoy this kind of consort practice, they must practice very hard the formal preliminary practices, including extensive practices to purify accumulated karma and one-pointedly supplicating the Guru as in Guru Yoga. After this, they should perfectly visualize the yidam deity and consort in *yab-yum* and accumulate a minimum number of mantras of the deity. Then authorized practitioners can engage in sacred sexual union while maintaining a deliberate visualization.

If you can genuinely emulate this approach with pure motivation, it certainly seems that accumulation of virtue must be the result. Indeed, it also seems reasonable to say that by mistakenly thinking that all this "mumbo jumbo" is absolutely necessary to realize your own nature, you would create obstacles to that realization. In any case, this is definitely not the best way to bring sexual activity to the path. We can experience the sacred reality within sexual union itself better with less symbolic distraction. Therefore, I will present below a new approach to facilitating a direct experience of the bliss of sexual union, called here "Preliminary Perceptions."

Preliminary Perceptions

Here is a summary of the five excellent Preliminary Perceptions for attainment on this Path of Desire, followed by a relevant explanation of each perception,

---

200 Even if you recognize that you are falling into this category, there is no need to give up. You can prepare and train over and over again, and even if progress is slow, you should be kind, and accepting of where you are; if you think you still need to develop much more understanding and integrate it into your practice, do not be worried or discouraged by your temporary limitations and go on as much as you can.

1. Perceiving this Path of Desire as a natural innate path.
2. Perceiving with certainty that all your temporary experiences of bliss embody the ultimate essence.
3. Perceiving that your temporary experiences of bliss are capable of increasing into limitless ones.
4. Perceiving that all the actions you perform on the path of tantra must be motivated by bodhichitta.
5. Perceiving the primordial, male and female aspects of non-dual *Dharmakāya* as the natural power of expression of your own nature.

Explanation

1. *This Path of Desire is an innate path* that develops both your incidental and ultimate natures. Perceiving that path as natural development involves perceiving that this is a much better path than one that is constantly fighting your natural emotions.[201]
2. Just as the taste of even a single grain of sugar allows you to know the taste of all the sugar in the universe, thereby granting you the ability to recognize it should you experience it again, so it is with your true nature, Sugatagarbha. *You, therefore, perceive with certainty through your practice that all your blissful experiences embody the ultimate essence of the path.*[202]

---

201 Such a perception has many levels, but you will begin to perceive it with certainty as soon as you experience the easing of conflict with the kleśhas that occurs when you bring them to the path. Those who reject this path as disgraceful say that until individual liberation practitioners reach a very high level, the merit they gain in their practice is proportional to the hardship they experience in denying their "shameful" natural urges. Is not it better to cultivate delight rather than agony?

202 You may think that this sounds like a very high realization, and wonder how such experience could possibly be considered as a "preliminary" to the Path of Desire. That is the same as wondering how the fruition can be the heart of tantric practice to attain that same fruition. If the experience of the fruition is a preliminary to tantric practice, would not you have to be enlightened before you could begin? That is exactly the mistake that most Tibetans make regarding the possibility of practicing tantra. They focus upon the fact that

3. Even if the blissful essence is perceived only briefly, through that experience, informed faith arises that such momentary experiences of bliss expand and join over time. When you perceive how glimpses of bliss are continuously maturing into the experience of your limitless, ultimate nature, *you also perceive that your temporary experiences of bliss are capable of limitless increase.* Your mind will be full of confidence in that regard.[203]

4. *You perceive that all the actions that are done on the path of tantra must be motivated by bodhichitta.* By actually traversing the path of desire you realize that your ultimate goal, the path's fruition, can only be fully actualized for the sake of establishing all limitless sentient beings[204] on that same level of immutable great bliss. This is because in order to go beyond dualistic fixations of *self* and *other,*

---

our self-perpetuating, saṃsāric karma encloses us in an impenetrable net of delusive perceptions and compulsive activities that block realized experience. According to this approach, pure perception of things as they are can begin only after complete annihilation of that saṃsāric network through realization that all its phenomena are empty of true existence as explained in the sūtras of the second turning. Only a few great beings can accomplish that in one lifetime, and the rest of us have no choice but to continue in our deluded perception of cyclic existence. The tantric path is based on the third turning view that ultimate reality is Sugatagarbha, which is compassionate Buddhahood. Compared to that eternal reality, the mechanism of saṃsāra is temporary and imperfect. Yet, our clouds of obscurations have frequent tiny gaps that allow us to glimpse the sun of wisdom behind them. That is how the conditionless grace of Buddhahood makes fruition practice possible for sentient beings.

203 This faith can be supported by you integrating in your mind a clear understanding of what the scriptures say about the *pure qualities of Buddha nature* and *pure perception of the Guru and the yidam deity* as exemplifying those qualities in the phenomenal world. In the Path of Desire, even temporary glimpses of bliss begin to dissolve dualistic illusions that we must seek ultimate fulfillment from something outside of ourselves in space and time. When you and your partner become the eternal reality of the non-dual deity and consort, you know the taste of eternal bliss, even if it was experienced for only a moment. Later, you will be able to rest in recurring flashes of that. As you do, you can actually see the reality of your glimpses expanding with no fixed limit.

204 Starting, for example, with your genuine appreciation for your partner or consort, who is your close companion on this profound journey.

you must abandon all selfish motivations. Therefore, you perceive with certainty that to genuinely practice that path, you must first generate bodhichitta.

5. *The primordial, inseparable male and female aspects of non-dual Dharmakāya are perceived as the natural power of expression of your own nature,* the changeless wisdom of great bliss. That wisdom naturally expresses itself as the two-fold father and mother, completely perfect in their great purity, with awareness that they contain the assembly of deities of the Victorious One's great ocean of maṇḍalas.[205] That may sound intimidating, but exactly that will be experienced as what you are if you eliminate obstacles by actualizing the previous conditions, then let it be there.

Conclusion and Further Advice

These five Preliminary Perceptions must be assimilated by practitioners who wish to progress on the Path of Desire. Thus, *if you really want to attain high realization in the Path of Desire, at the very least, make sure that all of these five are integrated* into your practice in gradual stages. If beginners remain mindful of these points, they can practice with whatever glimpses of the ultimate occur for them. If you are just starting, you need not be overwhelmed and intimidated by these five requirements. *Just perceive as much of them as naturally manifests to you with your current capacity.* It is said that by the Buddha's compassion, what you experience will always be just right for your level.

What about those who have no intention whatsoever to practice Tibetan tantra formally? Everyone has the same ultimate nature, and as it is my wish that they manifest as much of that nature as they can, this book was written with the intention that anyone would be allowed to read it. Couples who engage in little or no Buddhist practice might still learn to

---

205 See "yab-yum", "deity," and "maṇḍala" in the glossary.

appreciate each other more, and be less inclined to fight with each other by understanding how the masculine and feminine principles work together in all interactions.[206] That perception may produce many practical benefits in this life and lay down good karmic propensities for practicing the tantric path in subsequent lives, so, regardless of peoples' background or aspirations, there can be many advantages to learning these teachings, but certainly no disadvantages.

In any case, with minimal elaboration of the vast and profound points presented, this chapter has given instructions on just the essential meaning of the Path of Desire that all readers may employ according to their aspirations and capabilities.

Without adorning this topic with fine elaborations,
In preparation for the bliss of transcendent sex,
The indifferent appearances grasped by a personal self
Of small, inferior minds should be completely abandoned.
By grasping the value of pure appearance as changeless love,
You will come to enjoy the great purity of the ultimate,
With all its glorious qualities of limitless joy and bliss.

Engaging in the practice of the channels, winds, and drops,
Whose manner is necessarily autonomous,
Is described through a congregation of many pleasant words.

---

206 That too can be like tasting the nature of all sugar in one grain of sugar. Many women say their partners do not understand women's physical and psychological experience, so they do not know how to bring either of them to the true sugary taste. Following the instructions in this book can help resolve that problem. Many men need to learn not to rush things so that they can savor that taste properly; many women can benefit by becoming more welcoming to the masculine energy from their partners once a broader understanding regarding the interaction between the two principles is gained. All of this can take practitioners far beyond ordinary sex as this interaction manifests itself in all the deeper layers of our existence.

Though the secret means of the practice of desire,
With one's own and another body are difficult to master,
Beginning with the practice of the real thing is the point.[207]

If the qualities needed for the main practice are not complete,[208]
By assimilating these five Preliminary Perceptions,
Even without knowing the techniques of enjoying,
The four joys of bliss-emptiness that lead to the ultimate,
The pure level of great bliss will still be reached in time.

---

207 At the beginning of this verse, Rinpoché is referring to the completion stage yogic exercises that work with winds, channels, and drops of the subtle body. Most tantrikas believe that mastering them should be their focus, but excessive preoccupation with them can easily become a distraction from realizing the main points during sexual union. Instead, he encourages starting with the direct practice of the Path of Desire based on the preliminaries just described. The following quote from Shépé Dorjé in chapter 6 below will address similar topics.

208 This means actual, formal practice of Tibetan tantra, including the fulfillment of the formal traditional preliminary practices, empowerments, and higher levels of experiences such as the ability to control the movements of different types of *thiglé* in specific parts of the subtle body and so forth. Though most of us are not practitioners of this very high level, we can still rely on the Preliminary Perceptions described in this book as a solid foundation to build up our practice of the Path of Desire.

6

Clearing Misconceptions with Detailed Presentation of Different Types of Thiglé

Glorious Shépé Dorjé's *Eliminating the Torment of Sexual Desire* says,[209]

A HO! In emptiness, the nature of the vagina,
From the play of the penis, unobstructed appearance,
The baby, united saṃsāra-nirvāṇa, is born.
If that is known, all things are of the nature of sex.

The vajra being established as the ultimate,
Other than by this highest of means is impossible;
So, this naked offering of the practice of sex,
Is set out for a woman who is desirous of sex.

Now, arising in the form of a sun maiden,
Giving the yogins refuge, the vajra ḍākinī
Speaks in accord with the meaning of what was invoked by
    speech,

---

209 *Rgyo 'dod skye bu'i gdung sel*, f15b1. 15b6.

Through accumulations of the girl of vajra desire.

Pushing forwards and backwards and *trulkhor* exercises,
Ephemeral skills with the yogic winds and physical sex,
That people may think are wonderful are not found here;
But I know well the workings of crucial points of sex.[210]

---

210 This song presents poetically the profound significance of tantric sexual union. In the phenomenal world, the **nature of the vagina** is *prajñā*, **emptiness**, the feminine principle as the fertile source of phenomena. **The penis is the play of unobstructed,** non-conceptual **appearance** as the masculine principle, powerful skillful means. From the blissful union of the masculine and feminine principles, **the baby, united saṃsāra-nirvāṇa, is born.** That baby is a metaphor for enlightened experience of Dharmadhātu, the fundamental space in which all the phenomena of **saṃsāra** and **nirvāṇa** are **united. If that is known, all things are of the nature of sex** in the sense that all phenomena are produced by and as the union of the masculine and feminine principles. In practice, the indestructible **vajra** nature, Sugatagarbha, being **established as the ultimate** truth by the direct perception of realization occurs only through the blissful union of the masculine and feminine principles. Its occurring in any way **other than by this highest of means is impossible.** It is a **naked offering** — directly perceived as it is, without a conceptual context — of the blissful union of the compassionate enlightened mind with the consort of phenomena. This may be experienced by the **practice of** sacred sexual union, in which case, Shépé Dorjé, from his perspective as a male yogī, shares as an **offering of bliss set out for** any **woman** consort that a male yogī is fortunate enough to meet because such a vidyā consort who is open and **desirous of** engaging in this kind of sacred sexual practice is extremely precious. The analogous statement is true for female yogins, the yoginīs. The bliss of union is often first encountered by literal sex with a human vidyā consort or Karma Mudrā, but it may also be encountered or enhanced by working further with the same principles in the context of other, more refined kinds of mudrās. The next few lines are presumably reminiscent of practicing *tummo*, inner heat yoga. In that practice, both male and female yogins may each visualize themselves as a **vajra ḍākinī.** The heat of tummo rises four finger-widths below the navel, in the form of a fiery red sun of wisdom. Therefore this ḍākinī is **a sun maiden.** Her heat is **invoked by** A, the seed syllable of **speech,** to rise up the central channel and transmute ordinary phenomena into the true **meaning** perceived by wisdom. In the Path of Desire, the goddess may literally manifest as a **girl who gives** both yogins **refuge from saṃsāra.** The same is true for the principal deity. Then, **accumulations of vajra desire,** sexual bliss unattached to particular objects — leading to pure accumulation of merit and wisdom in the yogins' minds — go up the central channel and pervade the body, transmuting

Introduction to a Better Coordinated Understanding Regarding Thiglé

Many people think that if they want to practice the path of sexual activity at a high level, they have necessarily to master different physical *thrulk-hor*[211] exercises. They also assume that practicing the path of sexual union involves all kinds of wondrous sexual techniques that enhance the experience of the ultimate.

A very well-known technique that Tibetans talk about is called "drawing *thiglé* upward," but most people[212] who talk about this are speaking from the viewpoint of male practitioners of tantra. They have an old-fashioned, culturally conditioned view that men are the most important candidates as practitioners. They wrongly think that the sole meaning of thiglé is male semen. It can be inferred from that misunderstanding that they have never properly experienced the path of tantra and its fruition, the natural state.

Why? In tantric texts, thiglé often refers to a subtle nature, energy, or element (*khams*), present in the body that is synonymous with relative

---

all perceptions into indestructible **vajra** wisdom, the fulfillment of all **desire**. That vision is the ultimate **speech of the** ḍākinīs that is beyond words and concepts. In the process of manifesting this, there are three yogic processes of descending, holding, and "spreading what is spread," which will be shortly addressed later in the book. These can be enhanced by **pushing forwards and backwards**, through yogic techniques where the drops are pushed in various directions within the body, or through certain sexual positions that have the same effect. Yogic **exercises** known as **thrulkhor** or yantra yoga work with the inner energies of the subtle **yogic winds** and **physical sexual skills** enhance joy and bliss. Many **people think** these **ephemeral skills** are **wonderful**, but preoccupation with them can easily become a distraction from the realization of the main point. Therefore, explanations of these are **not found here**, but I, Shépé Dorjé, **know well the workings of crucial points of sex**, and those are what is explained in this song.

211 To control their inner winds and so forth.

212 Rinpoché is addressing here what practitioners in general think when they talk superficially about these matters rather than what genuine tantrikas who properly do these practices would think.

bodhichitta. That subtle element or nature feels like an energetic fluid that pervades the body and mind as oil pervades sesame seeds. In the ultimate experience of the fruition, absolute bodhichitta, *thiglé*, or *khams*, all refer to enlightened awareness that pervades all of saṃsāra and nirvāṇa.

If male semen, also known as *"kunda* element bodhichitta,"[213] really were the sole meaning of thiglé relevant to this context, there would be no causal connection between thiglé and relative and absolute bodhichitta, nor with the subtle white and red male and female sexual essences whose existence they support. Khams means element or nature in a general sense.[214] When used in a sense synonymous with thiglé, khams may refer to semen, but more often it refers to the subtler red and white thiglés of relative bodhichitta in the subtle channels, or even more subtly, to absolute bodhichitta, the absolute nature of things.[215]

Is it not then clear that equating these terms with semen alone in this context is completely fallacious?[216] Male semen arises and is stored in the testes. That is quite well known by Tibetans and verified by Western medical science. Gross physical semen cannot pervade the body. On the other hand, khams, in the sense of relative bodhichitta, pervades the entire body as can be easily known from personal experience. When we are about to cry or when there is any feeling of bliss, for example, as in sex,

---

213 *Kunda,* a jessamine flower, which is white and blossoms by moonlight, here used as a poetic term for the white male sexual fluid, or semen; sometimes the same word refers to a kumud[a], a white, night-blooming lotus.

214 For example, *khams drug* can refer to the elements, earth and so forth, of the *Kālachakra* system.

215 In the phrase, *khams bde gshegs snying po,* "khams" means the nature of things, Buddha nature or Sugatagarbha.

216 Material semen is not the substantial cause of subtler forms of bodhichitta, but some people superficially conclude that thiglé in this context means only the gross, physical, white and red sexual — essences, semen, and menstrual blood, which Tibetans believe is the female contribution to an embryo. A definition that ignores other relevant senses of the word makes more subtle presentations of this topic in texts impossible to understand.

there can be a sensation of a potent fluid moving within the whole body and energizing it. This is an experience of moving thiglé. Sexual union, in particular, has a strong potential to activate and move these "hidden," subtle essences. It is, however, important to know that such sensations can be achieved not only through sexual union but also through any strong and inspiring experience and especially through devotion to the Guru who opens the door to the genuine tantric path.

Summarized Presentation of Different Types of Thiglé

Now I will present a summary of the different types of thiglé:

1. If you want to engage in the proper sexual practice of Buddhist tantra, it is necessary to constantly generate relative bodhichitta through your love and compassion. This altruistic attitude and the feelings related to it have an impact on the subtle essences, thiglé, of your body.
2. In tantra, relative bodhichitta, or "relative indestructible thiglé,"[217] has semen as its substantial *sign* or indicator but not as its substantial *cause*. It should be understood to be the "actual" relative bodhichitta that is so highly esteemed.
3. "Primordial indestructible thiglé"[218] is absolute bodhichitta as the absolute nature of things, Sugatagarbha. Realization of this is accompanied by spontaneous, indestructible faith in it.[219]

---

217 "Indestructible thiglé" sounds like it should always refer to the eternal ultimate. However, it also refers to subtle, relative bodhichitta, which can be powerful and long lasting, but is not literally permanent. Similarly, when bodhisattvas first reach the first bodhisattva level, their relative bodhichitta is said to be indestructible from that point on. That does not mean that their relative bodhichitta will not change and increase further as they advance through the different bodhisattva levels.

218 In Tibetan, *khams bde gshegs snying po.*

219 "Indestructible faith" that what is experienced is truly the absolute nature of things and

Practicing the Path of Desire should be understood through understanding how these three aspects of bodhichitta arise and interact with each other. When all these conditions of their interdependent arising are complete, the wisdom of great bliss will certainly arise as well. When it does, it will continue to increase until complete realization is gained. Depending on that increase, opposing obscurations are gradually purified until none of them remain. That the liquids in the secret place of male and female bodies can be no more than a sign or condition of all these higher processes is easy to understand. Nevertheless, as so many people seem to be confused about them, I will analyze these points further.

When we speak about the white element and the red element,[220] identifying these as physical male semen and female menstrual blood alone is too limiting. As previously stated, these terms also refer to the sexual essences as subtle, secret phenomena. Both men and women have only their sex's material sexual essence — semen or menstrual blood — but scripture and reasoning prove that subtle red and white essences exist in both men and women. Identification of male semen alone as the white element and female menstrual blood alone as the red element obscures the causal relationship between coarse and subtle aspects of these essences and the subtle, secret levels of experience that occur when these two elements interact in Highest Yoga Tantra practices.

This mistaken definition seems to be a very significant sign of faults of not knowing the distinctions between subtle and coarse, support and supported, as well as appearance and reality in tantra altogether. When we do make the correct distinctions, our view will be accurate, our meditation unerring, and our conduct precise as well as other important and beneficial results.

---

one's true mind. Though, at first, this experience typically consists of temporary glimpses, the experiencer gradually gains stable faith that these glimpses are really experience of the eternal nature of things.

220 *khams dkar* and *khams dmar* in Tibetan.

Those whose understanding is divorced from practice and realization and whose minds are only led further astray by taking literally the words of their textual tradition usually ignore such subtleties. They draw the boundary between whether a tantric samaya is kept or broken simply by whether semen is ejaculated or not.[221] When people obsess over nothing other than not emitting semen externally, are they not displaying their ignorance of all other aspects of this profound subject?[222] It is clear to me that the presentation of such topics requires detailed reevaluation.

---

221 The fifth root samaya of Highest Yoga Tantra instructs that those practicing this system should not lose bodhichitta or thiglé. In the traditional text on the three vows, *Perfect Conduct*, by Ngari Panchen with commentary by Dudjom Rinpoché (pp. 118-119), it is said, "The fifth [samaya] is, with a desirous mind and at an inappropriate time, intentionally emitting semen, thus forsaking the bodhichitta generated for sentient beings." Then the commentary on that by Dudjom Rinpoché says that, "This also includes the abandonment of [the mind of] bodhichitta for any sentient being because [this] bodhichitta and the essential fluid are seen as one on the level of generation stage practice (of inner tantra)." Commentaries from other schools like the Gelug, explain this fifth root samaya according to this second meaning. Regarding exceptions, Dudjom Rinpoché says, "The appropriate times to allow seminal fluid to leave the body are during the secret empowerment as an offering to the deities, when increasing the family line of ancestral heritage, and when making special pills or other medicines [...]". Other traditional texts such as *Buddhist Ethics* (Jamgön Kongtrül,, p. 482) adds also, "...as a means to remove obstacles [to one's own life])," as a permissible exception based on the *Kālachakra*. In *Unveiling Your Sacred Truth Book 3*, the current author, Khentrul Rinpoché, presents the traditional approach to this and other *Kālachakra* root and branch samayas, along with issues associated with breaking and amending them, and addresses it while contextualizing its explanation to a modern audience. Additionally, he gave a more concise description in his booklet *The Seven Empowerments of a Growing Child — A Guidebook for Entering the Kālachakra Generation Stage* (Tibetan Buddhist Rimé Institute: Belgrave 2016). There, the description of this samaya focuses on encouraging practitioners to see "sex as sacred:" the advice is to avoid engaging in sex while dominated by afflictive states of mind or purely out of a fixated craving for ordinary pleasure of orgasm and so forth.

222 Serious practitioners at least know about these subtler senses of thiglé from reading about them, and some have experienced them directly by performing the relevant yogic practices. However, when they focus on this specific samaya of not losing thiglé, some seem to forget what they know, and they regard thiglé as meaning mainly semen. Rinpoché is directly challenging the limited interpretation of this samaya that has been fixated on over generations due to sticking too rigidly to a superficial understanding.

Examples from Scriptures and Extended Explanation Regarding Thiglé and the Proper Attitude for Engaging in Sexual Union

When the senses of thiglé are summarized in the *Guhyasamāja Tantra*, three classifications of thiglé or drops are taught, and other tantras have a similar intention. These are,

1. The thiglé of the absolute ground. This is equivalent to Sugatagarbha.
2. The relative thiglé of deluded ignorance.
3. Substantial, relative thiglés that include the subtle natures, khams, of the five elements.

No one who really understands the terminology and practice of Highest Yoga Tantra would say in any context that there are only two kinds of thiglé, semen and menstrual blood. Nor would they say that men and women are entirely without the other sex's essence. Those who think otherwise completely misunderstand what needs to be done in tantric practice.[223] As it is said traditionally,

Though the god is in the east, you prostrate to the west.
Though the demon is in the west, you throw wrathful *torma* east.

This is no different than ignoring a golden boulder lying directly in front

---

223 If both did not exist in both sexes, how could they be united as a non-dual wisdom element (*ye shes khams*) by yogic practice? For example, in tantric yoga of the channels, winds, and drops (*rtsa rlung thig le*), the red and white khams or thiglés are united in the central channel to generate the wisdom element (*ye shes khams*). When that occurs, yogins are able to overcome their obscurations and experience absolute phenomena. If males and females had only one of these two natures, and these natures could exist only in the sexual organs, that would not be possible. Tantric practice is intended to exalt the subtle red and white sexual essences to a level where both female and male practitioners share an experience of non-dual wisdom and bliss.

of you and placing a hundred times more attention and effort upon a little stone at its corner because you think it is much more important. The *Brilliant Expanse Tantra* says:[224]

On being motivated by bodhichitta,
Through thoughts of striving for others' benefit,
Bringing forth Nirmāṇakāyas is no fault.[225]

Shépé Dorjé's *Clear Points of the Path of Means* says,[226]

From following the vajra path, he arrived in the palace of a woman's womb, in the center of its luminosity, and, as he perceived he was staying there, by his emitting thiglé, the male and female semen and blood mixed, and from being transformed, they became the seed syllable of the yidam deity, from which he apprehended the appearance of the deity.

According to that and many other passages, there are situations where

---

224 As cited in Klong chen rab 'byams pa dri med 'od zer, *Snying thig ya bzhi*, img. 319. That text has *nyes pa med for nyes byas med* here. That e-text cites the source as *kun tu bar ma[g]po klong gsal nyi 'a'i rgyud a (sic)*. That may refer to the *klong gsal nyi ma'i gsang rgyud, rnying ma rgyud 'bum*, Dg.445, dr: BDRC scan UTIE0OPI7944B80B_I1KG12052.

225 The first lines refer to relative bodhichitta, not only as a wish to benefit all beings but as a subtle element in the body, which is subtle thiglé. The last line is ambiguous. It may mean that when the relative thiglés are retained and united, absolute thiglé is generated so that one becomes a Nirmāṇakāya Buddha. It may also mean that creating babies by ejaculating semen is no fault if this is done with pure motivation based on bodhichitta; moreover, loss of semen in this case may be accompanied by a net gain in relative bodhichitta. We could infer that even when it is not, occasional loss of semen is an insignificant setback as long as mental relative bodhichitta is being reliably accumulated.

226 The text has *thabs lam gnad* sel. It looks like sel should be *gsal*, making this is a reference to Shépé Dorjé's *thabs lam gnad gsal*, cited elsewhere in the text. However, we could not find this passage there.

the intentional emission of sexual fluid is the appropriate response for a tantric yogin. Generally though, when traditionally it is taught that there are seven occasions of losing thiglé, this mostly refers to the release of essential drops in the yogas of channels and winds. It follows that the correct sense of thiglé, and whether samaya is violated or not by releasing thiglé, must be understood based on the context.[227]

If some general principles governing the many points I have brought up here are encapsulated, doing a great deal of physical training with thrulkhor exercises and so forth is not the foremost focus of Highest Yoga Tantra. First, you must be guided by correct view, meditation, and conduct.[228] Otherwise, you will have a dualistic view that sees only this saṃsāric side. Then you cannot help being motivated by coarse self-centered desire. As a result, the ordinary bliss and joy generated by your ordinary objects of meditation will also be grasped with selfish dualism. If you only see in terms of the dualistic karmic formations of your coarse path of means, when you try to discriminate between keeping and violating samaya, you will not understand the main tantric samayas that are the essential point of practice.[229] As a result, you will tightly cling to less significant samayas

---

227 As thiglé is not semen alone, is it not clear that when semen is lost, thiglé as a whole is not necessarily lost as well? Even if semen escapes, it is sure to keep arising, so whether subtle thiglé or bodhichitta is also lost, whether its loss is beneficial or not, and whether overall progress in accumulating it is maintained even if a little is lost, depends on many factors like the view, attitude, motivation, and level of practice of the practitioner. Thus, if someone asks, "If, as you say, also other coarse substances such as tears can be regarded as a coarse sign of thiglé, and, in general, it is suggested to avoid losing thiglé, what to say about such faithful ones who spend long crying out of devotion"? That is another example of when emitting thiglé based on a good reason is appropriate.

228 These are presented by Rinpoché in *Unveiling Your Sacred Truth 3*.

229 The most important root tantric samayas according to Highest Yoga Tantra are to cultivate genuine devotion, pure perception, and so forth towards the Vajra Master and your own vajra siblings (those who took empowerment from the same Vajra Master as you, whether at the same time or not). Not keeping these main samayas properly, and grasping tightly at a literal interpretation of other less important samayas is like trying to keep healthy the small branches of a tree whose root has rotted away.

that you can understand as being the most important ones. Since you are completely missing the point, it will be impossible to realize the fruition properly. Even if you entered into it partially, you would still have a topsy-turvy, causal misunderstanding of it. Thinking that temporary phenomena cause the eternal fruition, the absolute nature of those phenomena, is as absurd as thinking that the sun and moon rise in the west and rivers run uphill.

Rather than following that ill-considered approach, try to establish a correct view, whose subtle purity is free from the dualistic grasping of the coarse mind. Have pure perception that knows your bodies to be full of maṇḍalas of deities. Illuminated by the unfabricated state from the beginning, open yourself to the feelings and perceptions of loving-kindness and compassion that arise innately from the pure ground.

Then, because you are pure of the coarse selfishness of a dualistic mind, you will be naturally directed only toward the benefit of others. *Due to generating the excellent nature of bodhichitta, your motivation will be pure. As the fruition of that, the red and white essences of the body will circulate well, and the eventual arising of the perfect ultimate will be certain.*

If this is the case, what is facilitated by the power of relative bodhichitta will be like ordinary objects in the world being heated when they are churned such as butter coming forth from churned milk. What occurs in tantric practice is as if seeds of absolute bliss were drawn out of the essence of ordinary phenomena through many actions of practice like churning, rubbing, and so forth. When those conditions support the ripening and melting of these seeds' coarse substantial nature, interdependent causal arising of a subtle level of mind that can experience the main point will then occur.

To understand this process, we must become familiar with the correct main points of the view, meditation, and conduct of the tantra path within our own continuums. If we do not, we shall be fundamentally mistaken about the source of these stages, and therefore, how we should practice to actualize them. On the other hand, if these excellent conditions are complete, we shall become supple, quick, and energetic as if we had performed the best of physical thrulkhor exercises to attain the physical dexterity of the Victorious Ones. By simply working with coarse, physical semen, this result is as impossible as being able to send semen as high as the top of a nine-story building through physical postures and mental intention. If such mistakes of impure understanding are made — as with the above example of people who discard the roots of tantra and cling to the branches — disappointment will be inevitable.

I shall give a little further clarification of what results from such mistakes. Such deluded individuals, after initial traditional training in tantra, may think, "I should manifest the Path of non-dual Desire;" but thinking this way does not preclude that their motivation is anything more than intense, self-centered craving. They may parrot lofty thoughts like, "My pure perception of my companion in means as worthy of the highest esteem must be flawless." Even so, due to their intense, self-centered desire to be gratified by phenomena of form, sound, smell, taste, and blissful touch, they are really guided by ordinary, craving desire. They may think, "I should meditate on my fresh, pure experience of the deities," and then actually contemplate them by rigidly focusing on stale clichés, concepts, and images that were fabricated long ago. In practicing the Path of Desire, they may think, "Losing semen is always a violation!" and practice an obsessive caricature of skillful means to retain every drop, never noticing how their intense hope and fear are draining all subtle manifestations of thiglé.[230] Such individuals are not really on the path of tantra. Since great

---

230 It is true, even from common sense observation, that men, in general, lose capacity and energy after ordinary orgasmic release. Rinpoché's point, however, is not that cherishing the "kunda element bodhichitta", coarse thiglé, is not important; but rigidly fixating on the idea of never losing semen in any circumstance — and therefore, disregarding other important points of the practice — is a narrow attitude that will not lead to realization. As he says, unfortunately, often practitioners misunderstand the intent of this samaya by equating it with mere technical skills of being able to not emit semen externally during

faults are likely to result from their misunderstandings, they need to be much more careful about their approach.

Some people who claim that they are abiding in the divine pride of the deity think that doing so makes all others inferior to them. In doing so, they pile up great errors upon errors. What is necessary in tantra, even in the generation stage, is *universal* pure appearance. To view all phenomena purely, practitioners must meditate on all appearances of themselves and others as equal in the universal purity that is the nature of things. Regarding others as inferior in any tantric practice hinders the very purity that one wants to experience; and all the more so when you view your consort as inferior in sexual practices. People with that viewpoint are not meeting even the minimum requirements for visualization in the generation stage.

When you are thinking about the actual practice of the tantric Path of Desire, if, through overbearing hubris, you think, "Now I will manifest the highest skills of the Path of Desire," by such conceited thoughts, you will never reach any part of that path.[231] That kind of conceit and powerful self-grasping will guarantee that a genuine experience of tantra never arises in your continuum at all, so take care to avoid it. This kind of greedy thinking is also a sign of an arrogant departure from awareness of the universal nature of human beings — the source of your capacity to practice tantra — to fantasies of your own superior incidental qualities. In that case, the fruition you achieve will have no more reality than the

---

sexual union. Unfortunately, traditional texts do not address clearly how and why the root samaya of not losing gross physical thiglé applies to women. Generally speaking, conserving and building subtle thiglé is just as important for females practitioners as it is for male ones. Involuntarily losing menstrual blood and other forms of coarse thiglé is not usually considered a samaya violation. Rinpoché says that, from a practical relative viewpoint, since orgasm does not inhibit women's energy for practicing the Path of Desire as much as it does men's, women do not have to worry much about that topic.

231 The problem is the arrogant attitude. If a sincere, respectful person had the same thought, it would be a virtuous one.

imagined causes.

Instead, remaining modest, recall proverbial sayings like, "Humility is the dwelling place of the forefathers," but also do not give way to despondent thoughts like, "This excellence excludes an unworthy one like me." Recognize that a wonderful opportunity has arisen. Thinking that your innate wisdom is hidden in the cocoon of your natural sexual passion as indestructible thiglé, feel a deep trust in your innate Buddha nature.

Those who are practicing the Path of Desire must enjoy sexual activity in the devoted manner of receiving the four higher empowerments from a companion in means who is higher than themselves as if they were devotedly serving a perfectly qualified Vajra Master. Being confident that pure perception is necessary and sufficient for actually receiving empowerment is important.[232] If you see your partner as an inferior to be exploited, receiving these empowerments will be impossible. In brief, when practitioners' conduct is driven by impure self-cherishing and a powerful dualistic view, even if a perception of the natural state exists from time to time within their practice, it will soon be destroyed by conceptualization.

---

232 Tantric practitioners train pure perception first by exercising it through Guru Yoga practice, then expand the same principle of "faith in purity" to themselves, to their vajra sisters and brothers, and eventually to all sentient beings. Here the advice is to train pure perception in relation to one's own consort who, like a Vajra Master formally bestowing empowerments during an empowerment liturgy, is now bestowing the same through direct practice.

Conclusion with a Summary of the Actual Prerequisites for Path of Desire

Here is a summary regarding the attitude necessary to practice the Path of Desire. These points should be adopted regardless of whether you plan to train formally in the actual completion stage.

1. If you have faith that absolute Buddha nature exists within everyone, both yourself and others, your desire to experience that is the cornerstone of your practice.
2. Then, make a habit of trying to perceive your body as containing all the maṇḍalas of the Victorious Ones.[233]
3. If the time has come to practice the sexual activity of the Path of Desire, do not stray into impure characteristics by debating the pros and cons of your consort's apparent ordinary faults and virtues. Rather, perceive your companion in means as incomparably sacred and priceless.

When these prerequisites are brought together, you are a person capable of sacred sexual practice. Even if you do not yet have the merit and good fortune of practicing the authentic tantric completion stage,[234] your sexual experience will still be greatly enhanced. If you are capable of spending your life in the happiness and joy brought forth by that, how could your sex life be non-virtuous? In spite of the harsh criticism that often accompanies these types of activities, being certain of their benefitting human

---

233 It is unlikely that beginners will have a full understanding of this prerequisite at first. If this is true for you, just relax and contemplate the idea of this and other prerequisites, and resolve to be open to the actual experience when it occurs. Then you will be able to progress step by step. See more in chapter 5 above, and "pure perception" and "maṇḍala" in the glossary.

234 See footnote 208.

life is important.

If the favorable conditions of view, perception, focal objects, and so forth are all correct, aspire again and again that you may have the good fortune of embarking on the great tantric path. As you make these aspirations, rely on constant mindfulness and vigilance, but let your sexual desire be as it is with some autonomy. Neither trying to forcefully direct it toward a "suitable" object nor to restrain it to conform to a preconceived moralistic ideal, think, "This is my innate wisdom!"[235]

In doing this, never let yourself come under the power of attached craving so that your mind thinks that fulfillment can come only from a certain external object. Also recognize that right now, as an ordinary individual, you have little autonomy; thus, if you are completely under the power of craving, you will not be able to control the resulting kleshas. Be aware of that; if not, you will not come anywhere near the tantric path.

By allowing yourself to experience the authentic taste of the tantric path, you will enter into that great reality. That is so because the previously listed conditions that make you capable of attaining the path to liberation are complete. On the genuine path that is not a mere imitation, pure appearance and divine dignity are produced. You must have a powerful resolve to traverse its stages. If you fail to do this, straying into a strong sense of craving for imagined objects that enchant you, you will quickly be enclosed in a dualistic lotus bud and carried away from the reality you glimpse. Those focused on such thoughts of hopes and fears will be unable to develop appropriate effort and other favorable conditions; thus, they will be unable to re-attain the fruit of the Path of Desire.[236] This kind of

---

235 At best, you will actually experience the taste of primordial bliss in the passion of your desire, but even if you do not at first, by letting it be, you will connect with that real nature over time as you recall former experiences of it according to the previous analogy of tasting a grain of sugar.

236 Unable to "re-attain" the sugar of the fruit while craving the "taste of sugar" experienced on a previous occasion based on feelings of hope and fear. Such kind of expectation eliminates any chance of success in the practice because it focuses on memory of in-

attached craving can *only* lead to failure.

> In worldly interdependence, which is the Conqueror's hand,
> Because of knowing the features of the support and supported
> On the path of Great desire, where Great desire is Great bliss,
> Inspired joy is enjoyed, as Great joy in its Great purity.

> From great[237] greed, the natural state cannot result.
> When there is great selfishness, its blessings cannot arise.
> By thoughts alone, the Path of Desire is not traversed.
> With non-attached non-thought, enjoy the Great Desire.

---

cidental relative appearances rather than openness to perceiving the ever-changing manifestations of ultimate reality. To really "re-attain" and increase the sugary taste previously experienced, hopes and fears need to be let aside.

237 In the first verse, "Great," in Great desire, bliss, and purity refers to qualities of the absolute fruition transcending distinctions of relative desire and non-desire. In the first line of the second verse, the same word is used to contrast these excellent qualities with what happens when there is merely a great deal of saṃsāric greed and selfishness.

7

Actual Sexual Union

Introduction to Sexual Union and its Proper Motivation

The *Guhyasamāja Root Tantra* says,[238]

By joining the two organs,
All things may be examined.[239]

The *Chakrasaṃvara Root Tantra* says,[240]

Praises have been uttered for the two sexes.
Tantrikas are united with the ḍākinīs.

---

238 BDRC D0443 Kangyur rgyud, ca 90a.1-157b7, f105.b.

239 In the relative, as Gendün Chöpel and Shépé Dorjé said, you can see how all activities are motivated by masculine and feminine principles. Moreover, proper practice of the Path of Desire produces realization of absolute phenomena, and so they too can be examined.

240 Quote //mtshan ma gnyis la bsngags byas te// sngags pa mkha' 'gro ma la sbyor// was not found in this work. Similar verses //mtshan ma gnyis la sngags sbyor te// mkha' 'gro dpa' bo gnyis med pa// were found in the *Abridged Cakrasaṃvara Tantra* D0370, vol. 77: 211b.1-244.b7, p. 235 a.

The ninth chapter of the *Abridged Chakrasaṃvara Tantra* says,[241]

> The sky-soarer, manifesting in the form of the king of birds, the garuḍa,[242] is, in reality, glorious Chakrasaṃvara with his face presently going toward the ḍākinīs, who are seen by the eyes of that face, and by former blessings, and so forth, an equal time is made of the three times so that all the realms are now pacified as bodhichitta and so forth, and they were also blessed in past time so that the divine ḍākinīs[243] and glorious Chakrasaṃvara are very excellently joined in great union in all activities. By that union, all valuable things exist in the palm of one's hand in a way that accords with their great glory and that inalienable reality cannot be ravished away by any thoughts that grasp at conceptual characteristics.

With the guidance of what is said there and in many other such passages, the principal evidence for the tantric realities of the sexual principles and their union can be fundamentally established. It is expressed in terms of intellectual understanding, non-conceptual experience, and liberation.

After the favorable conditions referred to in the previous chapters are complete, the actual sexual union may be engaged in. Upon reading the details below, there is a risk that my words may seem to suggest that it is only the actions and mindset of the man that matter. This, however, is not the case at all. What I mean to say is that on this path, there are many things that men must necessarily understand. Moreover, since I my-self have a male body in this lifetime, I have not directly experienced what

---

241 We could not find this text to provide an exact bibliographical reference.

242 Garuḍas are an entire race of unseen winged beings who exist in rivalry with the *nāgas*, serpent- or dragon-like sea unseen beings.

243 According to Rinpoché, ḍākinīs here in this context mean enlightened deities, like Tārā, but also other types of divine manifestations, like angels in other religions.

females need to learn. By first explaining the principal things men need to know, the essential meanings will mostly coincide with the next topic — things women need to know — and the explanation here can be received by making suitable adjustments. The fundamental points of the Path of Desire are appropriate for both men and women because both sexes are of significance for the tantric path. The great being Je Tsongkhapa says in his *Extensive Explanation of the Abridged Chakrasaṃvara Tantra:*[244]

> Though a man's partner remains a messenger lady,[245] through
> kindness and tenderness, like that for a sister, daughter, or wife,
> she should always be offered to with a very gracious attitude.

As taught above, whatever else a man may do in the Path of Desire, enjoying his consort as merely an object to be used for his own self-centered pleasure is completely wrong. He should instead have the great aspiration of offering his actions of body, speech, and mind to his companion in a manner that she will value and find immensely pleasing.

In order to do this, he does not need necessarily to perform formal chants and liturgies. His motivation should arise naturally from deep in his heart. Such a motivation must be nurtured with continuous and vigilant mindfulness in the beginning, middle, and end of sexual union. There is no need to speak in facile clichés that express no more than the ideas, feelings, and perceptions of an ordinary person, such as, "I love you so much!"[246] or "I remembered you this morning."[247] Do not depend on repeating the words of others. You can do much better speaking from the

---

244 *Rje tsong kha pa'i gsung 'bum,* 18 volumes, 8.10.f145a, Adarshah.org etext.

245 *pho nya mo,* another word for a female tantric consort.

246 In the sense where "love" is just a kissing word.

247 The attitude is what is most important, so a sincere person could say the same things.

heart. The *Tantra of Accomplishing Wisdom says,*[248]

> All the ocean of the Teacher, the Buddha's teachings,
> Combined and made available in experience,
> The reality of the great secret is this truth itself.[249]
> There is no liberation when this does not appear.

The *Guhyasamāja Tantra* says,[250]

> Though tortures of ascetic discipline,
> May be indulged in, nothing will be attained.
> Depending on all the qualities of desire,
> Is the way that attainment is received.

The *Chakrasaṃvara Tantra* says,[251]

> Thus, in bliss there is the essence of bliss.
> By that, the highest bliss may be established.

According to what is said there and elsewhere, if one of these days you are a man who is fortunate enough to engage in tantric sexual practice or sex altogether for that matter, when that day comes, focus your mind on actions that make the woman rejoice. A man who only wants to stick his *liṅga* in a woman's *lotus* right away is selfish and greedy and does not

---

248 *Ye shes grub pa'i rgyud.* The passage and text were not found to provide an exact reference.

249 The essence of tantric realization.

250 Quoted in the Precious Treasury of Doctrine, in *Klong chen pa dri med 'od zer gyi gsung 'bum*, BDRC e-text lccw.0424, vol 15: p.227.

251 Quoted in the *Precious Treasury of Doctrine*, in *Klong chen pa dri med 'od zer gyi gsung 'bum*, BDRC e-text lccw.0424, vol 15: p.227. Right after the previous.

know the nature of women. He is no better than a dog or pig, and such behavior can cause the woman to experience cruel suffering. Not only does it deny her the experience of bliss, it can also create such great physical and mental distress that for some, it cannot be forgotten for their entire lives. This is a very serious non-virtuous action that carries great negative consequences for all beings involved, in this and subsequent lives.

Unlike a man who can often be quickly aroused, a woman's desire is not usually directly accessible. It typically exists at a deep level and so, in general, it cannot blossom in an instant. Therefore, *before engaging in sexual union, it is important for a man to be competent in many kinds of means of arousing desire in his consort.*

These basic skills are undreamed of by many men in countries with inferior knowledge and education and to individuals with patriarchal or self-centered attitudes who have been brought up thinking that "real men" do not care about the feelings of women. That is not to say that such a systematic lack of compassion is not all too common in developed countries as well even though people there are supposed to be progressive. That speaks for itself, and there is no need to explain further why it is a problem. Nonetheless, for those who have the aspiration of practicing this Path of Desire of tantra, and for those who do not but still hope for a meaningful sexual experience as well, I shall briefly present some necessary points and basic, important skills of the Path of Desire. The lord of learned ones Gendün Chöpel says,

358. In brief, by a variety of activities,
     Until strong wishes for sexual union arise in women,
     Men should not engage in actual coition.
     That is the essence of all the treatises on desire.[252]

---

252 In the sense that high appreciation for the consort and consideration for their arousal are essential to the practice.

Sexual Practice in Progressive Stages and Further Advice

Introduction

The Highest Yoga Tantra path is one of great opportunities. This book is not only for the benefit of those who aspire to be genuine tantrikas. Even those who are not properly informed about the fundamentals of the Path of Desire and have no aspiration of practicing it as a path of liberation can still have great trust for what they can accomplish with the skills of desire taught here. For those of you who simply want to become genuinely courageous and skillful people, this book is for your benefit as well. Nevertheless, what follows is not for the benefit of those who are already very well-versed in sexual skills or for those who prefer the elegant language of the classical Path of Desire found in traditional texts.

Sexual Practice in Progressive Stages

When you are with a tantric consort, trying to have "fast sex"[253] like a "hungry dog wolfing down lungs"[254] is never right. When you are first with a woman who is a potential partner, spend a lot of time with her, engaging in a variety of activities until you establish her confidence and esteem for you. Remember that in general women tend to be more attracted to an appealing personality than attractive physical characteristics without such traits.

In the beginning, as you both savor pleasant conversation, court her by being a caring person who greatly appreciates her and is therefore eager to please with his attentions. Through your eagerness to please her with your attentions and by all this enjoyable and affectionate talk, you will begin to delight her mind. During all kinds of activities, possibly for

---

253 Analogous to fast food, where speed and convenience are more important than quality.

254 The point is not that the dog is so greedy that it wolfs down even disgusting offal. Tibetans consider fried lung a delicacy to be savored. The dog falls short by not taking his time. (Search "Tibetan lung," *lowa katsa*, for the recipe.)

a long time, and when that woman begins to speak in romantic phrases, and her facial expressions clearly show that she desires physical intimacy with you, perceiving that what you have wished for in your mind for a long time as precious and priceless is about to come true, slowly look at her face and welcome her with smiles.

First, speaking pleasant words and conveying your affection in other ways, gently touch the outside of her clothes, always remembering that underneath there is something priceless, powerfully and sensitively sacred. Your mind should be delighted at the good fortune of merely touching her clothes. Touching inside them right away, with anxiety and inner conflict about whether the time has come, spoils the mood. Enter into all these progressive stages thinking that they should be fully experienced as the preliminary stages of the profound Vase Empowerment and of the actual four higher empowerments[255] all together as described in this chapter.

Only after anticipation has gradually built, may you have the honor of touching her sacred body beneath her clothes. Do not try to place the jewel[256] in her lotus setting right away as this requires a very powerful and sensitive blessing. Thinking, "I am touching her," rest in one-

---

255 When Rinpoché speaks of "actual empowerment," he is pointing out the maximum level of experience that a fully prepared practitioner could attain on these occasions, while at the same time remembering that in the past, this was the actual process of bestowing higher empowerments employed by Indian mahāsiddhas. He does not mean that everyone who does this consort practice is sure to receive an authentic experience of empowerment by doing that regardless of understanding, previous training, and whether samaya with a lineage holder has been established. For those who are not fully prepared, the consort practice described here functions as a kind of "exercise," where you maximize your holy experience of sex as much as you can. Those who have already received a formal empowerment from a lineage holder can apply the principles learned earlier here and go deeper in the matter through direct practice. Such an approach makes this practice suitable for different levels of practitioners.

256 A.k.a. liṅga.

pointed meditative absorption.[257] This stage of touching is not concerned with touch alone. Smells, tastes, and so forth should be savored as well. Āryadeva says,[258]

> In acting to attain the fruition of great bliss,
> There is no skillful means but the bliss of great bliss itself.
> Through the means of invoking bliss of food, place, and so forth,
> Bliss possessing the eight great masteries is established.

As is taught therein "and so forth," touch different parts of the woman's body. Beginning in places that are not too sensitive, very gradually touch the neck, around the base of the ears, the nose, the mouth and other places where sensations are more intense. Also kissing those places, proceed to the mouth. While you are doing all that, remain in the same one-pointed meditative absorption on what is going on.

As you do so, let your expansive feelings develop spontaneously into the perception that all the Victorious Ones' maṇḍalas of deities in the entire universe are in every pore of your bodies. That really happens when things are just right, and that experience is not to be missed for the world. Being anxious to "fast forward"[259] to later stages like putting your liṅga in her lotus is never appropriate. To receive the authentic experience of empowerment, the later stages have to develop in natural continuity from the earlier ones like a rosebud gradually opening into a full blown flower.

Perceiving this chance to touch all the parts of the consort's body as a rare and precious opportunity, thinking that the auspiciousness of actually experiencing these first empowerments is very fortunate, let them

---

257 More instructions are given a little below.

258 Quoted in the Precious Treasury of Doctrine, in Klong *chen pa dri med 'od zer gyi gsung 'bum*, BDRC e-text lccw.0424, vol 15: p.227.

259 As you might skip forward to the best parts of a digital movie.

develop slowly and naturally. If you act with this perception, you may well experience the river of blessing of the actual Vase Empowerment.[260] *If you do not cultivate such an attitude of appreciation, ravenous attachment to whatever else you do will only carry you farther and farther away from the Path of Desire.*

Then gradually, with stable mindfulness of the highly sacred nature of this act, very slowly touch your partner's breasts and outer lotus petals. On these occasions, it is important and also necessary that profound perceptions and feelings of devotion arise. Your partner is now revealed as a manifestation of the holy Guru, endowed with the very powerful blessing of granting the four higher empowerments.[261] This blessing is highly sensitive and only functions if your attitude is worthy of receiving it. Recognize that finding yourself before such a being is supremely rare, and the precious karma of attaining these holy empowerments is supremely excellent. As you very gradually caress her breasts and lotus, recognize that these touches are sacred representations and empowerment substances.[262] As they merge into a single empowering activity, the totality of your experience becomes the actual *Vase Empowerment.*

Finally, not just lightly touching, slowly rub, press, and gently massage. Then very gradually, slowly massage the anthers[263] of the lotus. Touching and massaging these places is usually joyful for the woman. There is however no guarantee that the same action will always have the same effect.[264] Special, intimate knowledge between the partners must develop

---

260 See Appendix II for a scriptural reference regarding this and the subsequent empowerments.

261 See footnote 232.

262 This recognition helps you keep pure perception.

263 The surrounding area, and finally close to the clitoris.

264 The aim here is to remind the reader that even if these instructions work in most cases, when you are fortunate to be with your consort, you need to be empathetic enough to perceive whether they resonate positively with her or not. If not, try other ways that are

over time, and it is mistaken to think that there is a formula that will always work.[265] Joining this same advice to all the following instructions is important.

When your precious consort is fervently intoxicated with desire, her face flushes, and her nipples and lotus stiffen and swell. Never initiate actual sex until the *amrita* of great desire is flowing from her lotus. This nectar should be licked with the tongue and tasted. This is the actual *Secret Empowerment* substance. Know that tasting this holy, very powerful and sensitive empowerment substance is infinitely superior than receiving the empowerment substance of a symbolic empowerment liturgy.

If the consort, just from that, spontaneously moans or cries, soft sounds come from her nose, her face reddens with desire, and amrita flows from her lotus, you may then enter into the actual sexual activity of great bliss. At that time, as you are madly intoxicated with 100,000 joys, perceive with delight that you are about to have the good fortune of receiving the actual Wisdom Empowerment.

Now, with your consort's delight,[266] the vajra jewel or head of the penis is very slowly and gently placed at the mouth of her lotus. Finally, it is very sensuously inserted just a little and then pulled back. As you rhythmically repeat this action again and again, think something like, "E MA! What wondrous good fortune! The chance has come to offer this king of all offerings to this sacred human consort, who has the nature of prajñā." Also continue to recognize, with immense gratitude, "This is the good fortune of the actual *Wisdom Empowerment!*"

The arising of such remarkable perceptions as your body experiences these special sensations are the result of the activation of karmic pro-

---

more pleasurable for her. The same applies to women in relation to men.

265 For example, the sensitivity of the anthers varies widely. Sometimes, direct stimulation of the clitoris may be pleasurable only after sufficient buildup or not at all.

266 As general advice, check if your partner is enjoying it as much as you are. Acknowledge your partner, for example, by looking at her, and so forth.

pensities previously established at deep levels of your mind. The ripening of this incredible karma on this very particular occasion can only happen if you are resting properly in one-pointed meditative absorption. Turning a mental wheel that emits many discursive thoughts is not proper.

Now, as these perceptions naturally develop, while you remain in one-pointed meditative absorption, very gradually enter deeper and deeper into her lotus as far as it is pleasurable to her. As you do, be profoundly certain that by many millions of empowerment substances, you are attaining immeasurably many authentic Wisdom Empowerments.

Then, when the desire to do so becomes irresistible, very slowly churn the vajra in the lotus, pulling it back again to the lotus mouth. Every time you repeat this, with her delight, the vajra should go deeper inside. As you follow this rhythm, spontaneous feelings and perceptions that the ocean of maṇḍalas of the Victorious Ones is within your bodies[267] may gradually arise with increasing vividness from the depths of your mind.

Finally, when only these special perceptions and understandings occur in your mind, you will be able to enjoy them in a state of irresistible intoxication. This occurs because you recognize that you are experiencing the great wisdom of blissful suchness through the bliss of thiglé[268] melting. *If you are able to rest for a long time in just that, that is the path.*

If you can progress to this point of the Path of Desire, you are able to do what is difficult for many others. With no worries at all about what to do earlier and later, your profound feelings and perceptions are the wisdom experience of bliss. Do not let yourself be distracted for even an instant by thoughts of anything else. You are experiencing the actual wisdom of the transcendental fourth empowerment, the *Word Empowerment,* or something very like it. Recognize this as pristine wisdom without

---

267 Perception of your bodies and what they are feeling must be not lost or de-emphasized by trying to forcefully create a deliberate visualization. As your enjoyment is enhanced, you begin to experience naturally what is present on a deeper level.

268 Or khams.

dualistic grasping and free from elaboration. *Rest in it naturally, without fabricating anything at all.* With that, the basic steps of sexual activity have been taught.

Further Advice

The inexhaustible great bliss of the thiglé melting is experienced in the secret place, the *bhaga*, which is the source of profound bliss.[269] Yet, focusing and resting for a long time only in the secret place is not proper because you need to maximize your experience. The secret place bliss-protecting chakra's wisdom of great bliss must spread everywhere — outer, inner, and in between — with the apprehension of maṇḍalas of the Victorious One in all the chakras of your bodies.[270] If you focus too tightly on the secret place, you will lose control of bodhichitta, because your special feelings of bliss will be unable to spread anywhere else and they will be stifled out of existence. In that case, your experience of sexual union will only be one of an ordinary being and you will not have entered the path of tantra, even partially. *To experience the Path of Desire properly, there must be experience of the great bliss of melting being distributed throughout your body, outside, inside, above, below, and in between.*

Usually, in the texts of Highest Yoga Tantra, thiglé is said to descend, to be held without loss, and to spread; and that much can be easily understood. According to the extraordinary, direct instructions, though the

---

269 Rinpoché wrote "lotus" in Tibetan, meaning "bagha" in this case. Bagha literally means the womb, with the vulva and vagina. The female practitioner experiences great bliss in her sexual organ, as does the man as he unites with the bagha. Both also experience the subtler level of that experience as the primordial nature, which is the source of phenomena, another meaning for bagha.

270 Rinpoché says that when the wisdom of the great bliss of melting spreads, we spontaneously perceive our whole body as an enlightened maṇḍala. This is not a deliberate visualization or a conceptualized contemplation, it happens in the sense of recognition. Apprehension of phenomena of wisdom is maximized, and self-centered narrow saṃsāric perception is diminished.

descent of thiglé[271] may be superior, intermediate, or lesser in intensity, its descent to the jewel tip is comparatively easy. Though holding the concentrated thiglé at the jewel tip without ejaculating is a little harder, there are techniques for doing that, and it is not terribly difficult.

The hardest of the three is "spreading what is spread,"[272] but it is also the most important and beneficial; it is the king of instructions that brings all other instructions together and, if it is mastered, everything will be liberated. In experiencing the great bliss of the Path of Desire, "spreading"[273] "what is spread"[274] is the last stage in the sequence of all the events of sexual union. Nevertheless, how well or how badly all the preliminary and final stages of sexual union go depends not only on whether "spreading what is spread" is skillfully performed, but also on what practitioners were like in the first place, their preparation and motivation for practicing the Path of Desire, and so forth. And indeed, *if you build a solid basis by working with the main points outlined here and in previous chapters, this final stage will likely happen naturally.* The greatest faults of motivation that can occur are the fundamental faults of self-grasping and self-cherishing, which lead to impure saṃsāric view of only seeing this mundane side. *If your attitude is incorrect, no matter what instructions about technique you may receive, you will not experience these empowerments.*

---

271 In a man, as feeling builds toward the point of orgasm, there is a sensation of concentrated thiglé descending to the tip of the vajra jewel. Some in a position to know say that there is an analogous descent to the lotus anthers.

272 In Tibetan, *'grem bkrams,* a verb and its participle that have the same root meaning.

273 "Spreading" in this case is a process that occurs as the subtle drops expand from the vajra and lotus jewels to pervade all the chakras, and eventually all the of channels of the subtle body.

274 "What is spread" refers to the drops, thiglé, that are spread to all those places by that process.

Common Challenges for Men and How to be a Modern Warrior

There is never control at first over what the human practitioner's nature is like, including characteristics of age, capabilities, and so forth. *Since motivation is most essential, it does not make much sense to place too much emphasis on youth or skills*; otherwise, you would be discouraged from practicing the Path of Desire if you are an elderly person or if you are not very skilled in sexual techniques. Desire, including some form of sexual desire, is there as long as life is present. Also, with age comes an increased perspective in this regard.

Therefore, even if serious physical limitations keep you from the sexual practice described, simply do as much as your current capabilities permit. There is no doubt that by cultivating pure motivation and perceptions, you will certainly attain benefits and sow good seeds for the future. Since very few insurmountable physical impairments or mental deficiencies make all kinds of sexual activity impossible, most difficult problems can be worked through by practitioners adjusting their attitudes.

If we speak of only the physical requirements of sex for males, which have no exact equivalents for females, the greatest problems men can face are,

1. The liṅga does not become erect.
2. There is an erection but it is not sufficiently hard.
3. The erection stays sufficiently hard for a short time, but does not last long enough.
4. The liṅga is capable of staying quite hard for a long time, but it ejaculates somewhat prematurely.
5. The erection is very hard and long-lasting, but semen escapes almost immediately.

Many techniques are taught to remedy the first problems. For those who know the correct path of bliss, practicing it need not depend only on the liṅga. Using sexual bliss as a path to ultimate bliss is possible apart from normal coitus. If someone is wholly impotent, or cannot complete the sex union, but the principal conditions and prerequisites of the Path of Desire are otherwise complete, the experience of bliss is by no means forever impossible.

However, if semen is lost too easily, an important physical condition of practice is absent. As for the little that can be done, before meeting with his precious consort, the man may ejaculate semen whilst alone and be motivated by his own joy to drink and swallow it.[275] As a result, when he meets with the consort, his performance is likely to improve although the degree of benefit is uncertain and some men may lose sexual desire altogether for a time.[276]

In conjunction with the above suggestion, or as a remedy in its own right, when the vajra is churning in the lotus, rather than performing it as if it were a race to the finish, progress slowly and mindfully. If you are

---

275 It is said in *Kālachakra* that if the man loses semen during union, he should take it back from the lotus of the consort with his tongue. "Drinking" with joy the ejaculated semen shows an attitude of honor towards the physical relative bodhichitta, or thiglé, that is so precious in this path. Admittedly, a man's thiglé is not necessarily restored just by drinking it, but the instruction to do this is an important reminder that semen, "kunda element bodhichitta" or coarse thiglé, is closely associated with the body's energy so that losing it is not always inconsequential, like voiding urine. Āyurvedic and Tibetan medicine also have a longstanding tradition of conserving semen for health.

276 As an alternative method, working directly with your own mind can be very helpful. When the man can completely abandon the ordinary idea that sexual intercourse must always conclude with ejaculation, it may be much easier to avoid losing semen. With practice and patience, doing this may come naturally. (To improve this process, one can additionally practice exercises to develop stronger muscles in the pelvic floor, allowing for greater control of one's own body. These exercises can enhance erection quality and other skills as well, and so they have the potential to bring greater satisfaction to your consort in various ways. Mastering this group of muscles of the pelvic region is the basis for the technique of pompoir, traditionally practiced by women in Asia to stimulate the penis, although it has diverse benefits for both women and men. A similar technique is called *kabasa*, pressing, in Arabic, and *kabza* in Hindi.)

near to losing control of the thiglé and your goal is a practice that avoids orgasm altogether or at least premature orgasm, slow down even further or stop for a while, feeling the bliss spreading throughout the whole body. If that does not help, stop altogether and, while hugging each other, rest your minds in one-pointed non-thought and remain there for a while.

As another alternative, the hero's tongue can repeatedly lick and savor the heroine's lotus and its "anthers," the clitoris, and other places in turn. You can enjoy other variations like viewing, touching, rubbing, massaging, and lightly scratching the nipples. In such situations, mutually experiencing again and again the smells, tastes, touchable objects, and forms associated with your bodies, manifest a feeling of profound longing. In this way, such intervals between intercourse are not separated from your practice. Then join the vajra and lotus again, and churn for a while. Alternate with these other activities as suitable.

In any case, before engaging in sexual union, let go of other thoughts so that you are clearly ready to start. Sex should happen naturally, and it will if you let it. At that time, be without such rigid thoughts as, "Now this must happen and then that must happen," or "This should be done and this should not." Your mind must come naturally to a one-pointed state, so turning a wheel of discursive thoughts like, "Only this is so and this is not," just gets in the way at the time of union. Prepare to be completely without strong hopes or fears, like "I must do this," and "I really want to do this, but it would be shameful."

Whether your goal is sex that produces high tantric realization, or just meaningful ordinary sex, be familiar with everything that is required beforehand so that disruptive thoughts will vanish naturally. Hopes and fears about whether your actions are acceptable are especially problematic. If you must think about such things, get it out of the way beforehand,[277]

---

277 It may be worth openly communicating them to your consort prior to beginning as suitable.

and then, *during actual sex, make no distinctions of good and bad at all.* You can be at ease, carefree in spacious naturalness, being open to whatever occurs should spontaneously happen. *As your mind floats with no "task" to perform, in that lucidly wakeful, vast, all-encompassing expanse, let it stabilize that way.* Narrowly focused, self-centered goal-oriented awareness is never right, in this case. In brief, do not rely on deliberate thoughts about the presence or absence of any procedures, high and holy, or down and dirty. *The Path of Desire does not work when you focus on your expectations of enjoying desirable qualities.*[278]

That said, when you are having sex, the mind, eyes, and winds should never be focused only on the secret place. Instead, (1) *perceive the human consort with high regard* as extremely holy. Be without impure, ordinary attached appearances. If you can spontaneously experience your union as the union of the inseparable father and mother deities; for example, Kālachakra and Viśhvamātā,[279] that is best. If you cannot do that, (2) *produce a perception of offering* your body, speech, and mind to the consort before you as a Guru who can grant you the four higher empowerments. (3) At the very least, *try not to think, with self-grasping and self-cherishing, about exploiting your partner* to attain something for yourself alone.

If a man wants to have the best possible sex life, he must be willing to investigate to discover the best approach. To know what he should investigate, he needs to contemplate what sex is all about. In particular, he must understand that sexual union is at its best when both partners are intoxicated with desire. Therefore, becoming intoxicated with desire himself is by no means enough. He must definitely know how to make the

---

278 Craving the rich desirable qualities of the desire realm, 'dod 'dun, is sometimes classified as one of the five fetters to enlightenment, *kun sbyor lnga*.

279 When genuine tantrikas engage in "sacramental" union, their worldly bodies embody enlightened deities. They can manifest for example as Kālachakra and Viśhvamātā in union, as they create, sustain, and dissolve the universe that manifests their ultimate love and compassion. Such deities are the highest manifestation of the masculine and feminine qualities that create everything and accomplish all actions in this world.

woman intoxicated with desire as well.

In ancient civilizations, "warriors" were chosen primarily for their fighting skills and will to power since defend, battle, and conquer were chiefly their requirements.[280] Nowadays, the following two ways can be used to classify an exemplary modern warrior:

1. Whatever is done is done with daring and determination without fear or panic.
2. When confronted with others' powers, a modern warrior does not lose control over their own power.[281]

These ideals apply in all walks of life, including courtship and sexual activity. Unfortunately, many men of the "old school" continue to think about women only in terms of ensuring their own satisfaction. This bias is reflected in many older tantric texts that appeared in patriarchal societies. They have a lot to say about the deficiencies of various kinds of female consorts whereas the faults of the men who enjoy them have been deemed as beside the point. Therefore, in discussing this topic, I wish to focus here upon common faults of men to restore a balanced approach.

If they are in a position of power or trust relative to the woman, they use their status to pressure her into submission. If all else fails, they resort to outright coercion. These men are of the lowest kind, who merely contain the outer shell of a man. When they are with a woman, they rush to their goal of orgasm. As women say everywhere, "They want only one

---

280 The principles of ethics and human relations were decided on the same basis as exemplified with a bit of parody in this dialog from the film *Conan the Barbarian*, Universal Pictures and 20th Century Fox (1982): "Barbarian General: Conan, what is best in life? Conan: To crush your enemies, see them driven before you, and to hear the lamentations of their women. Barbarian General: That is good! That is good!"

281 For example, a male warrior does not lose his own powers in front of a woman whom he sees as attractive; he can still control his own powers without being overwhelmed by passion.

thing." Such actions are outward and physical signs of a man of inferior character, with no sense of finer possibilities.

Commonly, it is men who consider women to be less valuable than themselves who lose self-control in such a way as it is often the case in Asia. Their lack of chivalry in this area is a sign that they lack any compassionate warrior virtue altogether. Those who think highly of women do not lose control in the presence of a woman whom they see as attractive, but instead, savor the experience. This is a sign of a man with warrior virtue. In sexual activity, inferior men full of self-centered approaches rush quickly to their own orgasm, losing semen and interest altogether.[282] They are not interested in sharing deeper joy and bliss with a woman and so are more like animals in their behavior. Need I say that they deny themselves the good fortune of this wondrous path of great bliss?

Though many such people do not have the good fortune of traversing the Path of Desire at the present time, it is never right to proclaim that anyone is permanently cut off from tantra. There is no individual on this Earth who cannot improve themselves. With the willingness to train properly, it is possible for anyone to increase the enjoyment of themselves and their sexual partners. Hopefully, they will eventually prepare themselves so that, in the future, they are able to practice the genuine Path of Desire of tantra.

Stages of Actual Sexual Union for Women and Conclusion

In my opinion, though individuals may vary, women are more suitable for the tantric path than men. In general, women have the nature of prajñā, and their tendency to be more feeling orientated complements tantra's

---

282 Losing energy after orgasmic release is not abnormal for men. The point here is that this lower type of man thinks only of his own lust; he rushes in, finishes as fast as he can, and after that he loses any interest whatsoever, including empathy toward his partner's feelings and desires because his "purpose" has been achieved.

nature to work with emotions, empathy, creativity, and so forth. Physically, they are also more reliably suited to continued or repeated sexual congress than men. As they do not have to worry about the aforementioned problems that affect men, it is likely to be easier for them to practice the sexual activity of the Path of Desire.

That is not to say that women face no problems at all. Their most common challenge is that the effort and persistence required for thiglé to descend, providing proper lubrication as desire is aroused and brought to a peak, is usually greater than for men. Moreover, the strong hormonal changes of the menstrual cycle can also affect sexual desire and performance.[283] Even so, these problems are usually more easily and reliably solved than those of men, especially if the male consort can be supportive.

If you are a woman who is practicing the Path of Desire, before you get together with your consort, it may be helpful to first arouse your own desire. Open yourself to appreciate and embrace as much as you can all the masculine qualities he naturally possesses and delight your mind with the opportunity to be in union with him. If you do not feel such delight at first, there is no problem in entertaining appealing fantasies about being a sacred consort. Since the mind is very powerful, your potential for successfully evoking desire is likely to go well.

If the consort you have the opportunity to practice with is too old, physically not overly attractive, or just not very good at lovemaking, you may need to broaden your means of arousing yourself.[284] Sometimes, if

---

283 Comparatively, the vagina is more susceptible to inflammations, and when these occur, sexual congress may need to wait.

284 For example, a woman and a man could form a harmonious couple, be great partners in life, appreciate each other etc. and, even so, it could happen that there is no great sexual desire arising between them. Moreover, since not all men are skilled in lovemaking or courtship, certainly not all women are fortunate enough to meet a skilled one in this lifetime. In such case, if she wants to practice with the consort she has the opportunity to meet, she may need more effort to arouse her own desire (or help him arouse her), if not, the practice may fail. The Path of Desire does not work properly if both practitio-

you employ means of increasing desire when you are with the consort, it works, but if it does not, you will just be faking it, and then arousing genuine desire for the consort will be quite difficult. If you learn means of arousing your desire beforehand, your chances are much better.[285]

As for ways of continuing to arouse desire within yourself and your consort, if you touch his chest, thighs, and other areas while admiring and absorbing your man's nature and powers, you may both feel a deep longing. You may touch ever so gently very sensitive places that people usually do not touch at other times, for the same reason, but, if particular places on the man's body are extremely sensitive and ticklish, this will not work for arousing him, so do not touch him there. Otherwise, gently brush the man's chest, cheeks, lower ears, and so forth. Then, with your breasts, hair, and similarly with your mouth and cheeks, touch lightly again and again. Touch, for example, your partner by lightly pulling your breasts over his entire upper and lower body, but do not touch the liṅga directly at the beginning. First, touch and gently drag the nails successively over the different regions of the scrotum. Sometimes scratch lightly and drag all the nails, like claws in the same way, and so forth.

Many other things that both companions are likely to enjoy in delight are like those mentioned above in the instructions for men. If your means of arousing your partner arouse you as well, that is best. If some techniques arouse the other person, but you do not like them, or they are just an unpleasant chore for you, that is not good, so for now, it is better to avoid them in favor of other mutually agreeable alternatives.

You and your partner may utter all kinds of sounds of arousal, humming, purring, or grunting. You should feel comfortable to make whatever noises come naturally, even shouting out is fine. However, rather

---

ners are not intoxicated with desire.

285 Employing mental or physical techniques for arousing desire beforehand can certainly work, but it may also be worthwhile to openly communicate or show your consort what he can do physically to arouse your desire.

202 TANTRIC PATH OF DESIRE

than focusing just on what you do with your body, *you should do every-thing with your mind one-pointedly*, as described above, knowing that it is a mistake to forget that.

At the time of surrendering to these experiences, both the man and woman should avoid sanctimonious dogma, like "Now I will engage in the traditional means of kindling desire into sacred bliss, by which, succes-sively, the four joys...blah blah." Think of something more genuine like, "Giving ourselves to each other is the best practice of all, and now we have an awesome chance to do that!" While you are thinking that, know that by enhancing your own desire you have the means of giving as a gift the joy and bliss within you. If your motivation genuinely has this approach, it will never be lost on others or benefit only others and do nothing for you.

Within you are the means of producing the innate joy and bliss of sex. Since what makes you both joyful could not be more suitable to pro-duce, desire for what you desire is best produced through knowledge that it is what your partner wants as well. Then, when actual means of arous-ing yourself to mad intoxication with desire occur, you can be certain that your companion in means also feels that. That is the best way to actualize the passion of desire.

In brief, when you are practicing with another, grasping the other as the principal one is the best means of intoxicating you both with desire.[286] Advancing on the Path of Desire by you and your partner, and intoxicat-ing each other with desire is the best approach. *Whatever manifestations of the bliss of melting occur by doing that are most likely to lead to the wisdoms of the four joys and, ultimately, to the experience of the innate wis-dom of bliss and emptiness.* Both practitioners should understand this to be supremely important.

As for other means of enhancing the liṅga's erection time, after

---

286 "The principal one" means regarding your partner as a fully enlightened being, as your principal meditational deity, or as an emanation of your own Guru, who is going to be-stow on you the four higher empowerments, as already described.

many actions of touching parts of the body, finally, at the time of actually touching the liṅga, if other parts of the scrotum are touched at the
same time, that often helps. The shaft of the liṅga is touched by the hands
and so forth, but be cautious about touching directly the liṅga's golden
top ornament,[287] as it may be too sensitive. Sometimes it may be touched
when covered by the sheath of the foreskin if there is one or with some
means of lubrication.

Finally, gently touch the liṅga, then churn it in your mouth, if you
feel like it. If you enjoy oral sex, it is extremely helpful. If you do not, and
there are alternatives you prefer, by all means, use those. However, if it
is extremely difficult to get your consort's liṅga hard, if you wish, you can
try it even if you do not enjoy it so much at first if that seems to you preferable to complete failure.[288] If you decide to engage in this, collect quite
a lot of saliva in your mouth, make the liṅga wet, then perform soft, long
churning motions again and again. At first, do this very slowly with close
attention. Then, gradually increase the tempo, like an Indian raga, if this
works for him.

When both the inside and outside of the lotus are quite wet, it is
the best time for you to welcome your consort's liṅga at the mouth of the
lotus. Put it just a little inside, penetrating the mouth of the lotus with a
gentle stroke then caress the whole vagina as you slowly pull back. Do
this again and again. Finally when the passion becomes irresistible, put
the vajra jewel just halfway in the bhaga, pull it out again, and repeat this
again and again. If the consort cannot keep his liṅga erect for long, you

---

287 The head of the penis, also called the vajra jewel. The jewel is compared to a golden top
ornament on a monastery, whose shape it somewhat resembles.

288 If the woman strongly desires to enter in union with her consort but it is difficult for his
liṅga to get hard except with oral sex — and if she prefers this last method rather than
losing the opportunity to enter in union with her consort —, she may decide to try it,
even if she does not like it much at first, following her own decision. The same instruction goes for the man in case his consort enjoys oral sex as a means of arousal, which is
the case for many but not all women.

need not do this process any longer than he can keep his erection.

Either the man or woman may do much of what is described above. Arousing the woman's desire before sex is very important as explained above, but usually, it is less so for the man as the man's desire is typically on the surface and easily aroused. If practices that work for both can be done, that can be a condition of the man's desire going deeper and harmonizing with the woman's.

In particular, if the man is old or does not have much desire to start with, it is useful if his sacred consort employs such techniques of skillful means. What accords best with the needs and wants of each individual and each couple's desires, should be gradually learned by experience. This will obviously not be the same for everyone, nor the same for all occasions. There is much to be learned about each other's desires as you progressively move forward.

In brief, by the mutual techniques employed by the man and woman, if the descent of the woman's thiglé has been well accomplished, "spreading what is spread" will occur naturally and easily. Unlike men, women do not need to make an effort to retain physical thiglé during sexual union. Since, in general, women do not greatly deplete their thiglé in orgasm, they are capable of repeated orgasms, and so their situation is different. Aside from this difference, the view, feelings, motivation, perceptions, and so forth that the woman should have are like those for men, as outlined in the previous section.

In the best case, in these occasions of tantric union, both partners should regard themselves as the yidam deity in yab yum, such as Kālachakra and Viśhvamata.[289] If however you put so much of your atten-

---

289 Due to one's habitual perceptions, commonly one tends to visualize oneself as the deity of one's own sex, and the partner as the deity of the other. However, this can be reversed, and, even better, both can visualize themselves as both deities in union, yab yum. If you have properly done a fair amount of generation stage practice, this will naturally express itself in terms of pure perception, accompanied by the deities' divine pride.

tion into a visualization that it becomes a separate project from your actual union, there is the danger that the favorable conditions you have accumulated will not be actualized. *Awareness of union should be spontaneous, direct, and non-conceptual.* Forcefully projecting meditation models of the generation stage onto the non-conceptual experience of the completion stage is likely to hinder more than help. More important is cultivating a feeling of Buddha nature and the pure qualities like love and bliss that these deities represent.

Moreover, it is taught that real tantrikas should not stay in the temples and monasteries of people like logicians and literalistic scholars who do not enter into the mindset of tantra because their attitudes and activities will conflict with those practicing tantrikas. On the other hand, it is also said that sentient beings with a devoted attitude who see, hear, remember, and touch yogins who keep genuine tantric discipline will quickly be liberated from their own evil deeds. As the *Chakrasaṃvara Root Tantra* says,[290]

> By seeing and by touching,
> By hearing and remembering,
> They are freed from evil deeds.
> Of that there is no doubt.

Many other scriptural passages, such as the previous one from Shépé Dorjé, say the same thing. Thus, as you are resting in the ground whose virtue is beyond conceptual delineation, naturally contemplate it from the depths of your mind, but do not dwell extensively on it through the discursive, conceptual thoughts and images at the surface of your awareness. If you do so, your experience, enhanced to your full capacity and undertaken with all appropriate qualifications, can reach the experience

---

290 Found in the *Abridged Chakrasaṃvara Tantra*, p. 245.b.

of the actual completion stage.

Whether particular individuals can grasp it or not, this path traverses the entire completion stage. Deliberately generating rigidly conceptualized thoughts and images that would be appropriate for the generation stage is not suitable here. In the completion stage, entering into actual, non-conceptual absorption is the main thing; so, if you forcefully generate thoughts and images, you will only remain in its prelude, the generation stage as if it were your nest. The last thing you need at this point is to make an extra effort to do that.

It is also extensively explained in some traditional tantric texts that, to the extent that the consort has matured toward a measure of authenticity and capability in the techniques of desire, the consort may be said to be superior, inferior, and so forth. Such conceptualizations are more likely to hinder than to help the non-conceptual approach required by the Path of Desire, so I shall not address them other than to acknowledge their existence.

If we do not consider the ancient liturgies and textual tradition of tantra thoroughly enough, it may seem that only men can be tantra practitioners, and women are non-practitioners used to benefit these male practitioners. Such an approach is more an illustration of the prejudicial weakness of the society of the time those texts were written than one intrinsic to tantra. Tantric tradition teaches a very profound and stable nature of things in which all actions, including those of tantric practice, arise from combining the masculine and feminine principles. How could it fail to know the natures and qualities of both males and females? Both sexes are required to practice tantra, and it is impossible that one can do so and the other cannot. Moreover, the particular qualities of men and women are usually manifest in their own sex and are hidden in the opposite sex. They typically exist in a gross manner in one sex, and subtly in the other. Everybody has both kinds of qualities to some degree. These points must not be ignored in practicing tantra.

Some tantric texts say that tantra will spread much more widely in this Age of Strife.[291] By the nature of the Path of Desire, it will have to spread among both men and women alike. From the very beginning on the tantric path, sensitive feelings of both body and mind such as devotion and so forth are required. Like tantra itself, these qualities must be steady and continuous like the stream of a river that never stops. These requirements may be more compatible with those who have the present body of a woman. It is therefore unsurprising that while tantric practice may have been the domain of men in the past, some texts suggest that tantra is soon to proliferate among women.[292] Undoubtedly, this will be very good for the future of Buddhist realization.

If we think about what sorts of people enter the path of tantra, one kind puts intense effort into mastering the many sexual techniques taught in the classical Path of Desire, thinking, "If I know these, I know the Path of Desire." Often that approach leads to missing the main point. Introducing advanced sexual techniques and thrulkhor exercises is pointless, in that case. This would be like a peasant with a king's throne, royal cloak, crown, and seal. Having the costume of a king will not make you a king with servants at your command. Similarly, if you have a large repertoire of sexual techniques, your ordinary sex may be better, but aside from that, your sexual activity will not lead you to the wisdom of great bliss of the natural state. Even if your sex life is fantastic, ordinary sexual pleasure can never become world-transcending in this case.

Since the fundamental *view, meditation, and conduct, are necessarily the principal conditions of success in tantra,* those who focus on sexual practices

291 Five degenerations [of the Age of Strife], [*rtsod dus kyi] snyigs ma lnga*. Degeneration of: 1) lifespan, *tshe'i snyigs ma*, 2) time (wars and famines proliferate), *dus kyi snyigs ma*, 3) beings (becoming harder to help on the path), *sems can gyi snyigs ma*, 4) views (false beliefs spread), *lta ba'i snyigs ma*, and 5) negative emotions, *nyon mongs kyi snyigs ma*.

292 Female tantrikas in the West are perhaps already more numerous than male tantrikas if we look, for example, at recent rates of their participation in empowerments, teachings, retreats, Saṅgha volunteering activities, and so forth.

alone never reach the genuine Path of Desire where they could be applied.

> Indian Brahmins and so forth, and learned ones of Tibet,
> Say much of the qualities of authentic vidyā consorts.
> According to their thinking, for every man or woman,
> Developing their own qualities must be accomplished first.

> Also, men who are possessors of bodhichitta,[293]
> By holding women's dignity as important and sacred,
> Let them be consorts who manifest the excellent path of great
>   bliss,
> And not just the ones with physical youth and beauty.[294]

> Though the consort's required virtues are taught to be many,
> In brief, if she has great faith, aspiration, and diligence,
> And most of all, little jealousy for other women,[295]
> A woman is of the family of authentic consorts.

---

293 Meaning here that they are compassionate and considerate of others. By that, they create a situation where any woman can manifest as an authentic spiritual consort. Similarly, an insightful and compassionate woman can "make a man" of her companion.

294 Traditional texts often say that a perfect consort, from a man's point of view, is a passionate woman full of energetic youth. As explained earlier in the book, the most important qualities are mental. This is true for both women and men. Qualities like youth and beauty mentioned in the traditional texts are a bonus. If they are present, they can be beneficial, but they are not required. Consorts of varying ages have always been employed, and the *Kālachakra Tantra* even recommends broadening one's experience by doing so.

295 Faith and diligence in the Dharma and ideally no saṃsāric jealousy, especially towards other women. The required virtues of male consorts have been presented earlier.

8

Different Kinds of Mudrās and the Four Joys

Different Kinds of Mudrās or Consorts

Mudrā[296] is a general name for spiritual or "knowledge" consorts, also called "vidyā consorts" — *rig ma* in Tibetan. The point of practicing with them is that by properly relating to such a consort, we can come to know the bliss of pristine wisdom that realizes absolute reality.

There is a wide variety of teachings on different kinds of mudrā consorts such as the four mudrās; in relating them to different contexts of view and practice, these different teachings may seem to be bewilderingly unrelated to each other. Here I shall first briefly present how to identify the different mudrā consorts employed for the sake of bliss:

---

296 *phyag rgya ma*

1. Wisdom Mudrā[297]
2. Karma Mudrā[298]
3. Dharma Mudrā[299]
4. Mahāmudrā[300]

All the different kinds of mudrā consorts can be classified within these four. It is important to keep in mind that different lists of four are not arbitrary but are due to particular philosophical approaches or practices that are being considered. Thus, generally speaking, Wisdom Mudrā, Dharma Mudrā, and Samaya Mudrā have different aspects and qualities according to particular systems and levels of practice.[301]

Wisdom Mudrās

"Wisdom Mudrā" primarily refers to a deliberately visualized or gener-

---

297 *ye shes phyag rgya*, a visualized consort. When this is done in the generation stage, such visualizations are also called Samaya Mudrā, *dam tshig phyag rgya*. As we list the Wisdom Mudrā as the first type of consort, and the first to be practiced by beginners in tantra when they start practicing the generation stage, the name Wisdom Mudrā seems paradoxically high for such a pedestrian manifestation. Sometimes Lamas who have the same reaction substitute *yid rgya* (mentally imagined mudrā) for the *ye rgya* (Wisdom Mudrā).

298 *las kyi phyag rgya*

299 *chos kyi phyag rgy*

300 *phyag rgya chen po*, often translated as "the great seal."

301 In the Yoga Tantra class, for example, the four mudrās are said to be Karma, Dharma, Samaya, and Mahā. The various lists of the four mudrās can be also summarized under three, non-arbitrary principles taught in Tāranātha's *Brilliant Clarity of Union* as three kinds of compassion (*snying rje gsum*) that reveal ultimate bliss: (1) the Karma Mudrā is a "real" consort who presents the wisdom of bliss in human life; (2) the Wisdom Mudrā is a visualized consort representing a wisdom deity (the Wisdom Mudrā, in this case, includes all other kinds of visualized or generated consorts such as the Dharma Mudrā, Samaya Mudrā, and Emptiness Mudrā; here one begins with a conceptualized visualization of the bliss of union with a wisdom deity, and that initial visualization will gradually intensify); (3) Mahāmudrā presents the changeless bliss of the absolute wisdom of fruition.

ated wisdom consort, which, at least in the beginning, is a merely conceptual object visualized as a wisdom deity of the generation stage.[302]

Although many divisions and levels are possible, we could divide Wisdom Mudrās into three main kinds or stages in order of being successively closer to the goal of authentic wisdom experience.

1. The lowest stage of a Wisdom Mudrā is a purely imagined or visualized wisdom being deity created as a conceptual object in the mental sense. Any feelings of bliss and purity and any sense of motion and interaction associated with the visualization will also be deliberately conceptualized.[303]

2. The second stage of a Wisdom Mudrā is still a visualized deity made to arise as a conceptual object, but this kind of consort has a very clear and vivid presence for which considerable proficiency in the generation stage is necessary.[304]

3. The highest stage of Wisdom Mudrā is still a consort of habitual meditation in the generation stage, but it has such a high degree of vivid clarity and feeling of purity that it is almost indistinguishable from a real wisdom being. Such consorts may be objects of both seeing and touch, transmitting a profound understanding and experience of the deity's empty-form.[305]

---

302 Why is a conceptual visualization of the generation stage given the exalted title "Wisdom Mudrā?" In terms of the object, such a visualization — also called *samayasattva* — is a representation of an actual wisdom deity. Even though it is a conceptual representation, the visualized deity represents different aspects of one's own enlightened nature; identification with them supports the development of pure perception and helps the practitioner to lessen attachment to their own limited current human form. Other beings are perceived in the same way, and phenomena are purely perceived as the deities' environment.

303 Because it is not a perception of pristine wisdom, *ye shes.*

304 Here, perception, feelings, and the sense of interaction with the deity have a more spontaneous directness that begins to transcend conceptual limitations.

305 Generally speaking, the visualization tends to be deliberate and conceptual in the be-

For even the lowest of these levels, the visualization may be much more lifelike than a painted *thangka*. This needs to be mentioned because, unfortunately, there is a misconception that the practitioner should visualize the consort as a motionless two-dimensional representation, like a picture.

In short, a pure perception of the consort as an authentic wisdom deity is the goal of practice with visualized mudrās as it is of the generation stage.

Karma Mudrā

When we speak of the "Karma Mudrā," the term is said to mean that, by the power of *karma*, a tantra practitioner has the good fortune of union with a human *mudrā* consort, or that the practitioner engages in activity, *karma*, with such a *mudrā* of a "compatible family."[306]

According to another way of understanding these words, the object of the action (*karma*) of illusory relative union is the human *mudrā* that is engaged with, and there is a *karmic* connection with the specific *mudrā* consort. In this interpretation, even a "real" human consort is illusory, in the sense that all phenomena arising from relative karma are not phenomena of ultimate truth.

Many kinds of non-human beings, like ḍākinīs or ḍākas, manifesting with an apparently material body that is visible and touchable like that of a human being, can also be Karma Mudrā consorts. Such experience usually arises only for very advanced yogins. As actual beings, such consorts are a

---

ginning, but, as the practitioner's inner energies are invoked and refined into wisdom energy, the level of the visualization also tends to increase toward perception of the bliss of wisdom. That explains how conceptualized consorts classified as Wisdom Mudrās can manifest as realized experience in very high practices of the completion stage, as described in the next chapter.

306 According to Rinpoché, in this case, "compatible family" refers to the qualities of a human being like oneself, not to tantric Buddha families compatible with the practitioner's particular current dispositions.

very different kind of manifestation than a visualized mudrā.[307]

Dharma Mudrā and Further Classifications

When a visualized Mudrā is regarded as a mental phenomenon that is an object in the object-field of the mental sense,[308] that object is called a "Dharma Mudrā."

It is so classified because it appears as the content of a thought that describes the qualities of a certain imagined phenomenon, *dharma*, that was first visualized or generated as a *mudrā* consort in the field of objects of the mental sense.

As with the wisdom mudrā, although such a consort is deliberately generated at first, in its higher levels it manifests as empty yet "real," like the empty form of a mirage or a rainbow. It may manifest to you on many levels of experience, and the higher levels may involve more and more

---

307 Some say that the Karma Mudrā is the "easiest" type of consort to practice with and so it is usually the first to be practiced in the bliss-method of the completion stage. However, it does not necessarily mean that it is the student's first practice. If you are practicing Tibetan tantra, usually other practices are engaged in first such as the ordinary Wisdom Mudrā practice of the generation stage in order to establish a good basis before you can relate properly to the bliss of a Karma Mudrā. In ancient times, when Karma Mudrās were used in higher empowerments of Highest Yoga Tantra, the student would engage in sacred sexual practice with a human consort during the Wisdom Empowerment following the instructions bestowed by the Guru (see details in Appendix II). In this way, Karma Mudrā practice was employed as a direct and efficient way of invoking bliss. Generally speaking, working with a "real" partner minimizes the difficulties of visualization, but this does not mean that this practice cannot be elevated to high levels. For it to succeed, you and your consort must always maintain pure motivations and attitudes. Otherwise, physical union easily deteriorates into ordinary sex, with the usual saṃsāric, emotional dramas between the partners. The instructions given in the previous chapters should help you to avoid such obstacles. If you follow the instructions properly, there are no disadvantages and benefits are certain. In the future, if you want to go deeper, you will need instructions of the completion stage from your root Lama. Then you may experience higher levels of Karma Mudrā that precedes experience of other kinds of mudrās near the fruition of the completion stage.

308 *chos kyi skye mched*, dharma āyatana.

vivid kinds of sense experience, like hearing, touch, and so forth.

The Wisdom Mudrā described above is regarded as a generated visualization of a *wisdom* being as *consort*, while the Dharma Mudrā is regarded as a visualized mental *dharma* that is an image of a *consort*. They are named by the way in which they are classified, so that the same visualization might be successively a Wisdom Mudrā and a Dharma Mudrā, by changing the framework through which it is regarded.

When we list the different ways of classifying objects of the generation stage mentioned in traditional texts, there are the Wisdom Mudrā, Dharma Mudrā, Emptiness Mudrā, and Samaya Mudrā. "Mudrā," in such cases, always refers to a tantric consort. From that list, the one described here is the Dharma Mudrā. As each of these mudrās has higher and lower levels, and since it is not possible to reduce them to only one type of classification, which mudrās are higher or lower in a given case is likely to depend on the context.[309]

---

309 The Emptiness Mudrā is named from regarding one's visualization as empty-form. On the lowest level this is mostly conceptual. On the highest, it is the experience of the union of appearance and emptiness described in the Prajñāpāramitā Sūtras. The Samaya Mudrā regards objects of the generation stage from the viewpoint of tantric commitment. Practitioners commit to visualizing themselves as a tantric deity to overcome conceptual obstacles to pure perception. In the climactic moment of generation stage practice in Highest Yoga Tantra, actual wisdom deities (*jñānasattvas*) with forms similar to those of the conceptual deities one has first visualized (*samayasattva*) descend to bless the visualized deities, as the real thing. This descent of wisdom can be compared to hunters setting out wooden decoy ducks in a lake, in hopes that real ducks will see them and descend to join them. That experience is, at first, on a conceptual level like the original visualization. However, when authentic wisdom is experienced, it refers to the high samaya of perceiving all phenomena from the pure viewpoint of ultimate truth, emptiness possessing all the supreme aspects. As described in the next chapter in a quote from the *Kālachakra*, when the Samaya Mudrā is referred to in high levels of the completion stage, the level of perception may increase until it does not violate ultimate samaya.

Mahāmudrā

Mahāmudrā, the great consort or seal, is the experience of all phenomena as the power of self-display of Sugatagarbha, the innate nature of things. It is the absolute reality that is to be attained as the goal by the other mudrās.[310] Therefore, someone who accomplishes Mahāmudrā no longer needs these other mudrās because such a practitioner has already actualized the perfect union of the feminine and masculine principles. They may however be engaged with in a merely external manner as a requirement of particular practices which will bring benefit to others.

Summary of The Four Joys

When there is the experience of union with the mudrās, perceptions of pristine wisdom resulting from the four joys are brought forth. Whether they manifest in a conceptualized or non-conceptualized form, their presence purifies coarse and subtle, impure manifestations of saṃsāric karma. These experiences are therefore of incredible value on the tantric path. The four joys are,

1. Joy[311]
2. Supreme Joy[312]
3. Special Joy[313]
4. Innate Joy[314]

---

310 As Mahāmudrā is not a conceptual object, it cannot arise in the generation stage. It arises only from the highest levels of the completion stage.

311 *dga' ba*

312 *mchog dga'*

313 *khyad par gyi dga' ba*

314 *lhan cig skyes pa'i dga' ba*

Each of these is divided into four in turn, so there are a total of sixteen joys, from Joy of Joy, Supreme Joy of Joy, and so forth, up to Special Joy of Innate Joy and Innate Joy of Innate Joy. If these are presented in the traditional way, they are hard for most people to understand because they have no experience of the feelings involved. I will try to explain them in a somewhat easier manner to understand:

1. Joy is the changeable joy and bliss of melting of the relative *thiglé* or *khams*, as experienced by an ordinary person.
2. In Supreme Joy, that same changeable joy and bliss of melting is elevated and stabilized through meditative absorption on that joy and bliss; in that sense, it is not exactly the same joy of melting thiglé that ordinary people experience.
3. In Special Joy, that bliss of melting becomes "unchanging." It is not the joy and bliss of melting only, but the special or particular joy possessed when the khams or thiglé descends, is held, spreads, is distributed, and so forth.[315]
4. Innate Joy arises from the indestructible thiglé inseparable from the absolute space of Dharmadhātu. Its great bliss is an intrinsic aspect of Sugatagarbha. It is fully and constantly experienced only by a fully enlightened being. However, because all beings have Buddha nature, they can experience increasingly expansive glimpses of it on the path.[316]

These four joys are four actual different experiences of joy. They are divis-

---

315 To avoid confusion, the relative bliss described here is said to be "unchanging" because it lasts much longer than the momentary bliss ordinary people experience in an orgasm, for example. Special Joy is not literally permanent, and it is not unchanging in every sense of the word. This relative unchanging bliss may oscillate or increase.

316 The absolute bliss of the natural state is literally changeless in the sense that it is perfect for all eternity. It does not develop, diminish, or cease. However, here too, the experience of it on the path lasts only as long as glimpses of that absolute natural state replace ordinary relative experience.

ible into four totaling sixteen, as explained above, on the basis of the particular qualities of each individual joy. Yet, when they are divided we can designate no real object that is divided. The way that each of the wisdom experiences of the four joys is brought forth is traditionally explained, but there is no understanding of their shared origin that beginners could receive. As I have written this with beginners chiefly in mind, there is little need for elaborate details on this subject, and so I will not present them. Here this brief presentation of the four joys will suffice.

As readers of this book need to understand only what is essential for practice, many topics of tantra are not discussed here at all. For the subjects I have covered, extensive explanations with many textual citations have not been included as the beginning students for whom this book was primarily written have little need for such elaborations. I hope my readers will not be disappointed because of that.

When I was making the decision to write this book, I investigated whether the benefit and happiness produced would be sufficient enough to justify the effort required, and then whether by adding certain extra material, more benefit would result. My reflections confirmed the need to write the book but without the extra material. Then I knew the writing would happen in that way, and I never forgot it. At the same time, I began to hope that writing about the Path of Desire would be very beneficial, and so I aspired to that good fortune.

Even gods of Tuśhita lack such a path of delight.
Precious gold and indestructible shining diamonds,
Various priceless jewels and other precious things,
Do not amount to even a fraction of its value.[317]

---

317 The Tuśhita or Joyful Heaven is the highest abode of the desire realm. The future Buddha Maitreya is said to be dwelling there, until he incarnates on Earth as a Buddha. Aside from him or other high bodhisattvas who manifest in the form of gods, the gods born there do not have the good karma of tantric practice.

Not received by those anointed as mighty kings,
By purchase with great wealth this can never be gained;
Unfathomed by the analysis of great intellects,
Is this wisdom of great bliss without defilement.

The stream of the river of merit, from which good fortune flows,
From the essence of the earth, restores the youth of the Earth.
The innate pure essence of all worldly beings produces
The four and sixteen joys, as a spring to cure saṃsāra.

By looking, smiling, laughing, licking, sipping, and sucking,
The consort-dancer, with perfect abundance of dance and music,
Can touch, pull, hum, and churn, shake up, and hold what
     descends,
And spread what is spread, in a blissful circle of sixteen joys.

On the Earth goddess rich with gold with her oceanic
     garments,[318]
Mad with the heat of bliss-emptiness, the yogin couple,[319]
Drunk with desireless passion, make the seven-horsed god
Hide from unbearable shame in the covering of Varuṇa.[320]

---

318 When the elemental maṇḍalas of the world are visualized according to the *Kālachakra*,
   on top is the golden earth, so the **Earth goddess** is said to be a goddess **rich with gold**.
   Below that is the water maṇḍala, so she is said to wear **oceanic garments**.

319 The **yogin couple** practicing the Path of Desire become so crazed or **mad with the heat
   of bliss-emptiness** that they perform many joyful actions like those Gendün Chöpel describes in the verses presented in Appendix I.

320 The **seven-horsed god**, the Hindu sun god, Sūrya, whose chariot is drawn by seven horses, sees that as he passes over them. He is so embarrassed by their intoxicated joy that
   he must **hide, from unbearable shame** before the mountains where the couple dwells.
   Though the mountains are part of the earth maṇḍala, below the ocean of the water
   maṇḍala, they also rise above it, outside it, and at its center. Therefore they are called
   the covering of Varuṇa, the ocean god.

9

Supplementary Explanation and Conclusion About Mudrās Supported by Scriptures and Reasoning

My aim is that this book should be translated into many languages in a clear, straightforward style that can be understood by everyone, regardless of their level of education. Many people who might be otherwise interested in the Path of Desire are likely to misunderstand and reject my teachings if they are not presented in a way that they can relate to, and so I have used different styles of explanation in different parts of this book.

The traditional Tibetan way of writing uses many scriptural quotations to support logical proof of what is denied and established. Though it is not suitable for most of the readers I have in mind, I give at some points in this book a logical presentation to help those who are open to it. Some scriptures are quoted for similar reasons. Those with no interest in these aspects — such as what is presented in this chapter — do not need to worry too much about reading and understanding them, and, as stated before, they can just skip them.

If I mention particular sources of confusion I wish to address, when most Tibetans talk about how to practice the Path of Desire, they think it is wrong for practitioners to practice the different kinds of mudrās in different orders and styles, according to the practitioners own specific ca-pacities. Those in the Tibetan practice lineages understand these mudrās mainly from textual explanations. Most Tibetan scholars say that each of the four mudrās *must* be practiced in a particular order, and on particular levels of the path.

Though it is conceivable that some of them can explain clearly and con-sistently how to practice these four mudrās, I have seldom seen it. They talk about the starting point, the correct order of stages, and so forth in merely verbal terms that resist application in real practice. Those who can speak with confidence about the experiential aspect of the four mudrās are very rare. Those able to give clear and direct practice instructions were never nu-merous, and now they seem to be almost completely non-existent.

For example, when those who are supposed to be authorities on the subject explain what mudrā should be practiced at what stage of the Path of Desire, beyond performing a dance put together from phrases that they memorized from books, they give only scattered bits and pieces of direct in-structions about what to do. The clearest written instructions on practicing the Path of Desire are found in Gendün Chöpel's teachings, some of which can be read in Appendix I of this book. Ju Mipham also taught but just a little. Nevertheless, both of them wrote mainly about sexual techniques, without saying much about how to relate the sexual experience to the path and fruition. A complete "toolkit" of clear, directly applicable written in-structions with the steps of just how that practice should be done does not exist, as everyone concerned clearly knows.

Jetsun Tāranātha's secret biographies are very hard to access and understand; they are not suitable for beginners at all. They do not ex-plicitly list the stages of this path of skillful means, but if people who are extremely intelligent and knowledgeable have the good fortune to read them in Tibetan, they can understand what the real Path of Desire is like. Elsewhere in Tāranātha's extensive teachings on tantric texts, such highly intelligent people can also receive a correct understanding of tantra in general. Then, from that, a new chapter in the history of the Path of Desire may begin.

Nowadays, Tibetans who claim to be scholars think that the conditions for practicing with the different types of mudrās, as for practicing tantra altogether, require attaining an extraordinarily high level of attainment with the miraculous powers of a mahāsiddha. They seem to have the mistaken view that, as long as they do not have such powers, there is no way they can properly begin to practice with the Karma Mudrā and so forth. It is also a clear sign of their weak understanding of and lack of practical experience in tantra altogether.

These mistakes seem to have arisen from confusion about the nature, divisions, levels, and actions of practice of the first three mudrās. In explanations of the four mudrās that appear from time to time, usually, the main points of the teachings on the first three mudrās are improperly understood, and so confusion and inconsistencies occur. In general, these texts' classification of the three mudrās as higher and lower is acceptable, but when they present each mudrā's characteristics and the similarities, differences, and ranking of subdivisions, what they say is somewhat confusing.[321]

---

321 As said previously, the levels of the Wisdom Mudrā and the other mudrās of visualization go all the way from the ordinary conceptualized visualizations to glimpses of pristine wisdom. Scholars who say that ordinary people cannot practice these mudrās seem to have been confused and intimidated by textual passages that present their highest levels. According to Rinpoché, that happens because they have little or no detailed knowledge of how these highest levels are the fruition of gradual practice over the course of the generation and completion stages. Because they are sūtra practitioners at heart, such critics of tantra have spent their lives regarding sex as an enemy, and it is hard for them to accept the sexual elements of tantric practice at all. They think that only a great siddha could overcome the attachments of sexual desire and attain wisdom through Karma Mudrā practice. Such biases make it impossible for them to understand what really goes on in tantric practice. To give just one example, some monks criticize advanced tantric practitioners for practicing "endless" sex because they avoid orgasm and reverse the thiglé upward to the higher centers where it expands in blissful nondual absorption in which they rest for a long time. Being able to rest in the natural state

That the four mudrās assist each other is certain. Additionally, at their highest level, they manifest different aspects of the ultimate way things are. Therefore, if we consult the reasoned presentations that occur in texts that discuss these mudrās, they say that if one of the four mudrās is not accomplished, the next does not arise. They are to be practiced in accord with the interdependent relationships of their arising. That is true as a general rule, but these scholars do not allow for exceptional cases and multiple contexts of reference.

Generally speaking, the Karma Mudrā is the easiest to train, as explained in the previous chapters.[322] Since that is the mudrā most suited for beginners with no knowledge at all, it is suitable to be the first of the three mudrās to be practiced. However, nowadays, that is not what is usually heard in the speech of those who claim to understand tantra.

For the Wisdom Mudrā, many divisions are acceptable. Sometimes it precedes the Karma Mudrā,[323] and sometimes, it should be known to be

---

like that really does require a higher degree of accomplishment, so when they condemn doing that as greed and corruption, it is like an in-joke for competent yogins. What they think is contemptible is actually very praiseworthy.

322 In the practice of Karma Mudrā, practitioners move from the perception of ordinary sex with an ordinary human consort to sacred sex including the pure perception of oneself and one's consort as the principal deity with the experience of ultimate, great bliss. If you follow the instructions presented in this book, you can engage in this practice directly, regardless of whether you have practiced other kinds of mudrās before.

323 For those who are already studying and practicing the generation stage of Tibetan Tantra, a common sequence is to start first with a lower level of Wisdom Mudrā. Usually, such practice is permitted as long as the empowerment of the visualized deity has been received, but there are exceptions for specific cases and individuals, and depending on the system and level of practice. Rinpoché has a flexible approach which allows some of his followers to do such practices without formal empowerment in the case of specific individuals in specific cases as far as the benefit is considerable. According to him, even without the associated empowerment, if the reasons or personal qualities are good enough, that would be acceptable, provided the person has good motivation and, ideally, genuine aspiration to receive the associated empowerment in the future. His advice is to evaluate on a case-by-case basis. His own *Shambhala Dharma Kings* sādhana (Dzokden: San Francisco, 2022), displays a unique way of guiding the practitioner to

later and higher than the Karma Mudrā, depending, for example, on the level of Wisdom Mudrā.

Moreover, individuals who do not yet have sufficient ability or capacity to practice with a Karma Mudrā,[324] or have taken the vehicle of individual liberation as their *principal* path and commitment so that such practice would violate their vows, are allowed to begin by meditating with the Wisdom Mudrā practices.[325]

Which of the two is practiced first depends on the context and situation. Experience of the Karma Mudrā may be higher than experience of the Wisdom Mudrā, but it may also be lower. Why then do some scholars say that if the four mudrās are not practiced in strict order, the proceeding mudrā will not appear? This is the way of thinking of someone with limited understanding, so to run over and join their side would be a mistake.

---

self-generation practice without employing a specific self-generated deity.

324 The Karma Mudrā is relatively easier for beginners as it involves relating to a real person who does not have to be generated and does not primarily exist on subtle levels, even though, for the same reason, it involves more potential for complications due to craving, emotional attachment, and so forth, as explained previously. Therefore, for some individuals, preparing first with the Wisdom Mudrā will work better. This could also be the case for those who currently do not have the opportunity or conditions to practice with a human consort or because of health reasons, and so forth. The personal Karma Mudrā practice described in this book is available to anyone as an introduction to the Path of Desire. However, to do this beginners' Karma Mudrā practice, while pretending to be practicing the high-level Karma Mudrā practice of the completion stage, would be dangerously unrealistic. If you do not acknowledge that riding a bicycle in your yard is different from taking part in the *Tour de France*, you are in danger of a serious accident.

325 Monastics committed to the *vehicle of individual liberation as their main path* cannot practice the Karma Mudrā at all, as this is regarded as violation of their vow of celibacy. Other monastics who genuinely focus on the *tantric vehicle as their main path*, can practice the Karma Mudrā, as discussed in detail in Part Two chapter 6. Even for monastics who focus on tantra as their main path, sometimes Karma Mudrā practice may not be suitable to perform for various reasons such as the lack of supporting circumstances of their environment.

Regarding the traditional order of mudrā practice in the *Kālachakra* tradition, the *Kālachakra Tantra*, as quoted in Jetsun Tāranātha's *Brilliant Clarity of Union*[326] says,

རྒྱལ་བའི་ལྷན་སྐྱེས་བདེ་བ་འདི་ནི་འཕེལ་བའི་དོན་སླད། དང་པོ་ལས་ཀྱི་ཕྱག་རྒྱ་ བསྟེན་པར་བྱ། (5.73.1)

In order to increase the coemergent bliss of the Victorious Ones, first the Karma Mudrā should be bestowed.

According to this passage, practice with a Karma Mudrā is allowable and suitable for a beginner, so it is definitely not true that a practitioner must have reached a high level of the path to do so. This passage also establishes that such practice is allowed to develop potential on the Path of Desire.

In general, the way of the world is that, *whatever great goals you want to achieve, you must begin with the circumstances you have and what you can do with them.* If you think you cannot begin until something huge happens that has never happened before, your approach will guarantee failure. How could such a defeatist way of thinking ever be appropriate for the tantra path? Also, it is clear that the lower mudrās helping the higher ones is permissible, and that seeking strategies for doing that is always appropriate. Accordingly, the rest of that stanza from the glorious *Kālachakra*, with a commentary by Ju Mipham says,[327]

---

326   *Zung 'jug rab gsal*, BDRC scan W22276-v4, img559.5

327   Rime Lodrö tr., Ju Mipham, commentary on the *Abridged Kālachakra Tantra*, Chapter Five, p. 98. Note: Rinpoché quoted only the root text in his original manuscript, presented here in Tibetan characters, and in English in bold. As the root text is very intricate and difficult to understand, the translator thought it would be helpful to provide the readers a commentary on the root text written by Ju Mipham, which is inserted in plain text in the quote.

དེ་ནས་ཉིམ་འི་གཟུགས་ནི་ལུས་དང་གདོང་དང་རྐང་པ་གཙུག་ཏོར་ཡན་ལག་ཐམས་
ཅད་རྫོགས་པ་སྟེ། (5.73.2)

Then the mind-arisen goddess, the Wisdom Mudrā, a visualization of the variety consort who is like the brilliant form of the sun, should be relied on. This is done by meditating on her completely and perfectly visualized body, face, legs, crown, and all her aspects.

གློག་གི་དབྱུག་པའི་རྫས་མཐུན་འཕོ་མེད་བདེ་བ་སྐྱེད་པར་བྱེད་མ་མཆན་ཉིད་ཡན་
ལག་རབ་ཏུ་རྫོགས། (5.73.3)

Then, like a bolt, literally a stick or club, of lightning, when the fire of tummo blazes, she[328] is the creatress of changeless bliss. Having the characteristics of empty-form, this is Mahāmudrā, completely perfect in all aspects. She should be relied on to manifest the Samaya Mudrā. With that, in the jewel, the thiglés are changeless and unchanging.

ཏྟ་ཌྟ་རྣམས་ཀྱིས་རབ་ཏུ་སྣང་བར་བྱེད་མ་སྲིད་གསུམ་གནས་ལུས་ཆོས་ཀྱི་
དབྱིངས་ནི་དེ་ནས་གྱུར། (5.73.4)

Samaya Mudrā is the consort who makes the unobscured three realms fully and continuously appear as the ultimate realm. That changelessness is accomplished by means of the four vajras at the time of fruition. These vajras are of the nature of cessation, and in them, the drops of the four vajras of body, speech, mind, and wisdom are always changeless. Existing in the unobscured places of the three realms, body — the kāyas — is united with changeless bliss. Emptiness possessing all the supreme aspects, the nature of Dharmadhātu, is samaya, [as a commitment

---

328 Grammatically, "she" can only refer to the Wisdom Mudrā, but this highest level of Wisdom Mudrā is like a lightning bolt that can transmute ordinary form into the empty-form of Mahāmudrā with its intrinsic great bliss.

to apprehend all phenomena in terms of the ultimate.] By never going beyond that samaya, it **then becomes** the Samaya Mudrā that is never destroyed or disintegrated.[329]

In that part of Chapter Five of the *Kālachakra*, the stages of the Path of Desire altogether are also laid out, though we have not quoted those passages here.

In general, it is extremely important not to mix fish and filth in such explanations. If you do not know how to view the nature of things in such a way that you can distinguish truths from falsities about how things are, it is like mixing wholesome and rotten things together without knowing which is which. Not only will you be unable to recognize which ones are good, but eventually the rotten ones will corrupt the good ones.

When you want to accomplish an undertaking, many available tools might be employed. Taking into account the capacities that have arisen from your individual merit and particular abilities you may have acquired due to special training in this life, these tools may be selected and employed as needed. Similarly, though the first three mudrās are usually practiced in a certain order, the one most appropriate for your circumstances at a given time may not accord with that usual order. Jetsun Tāranātha says in the *Brilliant Clarity of Union*, [330]

> Moreover, while it is possible that the path of bliss of the Wisdom Mudrā may be practiced before that of the Karma Mudrā, in that case, Wisdom Mudrā practice is regarded as a prelimi-

---

329 In this unique presentation of the mudrās, Samaya Mudrā changelessly stabilizes Mahāmudrā, the experience of fruition, by means of the four vajras as the Buddhas' timeless fruition. Without that, Mahāmudrā would be merely a temporary glimpse of the fruition. This is another example of how the meaning of the mudrās can change depending on the context, level of practice, and so forth as here Samaya Mudrā has a much higher meaning than it does in the context of the generation stage.

330 BDRC scan W22276-v4, img559.5-560.2.

nary to Karma Mudrā, and so it is included within it;[331] when this is done, from after [starting] the yoga of Retention to the first part of Recollection,[332] it is in situations where the thiglé is [still] weak, or the faculties are [still] inferior[333] to engage in Karma Mudrā right away, but the path of Karma Mudrā still needs to be practiced.

Regarding other reasons, when forms and practices of the path that are unlike the usual approaches are employed to possess the fruition of practice, are they not special teachings of tantra in general or the wondrous, uncommon teachings of Highest Yoga Tantra in particular? Similarly, *in practicing Karma Mudrā, you have to begin where and when you can with the capability you have and gradually improve as you train.* Never beginning at all is just wrong. Never starting at all due to your hopeless fantasy that a high level with which you have no connection will miraculously manifest is a recipe for defeat. In the empty sky of the new moon day, the next day's crescent never arises. Gold, silver, and precious jewels never appear for no reason in empty space. If you still refuse to begin, are you not like an idle beggar hoping, for no reason at all, that one day he will suddenly be the king of the world with its oceans?

Regarding the higher stages of Karma Mudrā practice used as means to advance in the Six Yogas of *Kālachakra* to direct experience of the

---

331 According to Rinpoché, when the Wisdom Mudrā in this case is considered a preliminary to Karma Mudrā, it simply means a visualized consort, and not one on a very high level.

332 Retention and Recollection are, respectively, the fourth and fifth of the Six Vajra Yogas of *Kālachakra*, the general structure of which is outlined in Rinpoché's *Unveiling Your Sacred Truth — Book Three.*

333 According to Rinpoché, "weak" or "inferior" here means that the thiglé has not yet been sufficiently purified or trained. Though these are very high practices, within their context, this occasion is an inferior one.

fruition of Mahāmudrā, the *Brilliant Clarity of Union* says,[334]

[...] From (1) practice of Karma Mudrā at the time of needing to hold the winds forcefully, (2) practice of Karma Mudrā at the time of bliss without leaking, and (3) enrichment of resting in the essence on the path of Mahāmudrā as it develops into changeless, peaceful bliss, refers to the three occasions of (1) Controlling the Life Force with individual thoughts — this is the occasion where forceful union is needed to become familiar with nāda[335]—, (2) refers to the occasions of Retention,[336] (3) refers to the first occasion of Recollection.[337]

When difficult worldly actions need to be performed, you have to begin with what you can do. For example, when you first try to apply bodhichit-

334 BDRC scan W22276-v4, img560.2-560.5.

335 The third of the Six Vajra Yogas of *Kālachakra*, prāṇāyāma, *srog rtsol*. On this occasion, if you have practiced the first two yogas well, you can experience the nāda as a union of "sound," speech, winds, and so forth, which is difficult to describe but is clearly experienced as an all-in-one experience at this stage. "Forceful union" means that you hold and unite the winds forcefully, not spontaneously, through special breath and body exercises involving many repetitions of holding the breath for a long time with strenuous vase breathing to draw the upper and lower winds together; all of these are joined to meditation instructions. This forceful uniting and holding the winds supports gaining familiarity with the nāda.

336 The fourth of the Six Vajra Yogas of *Kālachakra*, dhāraṇā, *'dzin pa*. The accumulated thiglé in the navel is enhanced and this energy must spread to the upper chakras, moving and remaining in specific areas without dispersing. Practitioners learn how to dissolve their winds in their drops (thiglé), and the winds are experienced as inseparable from them. In its later stages, accomplishment will lead to full control of one's drops or essences and the beginning of experience of the consort of empty-form, which is refined and stabilized in the fifth yoga.

337 The fifth of the Six Vajra Yogas of *Kālachakra*, anusmṛiti, *rjes dran*. Here, practitioners deepen their experience of the self-existing fruition. In the later stages, the experience of Mahāmudrā will be attained, which is then fully accomplished in the sixth yoga. In the fifth yoga, only the first of the twelve stages of immutable bliss is attained.

ta, you try to accomplish small actions of the first perfection of generosity rather than trying to begin with the sixth perfection of prajñā. If you fail, you must keep going, doing your best to succeed, or you will be rejecting the bodhisattva path altogether. Similarly, in mudrā practice, you should know with certainty that practicing the highest level of each mudrā from the onset is not done. Tāranātha says further, in the same text,[338]

> In these cases, many situations of eliciting bliss occur through the Wisdom Mudrā, but they are aspects of Karma Mudrā. The middle occasion of Recollection, from the Six Yogas, is the occasion of intermediate thiglé and faculties. Here, the Karma Mudrā is [no longer] necessary, and Mahāmudrā alone is impossible. This is, therefore, an occasion in which the Wisdom Mudrā should chiefly be practiced, so this occasion is that of the path of [the highest stages of] Wisdom Mudrā [or Dharma Mudrā].[339] The last occasions of Recollection and Absorption[340] are occasions of strong thiglé and sharp faculties. This is the path of Mahāmudrā itself.

Is it not obvious that beginners are not qualified to actualize the high level of Wisdom or Dharma Mudrās required in this case? Is it not also clear that, in order to progress through these stages, it is necessary to perform Karma Mudrā practice? In brief, after seeing in detail, here and in the previous chapter, that the classifications of mudrās have many layers and levels of understanding, it is clearly inappropriate to have a fixated view on how they must be practiced.

The definitive meaning of the different mudrās is clearly taught by

---

338 *Brilliant Clarity of Union*, BDRC scan W22276-v4, img560.5-561.1

339 Until there is the fruition of Mahāmudrā as described in the *Kālachakra* quote above.

340 Samādhi, *ting nge 'dzin*, the sixth of the Six Vajra Yogas of *Kālachakra*.

Tāranātha, a māhasiddha who practiced them extensively, but the teachings of those without real accomplishment do not correspond to their real nature. They offer only deceptions born of ignorant fantasy, allegedly established by spurious logical reasoning. Trying to practice tantra according to mere scriptural descriptions is also like that. Tāranātha says further, in the same text:[341]

> Thus, the Six-Limbed Yoga includes the path of the first three mudrās.[342] To increase the innate [pure] phenomena of the deities, by practicing the Karma Mudrā, the empty-forms of the parts of their bodies, faces, arms, and all the other characteristics of their bodies are ripened by being increased and enriched; by enrichment of [the Wisdom or Dharma Mudrā as] a visualized substitute for the practitioner's own body, bliss arises from the union of yourself as the visualized deity with the consort of empty-form itself; then there are "the form of the sun," the father, *yab*, and "the similitude of a lightning club" and so forth, that teach the form of the mother, *yum*, [transmuting experience of the Wisdom Mudrā into Mahāmudrā.]

Such teachings present a summary of many other scriptural passages and establish clearly that adapting the sequence of each mudrā practice to fit the situation is allowed. Those who want to know more about this should look at such texts as Tāranātha's *Brilliant Clarity of Union*, his *Commentary on The Praise of the Offering of Bliss*, and his secret biographies. Those who want to experience the four mudrās in the context of the Six Vajra Yogas of *Kālachakra* should engage in the actual practice of them under a

---

341 *Brilliant Clarity of Union*, BDRC scan W22276-v4, img561.1-561.3

342 Samaya Mudrā is not included here because it is actually related to aspects of the other mudrās as explained earlier.

qualified Vajra Master's guidance.

Regarding only one kind of scripture as supreme,
Should not those addicted to the arid path of reasoning,
Rather than being bound by its rigid chains of discipline,
Enter into the freedom of the path to liberation?

Those unsatisfied with the approach of conceptual reasoning —
Obsessive analysis of "is" and "is not" in the scriptures —
Should be allowed to raise some pertinent questions regarding
Its hollow words about the profound completion stage.

Those thinking that, in tantra, only thiglé should be relied on,
Then holding as definitive the mistake that thiglé is semen,[343]
By a heap of contradictions concerning guarding thiglé,
In consequence, rob the Path of Desire of all coherence.

Unaware that the path of male and female awareness holders
Is an ocean of joy and bliss, preferring ascetic bondage,
Those of small minds and bad karma, clueless as they are,
Still want to enter the path of self-existing great bliss.

---

343 In the sense that they believe that thiglé is just semen or the cause of thiglé. Indeed, it is correct to regard semen as a sign of thiglé as its coarse manifestation. See detailed presentation in Part Four chapter 6.

PART FIVE

CONCLUDING CHAPTERS

Something being essentially poisonous is impossible.
Knowing how to use poison as medicine is sufficient.
There are no more enemies within saṃsāra.
Knowing how to turn foes to friends is the height of wisdom.

1

How Human Life Becomes Joyful by Understanding Tantra

How People Want to Attain Happiness But Are Not Successful

If you do not reach a proper understanding of tantra as explained above, you will not know how to make your kleśhas into the path. Thinking that you cannot practice tantra at all will also have a general negative effect on your mind. Moreover, when you do not know how to make your kleśhas into the path, you will not know how to enjoy true happiness. Nevertheless, you still have the capacity to achieve it, and you only need to discover how to actualize it. Therefore, I shall say a little more about how people can enjoy happiness even in difficult situations.

People who know how to make their kleśhas into the path can have outstanding temporal happiness, but that is not all. They can also achieve changeless, ultimate bliss like an ocean. How can so much benefit and happiness be attained in this life and the next as well as in the *bardo*? The short answer is that the more you practice and experience, as you gain familiarization, the more benefit and happiness are created.

Human nature is such that all people seek happiness. Since most people do not know how to bring their kleśhas to the path, they find misery instead. This has been so from the ancient past. The many strategies these failed seekers of happiness employ are all very similar and by imitating each other, they only make matters worse. They strive for worldly wealth, comfort, success, status or fame, and so forth, and, as is seemingly reasonable, they also employ strategies for avoiding the opposites of these. Those who seek enjoyment and comfort do not want hardship and misery; those who want respect and praise do not want to encounter condemnation and criticism, so, if they do not get what they expect, they are unhappy. Preoccupied with the eight worldly concerns, they scurry like ants in an ant hill or exhaust themselves like spiders with a ball of silk bigger than they are. In such hopeless futility, they wear out their lives.

At the time of death, most have paid little heed to their culture's religious counsel for death and the afterlife. As they do not know clearly where they will go after death, they do not know what they need to do. Not knowing what is happening and why, with no refuge or protector, their fear and anxiety are a thousand times worse than a blind man abandoned in the midst of an empty plain. They must pass away from their human lives into inconceivable misery, and there is no alternative. Because they have sowed only the seeds of worldly concerns, none of them want the harvest of suffering that they reap. It is clear that most people's way of seeking happiness is not the right one, because it produces no lasting happiness.

If you have a good example of how to live, even though you do not know when the time of death will come, you can die joyfully. If you also know what to do after death, you can be completely confident of attaining your goals. Walking on this earth and breathing this world's air becomes meaningful. However, for that to happen, you must view human life differently than most people because most people's lives are not in accord with the causes of genuine happiness.

If wealth and possessions, success and status, reputation and fame are not the causes for ultimate happiness, should pursuing them be forbidden? Obviously, everyone needs some wealth and so forth to live at all. There is no problem per se in pursuing good conditions. Nevertheless, pursuing only these is not enough to enjoy genuine happiness. "If I create wealth, pleasure, power, and praise, and also eliminate all their undesired opposites, then can I not enjoy real happiness?" That too is not enough. You will know in your sorrow that these goals are no better than insubstantial dreams. You can pursue them, but you need to know that *these goals are, at best, conditions of just a little temporary happiness.* If you also know that there is no certain guarantee of even that, you have taken the first steps in the direction of the real causes of happiness.

Example of How Working with the Kleśhas is the Path to True Happiness

Bringing kleśhas to the path is a strategy that can overcome all worldly problems. Rather than fighting enemies, it is a strategy for making enemies into friends.

For example, imagine that after a long time, with great effort and sacrifice, you finally attain immense wealth and enjoyment. Then, one day, your best friend, who is dear to you like your own daughter and trusted without question, steals everything you have through an unbelievably deceitful, hypocritical plot. Will you heroically attack her to get all your things back? Will you chant a saintly prayer, and offer the thief the little you have left? If no strategy helps, will you kill yourself? Spending your life in vicious hatred may kill you anyway.

I will say clearly what your response could be. As soon as you realize what happened, laugh while thinking something like this, "HA HA HA, I could never have imagined being totally destroyed like this. This is the result of my karma, and there is no avoiding it. It looks like bad karma, but if I think twice, it is actually an opportunity. If my friend had not created these unique circumstances for me, I would never have made this unique opportunity for myself."

"Opportunity" refers to unusual good circumstances. Finding an opportunity is rare and wonderful. If an opportunity occurs without your having to do anything or even think about it, that is immensely fortunate. However, you have an opportunity only if you know how to use it. If you do not know how to actualize the potential for happiness that it offers, you have no opportunity. You will continue in your present suffering.

People would usually think in this situation, "My treacherous former friend has cheated me out of all my wealth, enjoyment, and reputation. Now I am doomed to misfortune and misery." The result of this kind of reasoning will be long and excruciating pain, so try thinking differently. "My friend's despicable actions helped me to abandon a deluded way of seeking happiness that doomed me to suffering. I could never have broken my attachment to worldly concerns by myself. She created a disaster that forced me to pursue a better way of living. If I cannot figure out how to use that disaster as an opportunity, I will never go beyond being ruined, and the rest of my life will be an intolerable defeat. Rather than letting her ruin my life, I should begin a heroic struggle that can overcome all obstacles." With immense gratitude for your tormenter, think, "She has made me bigger and stronger."

The more dry wood you put in a blazing fire, the larger it gets. The more serious the challenge you face, the more heroic your mind must become to meet it. If your mind remains discouraged and low-spirited, defeat is inevitable. However, fear not. *Limitations of the mind are incidental and temporary, and so they can be eliminated. All true virtues are intrinsic aspects of the eternal primordial nature of the mind, so they can never be destroyed,* only uncovered and enhanced. When you come to this understanding, you are beginning to learn how to bring the kleśhas to the path.

Then, think further about the opportunity offered by your friend, "If I don't do this, because I think that such an unusual response would be madness, I am rejecting this wondrous opportunity. I am giving in to the disaster she created. There could be no greater loss. Though it was my friend who created this opportunity for me, the blessings of the Buddhas and Bodhisattvas could have done no better. In fact, my friend herself could be an emanation of the Buddhas and Bodhisattvas. Their kindness might have made this possibility exist for me so that I can progress quickly by overcoming such a challenge. What seemed at first to be terrible harm may really be compassionate guidance."

"Being so attached to my former wealth and possessions kept me away from all I really wanted and needed. Eliminating that attachment might be a blessing of liberation in disguise. If I view my situation as bad, my destiny will surely be tragic. If I view my situation as good, my future will be fantastic. Would I not be a fool if I fail to choose the view where my life will be good? The Buddhist teachings say that the way phenomena appear to us and the way they really exist are different. My present appearances of inescapable suffering are not appearances of the real way things are. They are delusive relative phenomena, so why do I cling to them?"

"In the way things are, good and bad are united as universal purity. There, my situation is indestructibly good. Now, this situation appears to be a horrible one that could not be worse. People call that depressing way of seeing things 'being realistic,' but if I am *truly* realistic, I know that giving in to such negativity will surely harm me for the rest of my life."

"What will happen if I accept the ultimate virtue that has only the nature of benefit and happiness, even though I wonder if it is too good to be true? What appears as suffering today will manifest as indestructible bliss tomorrow. I could be going from bliss to higher bliss, instead of from pain to perdition. Clearly, no one would say that eternal bliss is not better than endless suffering. If I have a real choice between seeing this situation as suffering or happiness, why would I not wish to see it as good? Should I believe the ordinary people who have failed to find happiness who call this positive viewpoint unrealistic, or should I believe the omniscient enlightened beings such as the Buddha, whose confidence in this viewpoint led him to perfect enlightenment?"

Often, catastrophic events make us re-evaluate our lives, and when we look back on them long afterward, we can see that they allowed us to make great progress. Often, situations that seemed good at the time are later seen to have led to great loss. Once we realize that being trapped in painful situations occurs only because we do not know how to look at all sides, it will be easy to change our deluded negative view into a true, pure, and positive one. Then progress will be easy because the pure view accords with the Buddha's realization of the way things are.

Now imagine that, after all, your best friend also steals your husband, or though she is supposed to be your friend, she is always competing with you, and she always points out how she is greater, higher, smarter, stronger, better looking, and more likable and in the competition between you, she always makes you look like an incompetent fool. With an ordinary viewpoint, you could not help being jealous, envious, angry, upset, and so forth. However, if you reflect that you have produced all these unhappy feelings yourself because you do not know how to deal with situations like this, you realize that *simply not being obsessed with her will end her being a cause of suffering for you*. On the other hand, if you carry your present self-destructive attitude any further, she will become your exclusive environment, causing you constant agony as though you had gone to hell.

Despair over the inevitable faults of the relative reality is the opposite of the tantric viewpoint. If you analyze the apparent calamities of ordinary life from this latter viewpoint,

1. They are deluded appearances of what does not exist intrinsically.
2. All your "painful" appearances are actually displays of the power of manifestation of absolute reality, and as such, they involve no faults or betrayals at all.

If we take jealousy as an example, when the pain of normal jealousy makes us want to compete with a rival, the goal is so limited that happiness is unlikely, even if we win. Once we understand that the unbearable pain of delusive jealousy is not the real way things are, jealousy will spontaneously expand into an appreciation of things as they are. Thus, the essence of jealousy will lose its former saṃsāric quality and direction. Nothing will seem to be a problem or obstacle for you. Perseverance in this joyful outlook will overcome your temporary illusion of competition. If you aspire to be victorious over rivalry, change your focus so that you no longer engage in malicious rivalry with the person who wronged you. Redirect your malice to the ignorant illusions of the kleśhas that caused every moment of your life to be steeped in suffering. To enhance your natural power, focus on the favorable conditions that will allow you to accomplish this great undertaking and welcome the vast fruition of your tantric practice.

When the kleśha of jealousy is handled like that, it will surely go to the side of virtue. Jealousy brought to the path will become a cause of enthusiastic courage and diligence, rather than suffering. However, it is naive to think that good results will be reached right away. Virtue will eventually prevail but challenging experiences may continue to appear as a way of keeping you honest because that is a process of learning and transformation. Even in the face of difficult outcomes, we should not let the jealousy that has expanded into far-sighted wisdom fall back into poisonous jealousy.

Whether people are superior or ordinary, they want to enjoy a happy life. In spite of this, due to their limited viewpoint, ordinary people think they must simply surrender to the continuous harm of the outrageous faults and transgressions of this world even though doing so will make happiness impossible. To attain true happiness, they must have a higher way of viewing their situation. *They need to learn how to experience relative challenges as ultimate opportunities.* A happy life is impossible when our ordinary view turns us into women and men of constant sorrow. On the other hand, with dependence on the extraordinary view, motivation, and pure perception of tantra, such a life will manifest. We never again need to experience a life of suffering, rather than happiness.

A Summary of How to Enjoy a Happy Human Life

If the conditions of genuine happiness are briefly summarized in steps, they are,

1. **Knowing the Conditions for Happiness**
    The real causes of happiness are certainly not those everyone believes them to be such as youth, good friends and agreeable spouses, success placed in your hand, wealth, enjoyment, fame, and so forth. At best, these are conditions for only a little temporary happiness. Knowing that they are not true causes of happiness includes knowledge that true causes of happiness must produce happiness that is long-lasting and free from its opposite. Knowing that the conditions most people seek such as wealth and so forth can only produce the lowest kind of happiness is the first step to attaining true happiness.

2. **Strengthening Awareness**
    Next, you need to accept that human life does not meet our expectations. Even when we manage to establish wealth, there is no guarantee that even temporary happiness will result. Sometimes, even a fruition of unhappiness is possible. Recognizing that saṃsāric strategies are unreliable and strengthening this awareness is the second step.

3. **Changing Perspective**
    We usually seek wealth, enjoyment, and so forth because we expect they will give us genuine happiness. Reflect on how that hope is like a dream that will never come true. Once you recognize that no strategy based on the faulty causes most people accept can possibly succeed, you see that you must look further afield to find the cause

of happiness. If the opposite of what you wish for happens, can you still make progress toward true happiness? Can you meet disaster without sorrow? When obstacles and hindrances that are the opposites of your expectations and desires occur, you do not need to feel helpless. When calamity occurs, you can still feel the essence of happiness because your Dharmic armor truly protects you. In brief, changing perspective by fully accepting that there is nothing you can do that will guarantee you will never experience unhappiness in saṃsāra, and then, renouncing your saṃsāric attachment, is the third step to reliable happiness.

4. **Identifying Opportunities**

By guiding us towards the knowledge that there is a way of making progress beyond the futility of seeking saṃsāric happiness, the "unfavorable" results we experience can become the favorable conditions of deeper happiness. If workable strategies to avoid carelessly falling into suffering are found, the probability of success increases. In particular, instead of using antidotes to destroy phenomena that cause you to suffer as employed in the sūtra path, turn such phenomena into opportunities. Recognize that in bringing your kleśhas to the path according to the tantric approach, what you need to reach your goal of happiness is already at your disposal. Identifying your opportunity to practice the tantric path is the fourth step.

5. **Gaining Confidence and Taking Action**

Once we know that through skillful means the causes of saṃsāric unhappiness can be transformed into causes of ultimate happiness, our former unsolvable problems become precious opportunities for spiritual growth. If, when you experience hardship and misery, joy and confidence arise at the same time because you know you can go beyond them, you have walked another step toward real happiness. In brief, the fifth step is gaining sufficient confidence to put the tantric path into practice. You will probably not get it right on the first few tries, so do not be discouraged. As with any new approach in life, we can learn from our failures and eventually become more skillful.

6. **Accomplishing Genuine Happiness**

When all these steps are fully comprehended and practiced, the mind can settle through knowing how to turn all unreliable relative causes into reliable conditions for eventually attaining ultimate happiness. For example, imagine that for your entire life, you have never harmed anyone and have always helped people as much as possible. And yet, not only does everyone disrespect you without any valid reason, the few faults you have are exaggerated and scornfully criticized. Furthermore, people delight in making up false stories that put you in the worst possible light. If you can in this and all such situations immediately react to it as happily as if they had given you praise and affection, you will have established genuine happiness in this life. That is the sixth step. Now you know how to bring both the circumstances that oppose delusive saṃsāric happiness and the resulting kleśhas to the path as unopposable causes of true happiness.

Verse Summary

If we want a million leaves of virtue to grow,
On the tree of a real and happy human life,
Not creating the karma that is created by all,
What is understood by none must be understood.

If we turn back from the path where everyone was destroyed,
To the pleasure grove of the rising sun of wisdom and kindness,
In a new youth adorned all over with beautiful flowers,
We can embrace the undying joy of eternal youth.

There, the maiden of prajñā in our own minds is happy,
To embrace her joyful companion, the warrior of compassion.[344]
The treasure of the highest, happy realm, Śhambhala,
With its million excellent qualities, is born from that sweet union.

344 Another way of referring to bodhisattvas.

Shar Khentrul Rinpoché's Root Guru the Precious Lama Lobsang Trinléy

2

A New Way of Viewing the Guru-Student Relationship

Introduction and Explanation[345]

This book offers a detailed analysis of tantra and its essence, yet, as the paths and means of tantra have very extensive elaborations, how could this explanation be fully complete? As this book re-examines the Tibetan tradition and criticizes distortions that have come to exist, I do not follow my tradition's usual way of formally presenting every detail. Nevertheless, how the good aspects of Tibetan tantric tradition can be retained and built on is also presented.

Here again, the way of entering into tantra is important. There are many people who regard tantra highly and yet do not properly understand the relationship with a tantric Guru. Consequently, they cannot truly enter tantra at all. As the beginning student is an ordinary person of

---

345 This chapter is just a summary presentation of this topic. Rinpoché wrote extensively about this e.g. in his previous books *The Hidden Treasure of the Profound Path* and *Unveiling Your Sacred Truth — Book Three*. There are also a vast number of available recorded teachings by him that can help the reader become familiar with his own perspective on entering tantra genuinely.

this side of relative reality who has yet to encounter the absolute fruition, the tantric path must also begin with ordinary, relative qualities and relationships. Teachers and students who fail to understand the vital importance of this human to human relationship waste the spiritual endeavor of hundreds of human lives.

Indian religious systems typically have great respect for spiritual teachers. Therefore, it is only to be expected that in the tradition of Tibetan Buddhism that originated in India, the teacher or spiritual friend is also held in high regard. Followers of the Tibetan lineages of tantra have great respect for the Guru, involving genuine faith, sacred outlook, dedication, and sacrifice, and this is described in detail in the Highest Yoga Tantra texts. Such a way of doing things was widely followed in Tibet though the ultimate point of doing so was rarely realized even intellectually and was only partially realized experientially in practice. Many practitioners merely followed cultural customs.

Unsurprisingly, not only many non-Buddhists throughout the world but also some Buddhists who follow other systems have negative judgmental views of the relationship between Guru and student in Tibetan tantra. In their eyes, the devotion of these faithful ones is excessive and their actions fall into extremes. These Buddhists claim that their own "correct teachings" do not provide even the slightest reasoning for accepting the validity of tantra. While I personally agree with the Tibetan tantric schools in the aspects of their view, perception, textual traditions, philosophical reasoning, and so forth, I disagree with a great deal of the way tantric students and present societies relate to these schools' traditions, their habitual way of doing things, and so forth.

According to the traditional teachings on Guru Yoga, the Guru must be regarded as a living Buddha, and whatever the Gurus says must be regarded as the holy Dharma. If the Guru appears to have performed improper actions, these must be viewed with pure perception as actions of compassionate skillful means. Students who view the Guru as having faults break their samaya commitments, producing immense obstructing karma that needs to be purified. If this is not done, the realizations that bring the path of holy Dharma to fruition cannot arise for such students. All their actions will be ineffective, and their lives will be short with considerable sickness. As soon as they die, they will be born in Vajra Hell, experiencing the most intense sufferings of all the hells. This approach is so common in tantric texts that almost all of them teach it at some point.

Traditional texts say that all the good qualities of a Guru must be complete within a genuine Guru and any faults that would invalidate these good qualities must be absent. Students need to analyze carefully whether particular Gurus have these virtues and faults before establishing samaya with them and regarding them with the required pure perception. The Guru should carefully evaluate would-be students.

Though this is taught to be necessary, Tibetans in general do not accept in practice that anyone other than the highest Lamas has the capability and privilege to evaluate whether a Guru has the required qualities. Therefore, ordinary Tibetan Buddhists never have an opportunity to evaluate whether a prospective Guru is suitable. If an ordinary person dares to attribute faults to a particular Guru, virtually no one else considers their judgment valid. Even when people draw such conclusions, very few have the courage to declare them publicly. If anyone agrees, almost none of them have the courage to say so. The result is that there is no effective evaluation of tantric Gurus by their potential students. That also happens because people strictly believe that such criticism would generate unspeakably bad karma. As is said,

> Those who, having received a single verse,
> Do not take the speaker as their Guru,
> After a hundred births in the form of a dog,
> Will be born as a worm in stinking shit.

Traditionally, Tibetans believe that everyone must follow these words literally if they want to avoid those consequences. Consequently, the Gurus are never questioned at all. Though it is taught that before you take someone as your Guru you should examine for many years whether that person is suitable, there is no clear procedure for doing that. If you want to examine reliably whether a certain Guru is higher than an ordinary person, you would have to spend considerable time in their presence so that a careful evaluation of their teachings can be made.

If you fail to do that, whatever observations you make will be founded only on hearsay and no such examination can be adequate. Even if others speak sincerely about their own examinations, they are only reporting their own personal experience. Since these experiences are due to their individual karma, they can never be a reliable guide for predicting your own, and so they are not sufficient grounds for evaluating a potential Guru. The words of others are not an adequate basis for choosing a refuge from saṃsāra in this life and later ones just as they do not suffice when you are searching for a spouse to be your life companion.

Such an important decision needs to be made properly. If you rush into such a relationship after just listening to the gossip of people around you, your approach is no better than a sheep instinctively running away when a dog appears. However, that is how it is done by most Tibetans. Since it is customary that they cannot reverse their decision once it is made, how can that be a workable strategy? Many choose their Guru based on their name or reputation. They never try to evaluate whether someone without significant status might be a realized being. Usually, they have no better means of evaluating potential Gurus than observing them superficially for a short time. When they are with a prospective Guru for this short time, they ignore the words of Dharma being taught and try to examine the Guru's qualities on the spot, but that cannot be a genuine examination. They have no other opportunities, so making a proper examination is hopeless.

It is almost impossible to properly choose a Guru like that. As a consequence, any respect they have for their Gurus is unavoidably a mere show of following cultural norms. If merely pretending to listen to the Dharma someone teaches and having no genuine respect for the Guru who teaches it are unavoidable, these students can neither understand nor practice the real meaning of what the Guru teaches. Moreover, Tibetans believe that if they received even a few words of Dharma from any teacher, they have to see that teacher as their Guru, and they are therefore supposed to do whatever the Guru says. How then can the necessary qualities of faith and confidence be genuinely established on such shallow foundations?

Unlike many others, as a student, I personally never accepted *involuntary* relationships initiated by any Guru. Why? When this happens, Guru and student have an inauthentic relationship that destroys the world-transcending power of their mutual Dharma practice. In this scenario, such people can establish only worldly qualities, they are forcefully excluding any genuine transformation. Therefore, I have also never involuntarily initiated such a relationship with my own followers.[346] As I have never accepted such compulsion that ignored the real situation already from the time I was young and of very limited capabilities, I have experienced intense hardships as a result. Since some of these "big" kings in a small valley[347] continue to abuse their self-designated subjects, progress is still needed. *Receiving teachings from a certain Guru does not compel you to be that Guru's student forever. The choice of a root Guru must come from one's own heart.*

---

346 As an example, Rinpoché himself does not offer the four higher empowerments of *Kālachakra* in public, but only upon individual application and after careful examination on both sides — from the student to him and from him to the student; commonly he advises some followers to wait and gather more conditions to make sure they are ready for establishing samaya. He does offer in public other empowerments such as the extended Vase Empowerment of the *Kālachakra* Empowerment or Initiation (*The Seven Empowerments of a Growing Child*). In this way, students and teacher can get to know each other before establishing a deeper Guru-student relationship.

347 Like "big fish in a small pond," who are not really very big at all.

On the other hand, many people, especially in the West, make another kind of mistake by falling into the opposite extreme of belittling the Guru. They think that a tantric Guru, or any spiritual teacher, is entirely unnecessary, arrogantly believing that reading books and surfing the internet is a sufficient basis for practice. This way of thinking shows that such people have concluded that the qualities of the Dharma path are no different than those of worldly subjects. However, the qualities of the level of perfect Buddhahood are limitless and go beyond the worldly sphere.

A Guru is necessary to make these qualities manifest in a student's continuum. A teacher who embodies virtuous Dharma is necessary for a student to be able to connect with it. Once the Guru's good qualities are perceived, only then can whatever confidence, respect, faith, and affection arise for the Guru and the Guru's teachings be directed towards the Guru's non-dual manifestation within the student's mind. *Nevertheless, in reality, the students' qualities are even more important than those of the Guru.* Whether or not students will perceive precious qualities of their Gurus does not depend primarily on the Guru's apparent qualities but on the student's own attitude and merit, and on the karmic connection between a certain Guru and a certain student.

When pure perception and devotion toward an external Guru eventually blossom, important inner conditions for great realizations are established. Such an internal relationship never develops from a relationship with dualistic, external objects like books, no matter how good they may be. Arrogantly thinking, "I can reach enlightenment on my own!" is a great mistake.

Moreover, other very proud and self-centered people say with dishonesty that they have established such a Guru-student relationship. Indeed in reality, such individuals associate with a tantric Guru, and then, pretending that the Guru is their intimate Dharma friend, they request many special instructions and higher teachings. Eventually, they say that they are better than that Guru, thinking that to acknowledge such an inferior as their Guru would be utterly inappropriate. Clearly, they never understood the meaning of a Guru-student relationship, or, insofar as they did, they never truly wanted to participate in one.

Some people make mistaken statements like, "I do not need an external Guru because I have the inner Guru of Buddha nature!" This is just the shameless talk of someone who does not know the first thing about relating with the outer and inner levels of a Guru, the basic distinctions between the two truths, and so forth. So that such people will not continue to harm themselves by their mistaken views, a reply like the following should be made.

Overcoming the Wrong View that a Guru is Unnecessary in Tantra

"Since your inner Guru does not manifest to you at present, you have only the unmanifest Guru of the ground at this point. In order to make the inner Guru manifest, you need a Guru to show you the path. Are you unaware that such a Guru is called an 'external' Guru?

As long as you are an unenlightened ordinary human, an external Guru is absolutely essential in tantra. How could you think otherwise? If so, there are some very presumptuous consequences. If an external Guru was not needed, then by the same reasoning it would follow that you also would not need to adhere to the external view, meditation, and conduct. You would have no need for the external manifestations of the self-radiance, wisdom, and compassion of your inner Buddha nature, or of the Victorious One's ocean of perfect Buddha qualities. The practices of kindness, compassion, faith, perseverance, mindfulness, absorption, and so forth that make such qualities manifest, would also not be needed, nor an external Buddha and sentient beings as favorable conditions for your spiritual progress. Such an attitude full of arrogant and false thoughts never led anyone to enlightenment.

If, as you say, people do not need to practice the path, a Guru in the world would be useless. If so, a Guru-student relationship would be useless, and everything explained in the associated textual traditions would also be useless. However, because the path does require a teacher, a Guru is taught to be the root of the path. There is no way that even a part of the tantric path can be practiced without one.

If enlightenment would not require practicing a path, then a Guru in the world would not be necessary. Accordingly, a Guru-student relationship would be useless, as would everything explained in the associated textual traditions. The need for a path, however, cannot be denied, nor the requirement for a teacher to guide the student on a tantric path. The Guru therefore is the root of this path and not a single step can be practiced without one.

At the time of fruition, not even a part of it is separate from the Guru. That is because, at that time, Sugatagarbha manifests as your enlightened mind, which is also the mind of the ultimate Guru and the mind of the Buddha. Though you perhaps claim that the path and fruition exist apart from the Guru, if you say that you do not want a Guru, you are automatically rejecting the path and its fruition. The Guru is necessary as the root of the tantra path and the very being of its fruition. If this is denied, both the path and its fruition are absurdly said not to be necessary."

As ordinary beings, we can only relate with relative truth. Ultimate truth can only be manifested by working first with the relative reality in which we are in at the present moment. We cannot jump directly to the absolute inner Guru without first relating to the relative external human Guru. If people's arrogance prevents them from relating to the human Guru, such a person can never experience the ultimate.

Clearing Other Misconceptions and Finding the Proper Balance

Many people wrongly think that the relationship between Guru and student in Highest Yoga Tantra must be a sexual relationship. That is a great misunderstanding perpetuated by people whose knowledge about the holy Dharma is extremely limited. The genuine practice of tantra is supposed to pervade the twenty-four hours of every day and be mixed with everything that is experienced or done. That means that sexual activity is an extremely small part of tantra practice, so believing that the path of tantra consists of nothing but sex is an extreme distortion. Saying that the relation between Guru and student in tantra must be sexual is even worse. This type of relationship only occurs within exceptional circumstances and individuals, and not otherwise.[348] Many special conditions need to be met for this to be suitable.

Even so, might a sexual relationship be the best kind of Guru-student relationship? The answer is the same. It is the best course only in very rare circumstances.[349] The relationship between Guru and student must develop from naturally present ordinary qualities. It is important to know that the transcendent aspects of these qualities develop from their worldly aspects. These are mostly qualities that are desirable in all personal relationships like trust and confidence.

An extremely important, priceless relationship that occurs between people has the basis of genuine love or affection. I am not talking about common cultural ideals of romantic love. Such notions may be a good inspiration for establishing a home and family, but mostly they do not evoke *ultimate* trust, confidence, warrior courage, and so forth. Countless defects and strings often appear later on, so worldly romantic love is not

---

348 Like Padmasaṃbhava and Yéshé Tsogyal, or Nāropā and Niguma.

349 The best kind of relationship between Guru and student is one that attains the best result. The best result is that the student's ordinary good qualities develop into the ultimate good qualities of enlightenment.

a sufficient foundation for a relationship aimed at realization. Nevertheless, that its qualities have sometimes evolved into something higher is clear to everyone.

Faith, appropriate pride, respect, and appreciation between people must be autonomous to be true, pure, ultimate, and indestructible. They cannot be manifested or conditioned by social pressure or custom. When qualities like that exist naturally within you, the internal conditions for the arising of the tantric path are complete. However, you cannot say these conditions are all-sufficient in themselves. Practicing tantra does require external relationships with an authentic Guru, an authentic lineage tradition, and so forth.

Instead of attempting to make worldly good qualities the sole foundation of your tantric practice, if heart-felt confidence arises that these transcendent, inner qualities are extremely valuable, like priceless jewels that cannot be surpassed by anything at all, the entrance to the tantric path and the Guru will appear before you.

Accomplishing a correct path of the holy Dharma by means of tantra depends on all these factors. When they are diligently analyzed, that a teacher of holy Dharma is also necessary is easy to know. Even for accomplishing worldly actions, good connections with reliable external objects that generate confidence are necessary. Much more so, for those desiring to attain transcendent Buddhahood, a profound relationship between Guru and student is necessary to make practicing the path of holy Dharma effective. In brief, *this connection is a precious chance to establish a relationship between the ultimate aspects of two human beings*. This foundation allows us to develop further perfect connections with further ultimate aspects of both phenomena and beings.

As discussed above, correct means of examining whether two individuals are suitable to be Guru and student are very difficult to find. Even if good means of examination were found, applying them would be quite difficult because tantra has pure perception as its ground and root. In listening to the Dharma teachings of any Guru, the right understanding depends on doing so with as much pure perception as you can. Why? Who is a Buddha and who is a sentient being is not known. Whom you have a karmic connection with is also not known. Good explanations may come even from the mouths of children.[350] Therefore, *having no preoccupation with reputation, status, and so forth is required to recognize the true amṛita of holy Dharma.* Since that is so, *relate with everyone to the best of your ability, and listen to as much of the Dharma that comes from them as you can handle.* This is my practical advice. In this way you will be able to progress on your path of searching, finding, examining, and choosing a root Guru. For some, this process may be very fast due to their previous accumulation of merit, whereas for others, it may seem to take a long time. Either way, when the student is ready, the Guru will appear.

In general, whether or not the Guru presently appearing to you can clear away your worldly problems, most importantly, *transmitting the experience of something better than the worldly objectives of this saṃsāric reality is necessary for showing a student the path to attaining enlightenment.* As much as possible, a Guru should teach and manifest such qualities. You should be able to perceive at least some of them for your mind to be enhanced by blessings. If you find a Guru who is capable of guiding you through this process and in whom you perceive and receive great qualities in your own mind, you must consider yourself to be very fortunate and feel immensely grateful.

If it turns out that a Guru definitely does not have sufficient good qualities to guide you toward enlightenment, and if you do not pretend to devotedly follow her or him to simply save face with others, *there is no valid reason why the Dharma should not allow you to peacefully leave and search further.* On the other hand, if you pretend that you have more

---

350 This is true in the sense that the blessings of a teaching depend on your own pure perception of others and in the sense that Buddhas and Bodhisattvas can assume any form, not just the form of great reincarnations with high titles.

respect than you do, your hypocrisy is likely to create problems. In short, if there is a Guru from whom you do not perceive any mental purity at all, you need not pretend otherwise.

However, generally speaking, unless continuing a relationship is hindering you considerably, *having merely no strong karmic connection with a Guru is not necessarily a reason why you must break it off completely*. As a general guideline, it is important to be honest with yourself as well as with your own Guru, and so search the right balance for your personal situation.

And what should you do if you encounter Gurus who appear to have saṃsāric pride that is a hundred times as strong as their good qualities, and hatred a thousand times stronger than their loving-kindness, and who also have excessive avarice, jealousy, malice, and oppressive coercion? All that is manifesting by the power of your own karma. Not seeing any necessity for rivalry and combativeness, transcend as much as you can the way that the world, in general, would perceive such conduct. Fighting or denigration are not appropriate responses. If the relationship is, however, a great strain on your resources and capabilities, if you completely stop relating to such a Guru, no great fault is established by logical reasoning. Moreover, your doing this in a non-harmful way will establish a good precedent because you honestly did what you had to do for your spiritual progress. Why continue to pretend if such a relationship brings nothing to your spiritual path at all? No one wise and capable could find faults with this as long as you act genuinely and without malice. If you do not give up on your spiritual path, sooner or later a suitable Guru-student relationship will undoubtedly arise for you.

If, the Guru tells you to kill, and you see it as Dharma,
Or pointing his finger east, the Guru says it is west,
And you eat that shit, it may be beneficial,
For those with the equal taste of saṃsāra and nirvāṇa,
But if others simply pretend, the effect will be the opposite.

Though irreversible faith and the highest pure perception
May not arise for you naturally in your own heart,
Worldly virtues grasped as foundations and made to increase
Are the start of a good relationship of Guru and student.

In the natural state, there are neither master nor servant,
But if, from the center of the self-arising essence,
Beings other than you are grasped as being of great value,
The natural joy and bliss of the natural state arises.

This kind of human joy is absent in the three realms,
Realization of this will accumulate white merit.
If that is gathered, we wake from the sleep of ignorance,
So aspire that all awake from that sickness of ignorant sleep.

Not bound by a life of slavery to bad traditions,
With heads not impaled on stakes of fools' exaggerations,
Be free of the prison of rigid discipline grasped as supreme.
KYE! Don't act like a lazy sheep toward liberation!

The Sublime Realm of Śhambhala

3

A Brief Summary of Liberation from Birth, Death, and Bardo

Whether making kleśhas into the path is fully mastered or not, how can anyone fail to rejoice in those who benefit sentient beings? Therefore, if someone has the courage to fulfill such a role but has yet to figure out how to go about it, it is of immense value to at least try. In order to do that, the path of performing benefit within all lifetimes must begin in this very life.

Yet, *a series of lives in the waking state is not all there is. This waking state is one of six bardos*[351] *that pervade the succession of our lifetimes.* When we know that, we are better prepared to deal with them and to bring benefit to others. When we fail to recognize that, we think our benefit comes from worldly qualities like glory, wealth, enjoyment, reputation, fame, success, or status. Actually, if we were to consider the entirety of our lives, enjoying these transitory gratifications is like enjoying happiness for merely one second out of an entire day.

Every person on this earth will die and pass away from this waking state. Therefore, that most people do not prepare at all for what will

---

351 This chapter is just a summary presentation of the topic. For more detail, see *Unveiling Your Sacred Truth – Book Three.*

262   TANTRIC PATH OF DESIRE

happen to them when they die is unfortunate because, if they did, they could save themselves a great deal of suffering. Death is not just disappearing like a fire that is put out or water that dries up. When our outer bodies are left behind at the time of death, our minds, together with all the karma of happiness and suffering we have gathered over our many lifetimes, are irresistibly drawn to one of the six realms of beings by its most powerful karmas of happiness and suffering. We must go there to be born once again in this continuous cycle of death and rebirth. The body certainly vanishes, but your mental continuum does not. Enlightened experience establishes this as fact, and that is not known only to Buddhists.

Therefore, people who think only of this life are like people who diligently prepare for today but ignore the other 364 days of the year. They are like people who, if they are happy for the first hour of each day, never think about the rest of the morning, afternoon, evening, and night. Ignoring the good and bad possibilities of tomorrow, they make no preparations. From that viewpoint, they are like fools. If we consider well, are not people who think of no more than this life suitable objects of our compassion?

Through days and nights, weeks and months, the years of this and later lives grind us down like a rolling millstone. Acting as if "tomorrow" will never come, most people make no prudent arrangements for the future, but according to the Buddha's clear and profound teachings about karma and rebirth, how can the next life and future lifetimes not come in their turn? Reincarnation is actually only a very small part of the vast subject of karma.

As summer, fall, winter, and spring always come in succession, the same is true of the six bardos, or "transitional periods" of life. These six saṃsāric movements between different states of our lives cycle endlessly until spiritual realization breaks the cycle of suffering,

1. First, we have the bardo of living or *waking state.*
2. Second is the bardo where the mind is absorbed in *one-pointed meditation.*
3. Third is the bardo of *deep sleep and dreaming.*

These first three are the *bardos of living.* Then there are the *bardos of death and rebirth*:

4. Fourth is the successive dissolutions of the elements in the *bardo of dying.*
5. Fifth, right after that, when all the stages of dissolving are complete, is the occasion of luminosity of death, the *bardo of Dharmatā.*
6. Sixth, after that, continuing until we are reborn, there is the occasion of receiving a birthplace, the *bardo of becoming.*

To know these six is to know that unenlightened experience consists only of cycling from life to life in ignorance and suffering without any choice. *The first three occasions are three critical times of preparation to fulfill temporal and ultimate goals* by learning how to prepare yourself for the future. *The qualities of the latter three naturally arise one after the other, depending on the first three.*

At this present time in the waking state, when we are free to act with many strategies, if we gain the understanding and mastery of how we can attain liberation in the latter three occasions, we can make perfect Buddhahood manifest. If we cannot, we may still be able to take birth in one of the Buddha or Bodhisattva pure realms where we can complete the path to liberation. If we cannot do that either, we can at least receive a good rebirth in the next life. Since success in these three last bardos or occasions depends on having correct knowledge of how to deal with them, I will try to explain that briefly, in a way that is easy to understand.

Throughout your inner experience of a day, during the time of the waking state, take care to keep your mind and thoughts always one-point-edly mindful and vigilant. If you clearly evaluate whether what you are doing is aligned with your goal, you will make good choices. By focusing single-pointedly on good choices, you will become accustomed to virtue and it will dominate your mind. You will then progressively move toward being exclusively virtuous and it goes without saying that the number of virtuous phenomena will subsequently increase in number and in purity.

As all such relative virtue is gathered into a single essence beyond *self* or *other*, however great your self-cherishing may currently be, it will eventually cease. By your example, other sentient beings will also learn how to think like that, and when they witness good results, they will desire to do likewise. All non-virtues intrinsically favor oneself over others, whereas all virtues make no distinctions between self and other. Thus, virtues do not need to be separated from self-cherishing, as they are naturally free from it. As a consequence, your self-centered rigidness naturally softens with a gain of flexibility in the mind.

To take it further, when phenomena in the mind are virtuous, we are able to meditate on these phenomena with a one-pointed mind.[352] This occurs because phenomena classified under "me" or "mine" are understood to be free from the dualistic, conceptualized nature they appear to have when tightly grasped by saṃsāric fixation. When the true nature of all phenomena is known to be non-conceptual, we apprehend that non-conceptual phenomena are linked to joy and happiness while conceptualized phenomena are linked to suffering. We gradually realize that the reason why conceptualized phenomena are associated with suffering is that apparent phenomena are wrongly viewed as independent entities separate from our individual selves.

Then gradual realization dawns as to how, in reality, phenomena

---

352 Such as the meditations on the Path of Desire described in Part Four chapter 7 as an example, yet the forms and levels of meditative absorption are numerous.

have no independent nature or selfhood. When I say, "no...selfhood," I mean that individuals and phenomena have no independent *self* in the way that is understood by ordinary individuals. I do not mean they have no selfhood in any sense. If that were true, we would also be negating the pure awareness of Buddhahood that is our *true Self.* [353]

Once we know that appearances in our minds are empty of existence as the independent real things they appear to be, the mind can rest in the true, blissful nature that remains when those appearances are seen as empty. Once we learn to rest in this way, we develop the ability to do so when entering and abiding in deep sleep and dream states. Then we are better prepared to be liberated when encountering similar states through the dying process, at the moment of death, in the bardos after death, or, for those highly fortunate and realized, already in this current lifetime. Here, "liberated" means that we fully attain freedom or autonomy.

Aside from this illusory, saṃsāric self that is always in karmic bondage, there is the absolute Self that is our real nature. At present, that true Self is perceived in our continuum only in rare glimpses that seem to be unreal or far away, but, when we realize how things truly are, Sugatagarbha, Buddhahood, is then recognized and experienced as our true Self. When we are near to recognizing that, glimpses of true reality can be received in moments of meditative equipoise. If these phenomena are recognized for what they are, that is excellent. Bringing them together and extending them into continuous meditative equipoise is possible. That universal continuity is the continuity of tantra. When our mind is lucidly absorbed in this continuity of ultimate truth, that occasion is the

---

353 Rinpoché wrote extensively on this topic in *The Great Middle Way: Clarifying the Jonang View of Other-Emptiness* (Dzokden: San Francisco, 2020). For a traditional commentary, you can refer to Dolpopa's *Mountain Dharma: The Ocean of Definitive Meaning* (Dzokden: San Francisco, 2023). Recently, in order to avoid confusion between the two truths, Rinpoché suggested capitalizing "Self," when it refers to true, absolute Selfhood, but not when it refers to the false, dualistic self of the relative.

bardo of meditation.

If familiarity with this absorption can also arise at the time of deep sleep, there can be the especially exalted experience of being able to recognize "the shining forth of luminosity." When waking, meditation, deep sleep, and dreams can all be experienced as aspects of Sugatagarbha, we know that our real Self is what we are experiencing. In this way, everything is transformed into unerring enjoyment of the true nature of the whole universe, the value of which is incalculable. If we cannot perceive it directly, by making the effort to cultivate at least a good intellectual understanding of it, or by having a strong intuition or faith within that truth, practicing the path will be sufficient to manifest it in the future and eventually, we will enter that enlightened world.

If I give a clear summary of the stages of the elements dissolving into each other before the moment of death, rather than involving this coarse body experienced by touch and sight, those stages involve an experience of subtler aspects of the body dissolving and vanishing. In fact, all the phenomena of our external and internal bodies vanish from our awareness every moment. These tiny deaths of which ordinary people have little awareness continually occur. One obvious example of this happens every night when we go to sleep. Except for this little death being smaller in its length of time and scope of phenomena than the "big death" between lives, this too is real death. Why are we then not afraid of it? There is no fear because we have faith that tomorrow we are going to wake up again. If, when we went to sleep, we certainly knew we would never wake up, we would probably be terrified.

Similarly, when we are about to die, once we are sure that we will be born again, as if we were waking up from sleep, not even a speck of fear will come to us. Except for death being bigger in scope and longer in time than sleep, they are the same in all other ways. Everyone knows that when we go to sleep, the eyes, ears, nose, tongue, and whole body lose the ability to experience forms, sounds, smells, tastes, and touchables. This happens because the sense consciousnesses dissolve into the mental consciousness. Then, the mental consciousness becomes subtler and subtler, until finally, it too dissolves into the foundational consciousness.[354] This sequence also happens when we die.

When a limited degree of coarse consciousness appears again, that is the occasion of dreaming and it has much in common with the transitional period between death and rebirth. Though most people do not understand it, the subtle aspects of the elements dissolving into each other to produce deep sleep arise again in reverse order to give rise to dreaming. We then seem to experience our bodies and their surrounding environment as we do in the waking state. Since these are just subtle phenomena, our dreams usually lack the phenomena of touch, and dreams do not appear to ordinary beings other than the dreamer.

A similar scenario takes place at the time of death. Though the coarse body does not dissolve before death, its subtle aspects that are the essences of the five elements do. Gradually, one by one, all the elements are dissolved into each other. Just as when we go to sleep, when we die, the five sense consciousnesses associated with the five elements dissolve into the mental consciousness. The mental consciousness dissolves then in the foundational consciousness, a very subtle but still dualistic consciousness where all our individual karmic propensities are stored.

When even that subtle duality is transcended, herein lies the limit of saṃsāra. On this level, at least for a short time, there is an opportunity to experience our true, liberated Selfhood. That experience allows us to directly recognize that our true nature is fully enlightened. Ordinary beings call this "death" and perceive it as an object of immense terror. However, if the limit of saṃsāra is recognized for what it is, it is recognizing our true, enlightened Self. Those who have trained before will recognize it

---

354 *kun gzhi*, ālaya, the foundational or base consciousness where karma is stored. When its impure aspects are eliminated, the all ground wisdom manifests, *kun gzhi ye shes*.

just as a child recognizes the mother. There is no more important and delightful occasion in this universe. When our true Self is fully recognized, what ordinary people call "death" is realized as Dharmakāya. We realize that we are the wisdom that perceives reality as it is. After that, never again does death need to be an object of anxiety and terror.

If we cannot become that essence of supreme liberation, various appearances of *Sambhogakāya* arise from the Dharmakāya's energy of manifestation. Should we recognize these appearances for what they truly are, we still have the opportunity to be liberated, but if we are also unable to do that either, by the power of the roots of virtue collected in all our lives, and by the power of familiarity with the bardo between lives, we can still be born in a pure realm. If our roots of virtue and power of aspiration are great enough, we can be born in one of the pure realms of the Buddhas like Amitābha, who are the lords of the five tantric families. If this is not possible, it is somewhat easier to be reborn in a bodhisattva pure realm, like the realm of Avalokiteshvara. In particular, the sublime bodhisattva realm of Śhambhala has a special karmic connection with all of us living on this Earth, and that makes it easier for us to be reborn there. By the inconceivable compassion of the bodhisattva Dharmarājas and Kalkī Kings and Queens of that pure realm, and through the good karma of our own devotion and pure aspirations, it is certainly possible that we can take rebirth there.[355]

---

355 For that purpose, Rinpoché wrote diverse Śhambhala aspiration prayers which describe in detail also the stages referred to in this section. For understanding more about Śhambhala and its karmic connection with our planet, you can refer to *The Realm of Śhambhala: A Complete Vision for Humanity's Perfection.*

4

Conclusion with Auspicious Verses
and Colophon

Even though I am the one who wrote this book, the inner meanings of these topics were taught by the Perfect Buddha in the glorious *Kālachakra Tantra*. All the explanations here are related to the Buddha's teaching in that King of Tantras and other texts that teach the same meanings. Therefore, requesting the *Kālachakra* Empowerment[356] and listening to teachings associated with that tantra will be very helpful for understanding what I have written.

It is taught that, as we all train on the path to liberation and omniscience, the Buddhas and Bodhisattvas provide the experiences that we need. In particular, the Dharmarājas and Kalkī Kings and Queens of Shambhala, who have already realized the fruition of this path, have vowed to remain in apparent existence to help all sentient beings. From time to time, with their bodhisattva retinues, they manifest on this Earth, and eventually, they will guide the whole world to a second Golden Age

---

356 Also known as *"Kālachakra* Initiation" though Rinpoché prefers the translation *"Kālachakra* Empowerment." He and other Vajra Masters offer in public at least the *Seven Empowerments of a Growing Child* which is the extended Vase Empowerment of *Kālachakra*.

of peace and harmony. Now that you have read this book about the secret essence of Highest Yoga Tantra and the direct practice instructions for attaining it, all you readers, dear vajra sisters and brothers, will be able to enter, in varying degrees, into the profound levels of mind taught by these high beings.

How to rectify faults in the prātimokṣa vinaya,
And its traditional notions of how to tame desire,
Were explained by me before, but no one took it to heart.[357]
The burden of this defeat was heavier than a mountain.

Many well-known vinaya-holding sthaviras,
Discarding the root of prātimokṣa, grasped the branches;
But for those who practiced tantra, that occurrence[358]
Was understood as a timely rain that was heaven-sent.

As for this vast and subtle essence of tantrayāna,
Millions of stars of learned and accomplished ones,
Following their traditional paths within the sky,
Never intersect with its many lunar mansions.

---

357 In the past, Rinpoché devoted great effort to thorough study of the vinaya and its commentaries. He found the way in which Tibetan monasteries were applying the vinaya needed correcting, for example their ignoring procedures for amending the thirteen offenses with remainder, as discussed in Part Four chapter 3. With great disappointment, he realized that most people did not care much about these points because they were mainly concerned with following traditional customs.

358 Rinpoché means that many monastics who focus on the path of individual liberation ("sthaviras") were actually not focusing on the root vinaya vows but on its branches. For example, they focused on whether monks were carrying their robes with them, but tended to look the wrong way if they subtly cheated people through misrepresentation. After a long time of observing this happening everywhere, he eventually came to the conclusion that these problems monastics were having were actually a heaven sent opportunity because tantra was a more suitable path for them.

Why would they heed the words of this lowly wanderer?[359]

No king ever gave me high status, to wear on my chest as a
medal.
No high Lama has ever pulled me down a throne from heaven.
I have no great community, with servants to support me.
What kingdom's subjects listen to simple wanderers?

Yet, as even old farmers and nomads are experienced in their
trades,[360]
What is the fault if I truly describe the experiences
Of the karmic patterns of my many lifetimes,
Gathered in my own family of tantric nomads?[361]

---

359 According to Rinpoché, many learned Tibetan scholars and famous accomplished Lamas
of the past, here referred to as "millions of stars...following their traditional paths..." were
preoccupied with traditional approaches to the teachings. Therefore, they did not explain
the essence and practice of tantra in a practical and approachable way beyond academic
learning, and they did not put much effort into dealing with the challenging issues pointed
out by him. Rinpoché is not judging single individuals for what they did or did not do because we cannot know the exact circumstances of their time. It does seem clear that most
Tibetans who venerate the famous Lamas of the past as being wonderful seem to be interested only in traditional ways. They do not respect modern presentations of the teachings
that try to deal with contemporary problems. Regarding the next metaphor, as the moon
orbits in the sky, it always passes through a series of constellations of the lunar zodiac.
If those lunar constellations are said to represent points in the genuine understanding
of tantra, we could say that these learned ones are like stars whose motions in the sky
never come in contact with them. Rinpoché, describing himself as a "lowly wanderer" in
the world, tried to explain the essence of tantra very clearly because these issues must be
addressed; nevertheless, many people seem uninterested as he does not have the great
status he describes in the next verse.

360 Tibetans tend to see them as lower, uneducated people, but they are masters in their
own fields.

361 Though many high ranking Tibetans may dismiss Rinpoché as a mere wanderer because his status is inferior to theirs, he knows well his accustomed field of tantra, by
having related to it in this life and many former ones.

From delighted attachment to words, exaggeration can follow;
From the ignorant scorn of fools, deprecation follows as well.
As sheep flee dogs without thinking, or rabbits flee splashing
    sounds,[362]
Let everyone do as they will, in the happy glory of freedom.[363]

For me as well, many stupid, erroneous practices,
Were rigidly grasped too long, and glorified as righteous,
Not making authentic consorts my daughters of insight, and
    so forth;
Though I regret it now, who can rectify my lapses?[364]

Men and women who love awareness yearn for wisdom,
They aspire to benefit friends who have a similar karma;
With confidence in others who share the same good fortune,
They act to free their fellow disciples of destiny.

Though I longed to write on how to traverse the limitless paths,
Of secret tantra that is so vast and so profound,
If there had been no signs that the time had come to do so,[365]

---

362 None of these problems will be corrected if people simply proclaim and defend their
favorite doctrines and do not think about their basis in experience. In that case, they are
like a sheep that flees from a dog by instinct, regardless of whether the dog is dangerous
or not.

363 Whether or not readers approve of what is said in this book, they are welcome to make
their own evaluation.

364 Rinpoché makes the poetic confession of now recognizing that he wasted too much time
following strict monastic discipline, making no effort to join authentic consorts, or to
cultivate his own family lineage.

365 Although the insights shared in this book have been in Rinpoche's mind for a long time,
he only wrote it after he perceived signs or indications that the time had come for the
spreading of tantra that will lead to the second Golden Age.

Getting old and dying in silence, I would just have enjoyed my
   ease.

May the water of this merit,[366] like the mother of the moon,[367]
Filtered by going through the golden ground,[368]
And mixed with the sky of enlightenment, as floating clouds,
Grant us in all our births a rain of holy amṛita.[369]

By this merit, becoming the trusted messenger,
Of the Kalkī Bodhisattvas of Śhambhala in the north,
May I carry out their Buddha activity,
By announcing the good fortune of a new Golden Age.

May those with bad thoughts who exaggerate seeing and
   hearing with words —
All treacherous words that solidify things as good and bad —
Attain the goal beyond words that is the four kāyas and vajras,
By learning how to bring their kleśhas to the path.

Even if they are unable to accomplish
The Conqueror's level of the four kāyas in this existence,
Those with deep faith, aspiration, pure perception, and love,
Will be reborn in the highest tantric field, Śhambhala,
Where they will traverse the levels of tantra in one life.

---

366 The merit of writing this book.

367 A poetic expression in Tibetan for "ocean."

368 As water is filtered in the ground of the earth, may relative merit be filtered by association with the absolute nature of the pure ground.

369 By mixing this pure merit with all the merit of the bodhisattvas of the three times, "clouds"
of the holy Dharma can arise, which can rain their blessings upon sentient beings.

Colophon

The author, a vajra holder who keeps the three vows, one known as Shar Khentrul Jampel Lodrö,[370]guided by many special experiences and realizations, evaluating the situation of the holy Dharma in many parts of the east and west of Jambuling and the situation of the teachings of the Victorious One in the Snow-land of Tibet, starting again in 2021, after working on extensive sketches in 2019, wrote certain parts of this book, but due to many undertakings and activities, did not have the time to finish it all at once. Though for a long period, it appeared that the time was not ripe to conclude this writing, in 2022, on the fourth day of the second Western month, in the 12th month's 4th day of the Tibetan Metal Ox year, on an auspicious day where there was good synchronicity, this work was completed in the Australian region of Melbourne at Tongzuk Dechen Ling.[371] May all the vajra brothers and sisters in the whole of Jambuling attain the empowerment of bringing kleśhas to the path. Sarva mangalaṃ!

Arising from the cause of discordant, dissimilar views,
With its conditions arising from various different habits,
And these habits themselves arising from different customs,
What is praised as true by one is reviled as false by others.

Many view things that are good as being very bad.
What some praise as perfect, others call confusion.
On the eyes of karmic appearance are distorted lenses of bias.
Who can give rise to hopes of pleasing everyone?

---

370 Another name for the author, Khentrul Rinpoché.

371 Another name for Rimé Institute, or Tibetan Buddhist Rimé Institute, in Belgrave.

APPENDICES

Gendün Chöpel

Gendün Chöpel's Passages and Concluding Verses

Homage to Gendün Chöpel by The Author

Though he was far from just repeating what others said,
He knew how to receive all good explanations of others,
Like a bee that drinks slowly a lotus's deathless essence;
Warrior of insight, I pay you reverence!

From the nurse that is the jewel of your excellent explanation —
A kind of priceless jewel that is free from earth and stones —
As our life-force is refreshed with self-risen understanding,
Only faith, aspiration, and respect are received.

Like miraculous retrieval of nourishing milk from water,
From the rich ores in the earth of your well-said teachings,
By those who know how their deeper meaning should be retrieved,
Not just sex but its essence of wisdom is enjoyed.

Gendün Chöpel's Selected Passages

Though there are quite a few Tibetan books about sex, I have not written about them in this book, so that there will not be too big an accumulation of words. Those who are curious can look at some of the verses written by Gendün Chöpel in *Treatise on Desire*[372] or search for the whole text if they prefer. Those who want to know more yet can consult persons who are knowledgeable and experienced on the subject. Those who would still like to know more about sexual techniques in other cultures can consult widely available classics such as the *Kāma Sūtra* and the *Perfumed Garden*. My own book has no pretensions of being a manual for sexual expertise like these. With the greater benefit of progressing on the Path of Desire in mind, just the essential points have been presented in my book so that everyone can apply them according to their own capacity.

Below are some relevant passages from Gendün Chöpel's *Treatise on Desire*[373] regarding the significance of the union of men and women[374] that present the essential meaning of that work.

6.[375] In the *Aṅguttara Sūtra* of Simhala,[376]

The following words were taught by the Blessed One himself,
Among all forms, the ones that are the most beautiful,
Are the forms of women in the eyes of a man;

---

372 *'Dod pa'i bstan bcos, Kāma Śhāstra.*

373 *'Dod pa'i bstan bcos, Kāma Śhāstra.* For a translation of the entire work see the bibliography.

374 Not only is this union biologically necessary, the interaction of masculine and feminine principles is central to Tibetan explanations of human psychology and existence altogether, as described in detail in the present book.

375 The verse numbers are not present in the Tibetan, and therefore, are a somewhat arbitrary device for convenient reference, dividing the equivalent of paragraphs, and showing where verses are left out.

376 Śhrī Laṅkā.

7.   And the forms of men, as seen in the eyes of women.
     I have never seen any more beautiful than these.
     Among all sounds, the ones that are most melodious
     Are the sounds of women in the ears of men;

8.   And the sounds of men, as heard in the ears of women.
     No sound of any kind is sweeter to hear than these!
     Similarly, for smells and tastes, and touchables,
     The three most desirable qualities are said to be established.'

11. In certain sūtras that teach the eighteen sciences,
[a-b] One is the science of kāma, sexual techniques. [...]

12. The *Lalitavistara*[377] says, when it gives a list
     Of qualities that are suitable for a bodhisattva's consort,
     'Versed like a courtesan in the skills described in the treatises,'
     Sexual proficiency is counted high on that list.

13. When also there is a reference to, 'a woman,who knows the
        treatise,'
     The name of the treatise referred to is the following,
     Originally composed by the master Surūpa,[378]
     The *Kāma Śhāstra*, of which there is a Tibetan translation.[379]

---

377 *Lalitavistarasūtra, The Vast Expanse of Play.*

378 *gzugs bzang zhabs*

379 See bibliography.

14. The son of a Kashmiri king called Paribhadra,[380]
Who was a learned Brahmin by the name of Koko,[381]
Composed a treatise with the name the *Joyful Play,*[382]
That was never translated into the Tibetan language,
But a few Sanskrit fragments survive at *Ngor* Monastery;
One by Nāgārjuna[383] is also said to exist.

15. In the country of India, very famous at present,
Are the *Kāma Sūtra,*[384] and *Treatise on Desire.*[385]
The great and small texts combined amount to more than thirty.

76. To give a woman to a desirous man,
Among all gifts is said to be the best.[386]
This is taught in the *Practice Chapter* of the *Kālachakra.*
If you don't believe it, look! It is taught very clearly.

77. Like impoverished people who wrinkle their noses[387] at gold,
Or hungry, starving guests who despise and spit on food,

380 *zhi ba'i blon*

381 Kokkola.

382 The *Ratirahasya.*

383 *klu sgrub zhabs*

384 The *Kāma-sūtra, Discourse on Desire,* variously dated 400 BCE - 300 CE, is a Sanskrit text on how desirable and undesirable manifestations of sex and love contribute to emotional fulfillment in ordinary life. It is attributed to the brahmin Vātsyāyana in the colophon. The author notes that *kāma* is regarded by Hindus as one of four *Puruṣhārtha,* proper goals of human life. The other three are moral values (*dharma*), economic values (*artha*), and liberation from saṃsāra *(mokṣha).* The *Kāma-sūtra* was first translated into English by Sir Richard Burton in 1883.

385 By Maheśhvara.

386 And vice-versa, as in the verses 6 - 8 just above.

387 Like "turning up one's nose" in English, a gesture of contemptuous rejection.

Everyone thinks that they should deprecate sex with their mouths,
But in their minds, it is the source of all their joy.

78. Gold, silver, horses, and elephants are attained by only the wealthy.
Sex can be enjoyed by everyone, high or low,
As wind and sunlight, earth and water, and the like,
Though they are precious, are there for everyone in common.

79. All the wonders on Earth have been accomplished by humans;
Humans come from sex, between a man and woman.
If one thinks like that, what act could have greater value
Than to unite a man's penis with a woman's vagina?

80. So that this important deed may be performed,
No diligent exhortation to hardship is required.
All men and women, by their nature, want to do it.
This is the legal tradition of the King, Interdependence.[388]

81. Not depending on studies of workmanship and reasoning,
By the practice[389] of lying down for half an hour,
A living statue of Dharma lord *Butön*[390] was made.
Doesn't the way they accomplished it astonish you?

---

388 In the sense that unfailing interdependence naturally governs relative reality like a "king".

389 *sbyor ba*, the Tibetan for "practice," also means "union," either yogic union with the natural state or sexual union with a consort.

390 Buston (1290-1364). Fourteenth century Tibetan master, scholar and historian, early compiler of the *Kangyur* and many texts on Sugatagarbha. He wrote extensively on *Kālachakra*.

82. The miraculous joining of cause and condition is wonderful,
     The union of men and women is far more wondrous still.
     That this wondrous science is known by nature by any fool,
     Without any need for study, is the highest miracle.

83. Not holding such a wonder to be wonderful
     Is taught by the *Sakya* Paṇḍita[391] to be a sign of a fool.
     Though, I am, of course, completely mad these days,
     Those who are not mad will laugh out loud to see it.

84. The experience of bliss is surely no small benefit;
     Creating a family lineage is also no small benefit.
     If you can guard the Path of Desire in bliss-emptiness,
     How could that be of less benefit than the other two?

85. For every woman there is a man available;
     For every man there is a woman near at hand.
     In the minds of both, there is desire for union.
     What, do you think, are their chances of remaining chaste?

86. Even when worthy actions are visibly forbidden,
     Since, surely, unworthy actions still are done in secret,
     How can this unfeigned desire of human beings
     Be suppressed by the laws of religion or the world?

87. In the vajra city that possesses six essences,[392]
     In the apparatus of channels, with its ornaments of five chakras,
     How can the bliss that is naturally abiding there,

---

391 Head of the *Sakya* school.

392 Corresponding to the six elements, tantric families, senses, and so forth.

Being grasped as a fault and forbidden ever be what is right?

Regarding this subject of desire and appraisal of partners, which is so profound and important, Gendün Chöpel says,

88. Love for what is desired is passionate attachment;
So love for what is desired is also faith in that.
Fear of what is undesired is known as aversion.
So fear of the undesired is renunciation of that.

89. As desire and lack of desire are intrinsic mental phenomena,[393]
They can be transformed, but can never be abandoned.
For that reason, making the kleśhas into a path,
When we analyze in detail, is the way of all the vehicles.

90. One's personal benefit, the benefit of the country,
The king's dominion, and the beggar's means of life,
And any actions, great or small, that are performed,
Whose absence would be lamented, are indispensable women.[394]

91. The meaning of desire is making aspirations,
And making offerings to your yidam deity.
If men practice these with women,[395] it is said
The non-deceptive fruition will ripen very quickly.

---

393 In the sense that they are aspects of sentient beings' minds.

394 The Tibetan word for women, *bud med*, literally means "indispensable," as explained in Part Four chapter 2.

395 And vice-versa.

92.   This vast world is like a fearful, great desert plain;
       By the burden of too much karma, people are sure to be saddened.
       Able to bring refreshing joy that situation,
       A girl-friend as a playmate is like a karmic avatar.

93.   She is a goddess of form who delights your mind when seen;
       She is a field for growing your excellent family lineage;
       She is a nurse who takes care of you in the pain of sickness;
       She is a poetess who restores your grieving mind;

94.   She is a serving girl who does all of your housework;
       She is a loving companion who supports you for one life;
       The wife who is linked to you by formerly gathered karma,
       Is an embodiment of these six desirable qualities.

95.   'Women are very fickle and inclined to cheat.'
       The men who keep saying that are telling a groundless lie!
       Women and men are no different in cheating on their spouses;
       If you think carefully, nowadays, it is the men who are worse.

96.   Even when a king has taken a thousand queens,
       This is still proclaimed as if it were a virtue;
       If any woman were to take a hundred husbands,
       She would be defamed because it is 'not done.'

97.   If that king has sex with each of his thousand queens,
       How would he ever receive the name 'adulterer?'
       Since sex with one's own wife cannot be regarded as cheating,
       How can adultery be attributed to the rich?

98. A rich man who is very old with snowy hair,
Selecting a tender maiden, gladly pays her price,
Regarding her as only a purchased piece of goods.
Kye ma![396] For women, there are neither friends nor protectors.

Now, regarding ripening consorts, their characteristics, and so forth:

129. The outside of a rolled-up piece of cloth, like cotton,
Is covered with lubricant, so that its small tip is softened.
Every day, once desire has been aroused,
Put the cloth a little way inside the bhaga.

131. If the liṅga is churned on the skin between the thighs,
It is said that the bhaga naturally grows and ripens.

151. As for the desire of a teenage girl to have a man,
A thirsty man's craving for water can never rival it.
As for the lust of a man who wants to have a woman,
A hungry man raging for food can never rival it.

152. Being imprisoned in a dark pit is not comparable,
To young lovers kept apart by their righteous parents;
Being locked in stocks is not comparable,
To strict religious laws that make sweet love a crime.

153. However perfect the power of a renunciate attitude,
As water still flows in a river that is blocked by a dam,
When an unwanted religious tax is levied on sex,
It is like constantly pushing a boulder up a hill.

---

396 An expression of lamenting, showing his compassion for women in this situation.

154. Spouses, established as such by each other's karma,
Made companions as dear as their lives, by sharing kindness;
Abandoning deception and adultery,
Is the highest peak of all commitments of discipline.

155. With exhausted sexual essences and minds at rest in peace,
A man at the time of gray hair, with his beloved wife,
Strive on the Dharma path within their forest retreat.
That was the conduct of gentlemen, in bygone times.

156. As long as the horse of their faculties was running wild,
And had the power to ride through the realms of their desires,
Though they indulged that long in enjoyment of their passions,
How could a couple be blamed for that by thoughtful people?

158. If different terrible sicknesses are made to rise,
By relating to women such as prostitutes,
Making faults occur in the causal conditions of semen,
One's family lineage being forever cut off is certain.

159. To such stricken parents, children never can be born;
Even if a hundred were born, they would quickly die.
And though they died, one's body would still be sullied by faults;
And so, a path of more careful conduct is required.

161. If material things possessing form are churned and rubbed,
It is in their nature to release their essence;
When clouds are rubbed by wind, a stream of rain descends.
When sticks are rubbed together, flames of fire rise upward.

162. Similarly, butter, which is the essence of milk,

At first, exists in milk, inseparably mixed;
However, when it is poured into a container and churned,
After heat slowly rises from the parts of the milk,
Bits of its inner essence are drawn out and separate.

163. Similarly, thiglé, which is the essence of blood,
As first exists in a state of being dissolved in the blood,
But when there is the churning of a man and woman,
By the power of passion, heat rises in the blood,
And the essence, is drawn out, as butter is drawn from milk.

164. By just seven drops of the essence of food,
In the human body, a drop of blood arises;
From a cupful of these gathered drops of blood,
A single drop of the subtle essence is established.

165. Because in women, their menstrual blood descends each month,
Their physical strength is less, and their flesh more relaxed and soft;
Because the skin is thinner, it is very sensitive,
And, when they are old, their bodies accumulate many wrinkles.

166. Nevertheless, aside from such mere external details,
The bodies of men and women are without difference;
Not one thing that is found in the body of a man,
Is not also found within a woman's body;

180. But a man's desire, on the surface, is easily awakened,
While a woman's runs deeper and is harder to arouse;
Therefore, a variety of techniques of passion,
Must be employed to arouse the passion of a woman.

181. The anthers of the bhaga and its inner parts,
     Similarly the labia to its left and right,
     The mouth of the womb, as well as the tips of the nipples,
     When passion has arisen, are said to swell and shift.

182. For men, what is sensitive is the entire liṅga,
     Up to the crotch, and right to the edge of the hairs,
     When desire arises there, the touch of bliss inflames;
     The heart of it all is the jewel at the end of the liṅga.

183. However, the different kind of bliss that is found in women,
     Is spread out pervasively, without any definite focus;
     From underneath the navel to the roots of the thighs,
     Inside the bhaga, and also at the gate of the womb,

184. The anus, the large, soft surfaces of the buttocks, and so forth;
     In brief, all the outer parts of all of the lower body,
     Are pervaded by sexual bliss, and in completing that process,
     It is said that a woman's whole body becomes her lotus.

188. In whatever faculty the power of the mind is focused,
     By the channels of that power being drawn together,
     The fluid within them is squeezed, and it comes out externally,
     As when tasty food is recalled, saliva moistens the mouth.

189. When the body is burning with shame, it is covered in sweat.
     With passion, a mountain stream will boil out of the lotus,
     As with strong joy or sorrow, tears are shed by the eyes.

190. Therefore, when emotions such as passion and anguish
     Are stopped as they are first arising in the mind,

There is no problem, and doing so may be very good.

191. However, when they rise fiercely, and their power is great,
     Forcefully stopping them goes to the winds of the heart, and so forth;
     Though, looking at them externally, it seems that nothing is wrong,
     Excessive wind in the heart is the cause of mental illness.

192. Even if women have the equivalent of semen,
     It comes in a gradual flow, like water from a glacier,
     Rather than a great deal coming all at once,
     And so the way of it is not as it is for men.

193. As soon as it is emitted, from that instant, like men,
     Women are not satiated, losing all interest;
     If coition continues after their fluid is emitted,
     They do not feel a jarring, unbearable sensation.

Sexual techniques from the preliminaries to the main activity:

321. By engaging with savage fury, as soon as they meet a woman,
     Then depleting their semen, as soon as they engage,
     With a ravenous manner, like a dog that wolfs down lungs,[397]
     Not even a tiny spark of bliss will be obtained.

322. Whoever desires the fire of passion to reach the heights,
     Enters into the shrine of the pūjā of desire,
     Where the beautiful lady is set out as a drill-stand,[398]
     On the bed prepared for the sake of the joy that is soon to come,

---

397 See footnote 254.

398 *gtsub stan*, a stand for a fire-starting drill used in a Vedic fire offering.

323. Her right foot is positioned on her partner's shoulder,
     She lets her breasts and bhaga be clearly visible;
     After she has lubricated the palms of her hands,
     They should be used to strike the center of her birthplace.

324. Then, like a holding *phurba*[399] that is used in secret tantra,
     That is otherwise always concealed, in various different ways,
     As she grasps his organ to manifest flowers of joy,[400]
     All the intense enjoyment of passionate play begins.

325. Firmly embracing her partner's neck, with her left hand
     She kisses her lord and master[401] again and yet again;
     Extending her right arm, she grasps the shaft of his liṅga,
     Then should milk it, as she would the teats of a cow.

326. Likewise, she rolls his liṅga between the palms of her hands,
     Moderately pulling, she twists it right and left;
     Having grasped its root, by shaking it back and forth,
     She strikes it against her thighs, and then her lips and teeth.

327. The liṅga of the man, which has fully risen,
     She squeezes between their bellies, as a way to massage it;
     Sometimes holding it between her thighs,
     She rubs it repeatedly against the mouth of her bhaga.

---

399 A triangular ritual dagger or kīlaya.

400 *mngon par dga' ba*, also the name of the First Bodhisattva Level.

401 As noted previously, it is wrong to regard one's consort as subservient. When a woman is said to regard her consort as her master or men to regard his consort as his master, both are encouraged to highly value each other as being very precious as described in detail in Part Four of the book. Then, with a clearly established attitude, all kinds of consensual joyful play naturally flow.

328. Then when she has placed his liṅga in her fingers,
     She should look at it with eyes intensified by desire;
     With her palm around his scrotum, taking hold of it,
     She rubs the large veins of his penis, massaging again and again.

329. While she strokes the buttocks of the man with one hand,
     Around her navel[402] and throat, and beneath her arms,
     Places where the itch of passion is engendered,
     Should be touched and dragged, using the tip of the liṅga.

330. The hole in the liṅga from which the seed of a man arises,
     Is touched with the tips of the nipples and run over by the fingertips;
     When the man is trembling maddened with his passion,
     The hole should, in turns, be sucked and dragged over by the
        tongue.

331. In the area of the root, she scratches with her nails,
     And then, as she pushes the soft jewel with her hands,
     She plants it at the mouth of the bhaga again and again,
     Putting it halfway inside, then pulling it back again.

332. Because they bestow fine progeny and glorious joy,
     Because they are of the nature of life and the absolute deities,
     When it comes to ecstatic activities in these occasions of joy,
     To hinder them even a little is called a sacrilege!

---

402 Literally, the kidney area, which is not particularly sensitive. The meaning is that particular level of the torso, including the hips.

334. The woman who gives worship to the self-risen liṅga,
With an offering of the petals at her lotus mouth,
Through the source of bliss, Mahādeva,[403] being pleased,
Will attain glory, wealth, and the best of children.

335. All that reveals itself in the play of their powers;[404]
Thus, the hearts of both are made to tremble with bliss.
Looking into the other's flushed face, they totally lose their shyness!
Then she guides the jewel of his power with her hands,
Offering it to the aperture of her eager bhaga.

336. Inserting repeatedly just the tip, she pulls it back;
Again and again, pushing halfway in, she pulls it back;
At last, she joins them together, up to the very root,
The liṅga is made to point upward, for a very long time indeed.

337. By the woman's legs being raised and drawn backward,
They are made to spank the buttocks of the man;
By making her knees to touch, below her partner's armpits,
He is held by her thighs and calves, as they gently rub downward.

338. When, from time to time, the liṅga is drawn out,
The woman, after softly caressing it in her hands,
Releases it, then puts it inside her bhaga again,
At first a single finger's length, then two or three.

---

403 Śhiva. The self-arisen liṅga is his emblem. Here and elsewhere, Gendün Chöpel relies on Hindu sources to enrich his Buddhist background. By the woman offering herself to him as a flower offering as the man offered himself to her earlier, she manifests as his consort Śhakti, the cosmic power of desire. Union with the Śhiva principle of cosmic mind manifests the ultimate level of fulfillment, overflowing as a universal blessing for beings.

404 On the physical level, in the play of the liṅga and bhaga.

339. Gradually released, it is sent to the innermost;
      When it has completely vanished in the mouth,[405]
      She rocks the haughty testicles softly back and forth.
      Grasping at the root of the liṅga, with two fingers,
      Squeezing it well, she agitates it in the bhaga.

340. After two or three shakes, wrapping the tip of the liṅga,
      She brushes it with soft silk, doing it again and again;
      By that, it will be made extremely big and hard.
      Sometimes, she should also rub the gate of her bhaga.

341. Lubricate the liṅga all around the root,
      Then the tip and shaft are rubbed repeatedly.
      Companions who seek enjoyment in the power of bliss,
      Need to learn these special instructions very well.

342. Then as they are blazing with craving for sexual union,
      As they teasingly twine their limbs, the man enters her from below;
      From one end of their big bed, all the way to the other,
      In their mutual embrace, they travel, and roll about.

343. The more their longing, the more they weep on its fulfillment;
      The more they were silently mindful, the more they want to talk.
      When all barriers of shame have been completely transcended,
      The nature of bliss becomes extremely powerful.

344. By their performing in every way just as they like,
      The techniques of desire will manifest their nature;
      Just as they are explained in various treatises,

---

405 Mouth of the bhaga.

All the different kinds of joy will be experienced.

345. No intimate proficiency is required for this;
     If both are intoxicated by passionate ferocity,
     When it comes to sexual union there is no 'what goes where?'
     Go all the way, omitting nothing, all in all!

346. It is inappropriate for any third person to see this,
     Nor for anyone's ears to hear a menu beforehand;
     Such extraordinary, secret relationships as this,
     Are between only the dearest soulmates in the world.

349. When a man too quickly starts coition from the first,
     Since the woman being satisfied does not occur,
     Those sufficient in power and their supply of semen,
     Will have to do it twice or maybe even three times.

350. Also when a man's semen is quite near to coming,
     Delaying his motion, he can let his bliss spread out;
     Then, when desire is re-kindled, he can resume his attentions;
     Union in this case too, must occur two times, it is said.

351. As soon as the semen comes, the penis of the man,
     Not removed, should remain within the cave of the bhaga;
     As long as the woman continues in her motions of need,
     Until her bliss is complete, he does as she desires.

352. If even when that is done, her bliss is not complete,
     The man puts two fingers in the bhaga and vibrates quickly;
     Before having sex, in general, the man should make it a point,
     To rub and caress the hole of the bhaga with a finger.

353. Moreover, first having taken a penis made of wood,[406]
Men rub it again and again, inside a woman's birthplace;
When the woman is drunk with pleasure, union can begin;
In southern regions, this tradition still continues.

354. When their husbands have gone elsewhere, taking the same device,
Women deal with their absence by using it on themselves.
Of gold, silver, copper, and other precious metals as well,
It is said that such implements are made for the use of the rich.

355. Most of the women, in the country of India,
Certainly have knowledge of only their own husbands;
Since sex that satisfies their minds is all too rare,
They have many secret methods like that above.

356. Retinues of queens who are guarded by eunuchs,
Similarly rely on techniques such as these;
They occur in traditional tales told in every country,
But these are taught in the *Kāma Sūtra* as instructions.

357. It is said that the bride of a premature ejaculator,
Will experience sexual bliss not once within three years;
Men having no idea of their life companion's experience,
Would be an excellent reason for taking ordination!

358. In brief, by a variety of activities,
Until strong wishes for sexual union arise in women,
Men should not engage in actual coition;

---

406 Old form of a dildo.

That is the essence of all the treatises on desire.[407]

410. As couples engage in joyful play until satisfied,
[d]

411. Clouds of old hopes and fears vanish into the sky;
The moon of the self-arising nature melts into milk;
The great bliss of space that is clear and non-conceptual
Then arises as medicine; give that gift to women!
That was the chapter on actions of moving and piercing.

Other sexual techniques:[408]

423. A woman braces her feet underneath a man's armpits,
Then she mounts him, while her head is facing backward;[409]
Bending her upper body, with her right and left hands,
The man's two ankles should be held and leaned against.

424. Then she successively moves her buttocks forward and backward,
Pulling upward the liṅga within her and pushing it down.
To the right and left, to the front and back of the bhaga,

---

407 See footnote 252.

408 This section is quite extensive and can be tiring to read all at once. It can be regarded as a wealth of possibilities and you can, for example, read different verses each time you open the book. Should you choose to skip ahead, be sure to read the concluding verses that touch on the profound meanings of the Path of Desire starting at verse 557 below.

409 Toward his feet, in a variant of reverse cowgirl. Rinpoché has chosen passages from Gendün Chöpel where the woman is encouraged to be on top of the man during sexual union. This is unusual in Tibetan customs, where women are seen as inferior and always below men, even during sex. One of the reasons for choosing these verses is because Rinpoché wants to contradict this antiquated and narrow cultural view. (Old-school Tibetans can take comfort in the fact that this approach makes the woman do all the work.)

Like a stick, she presses it and then releases;
This brings joy to a vigorous man with a rigid liṅga,
And, at the very same time, to his passionate partner.

425. On a long bed, equal in width to the length of a body,
Or on a pile of cushions that are long and thin,
Above, the man lies supine, and the woman
Mounts him as before, facing away from him;

426. She positions his liṅga well inside her bhaga,
And places her two feet, to the right and left, on the ground.[410]
Then, as before, the woman lustily churns her buttocks;
Sometimes, as she rides, she changes her gaze to the front.[411]

427. Both the man and woman are sitting on the bed;
The woman's left thigh is pressed by the right thigh of the man,
The man's left thigh is pressed by the right thigh of the woman;
They unite with their lower bodies angled a little apart.

428. They mutually embrace while the right legs are on top;
From time to time, they exchange which thighs are above the other.
With this crossed technique of sexual union as the basis,
Further standing and lying positions are assumed.

429. With the man's buttocks being placed upon a chair,
The soles of both his feet are placed upon the floor;
The woman sits in his lap; as they embrace each other,
The woman wraps her legs around and behind the man.

---

410 This is the main difference from the last.

411 She faces toward the man, in regular cowgirl.

430. As the man's two hands are holding the woman's waist,
     He lifts her body upwards and presses it down again;
     Sometimes, by rotation of the woman's pelvis,
     Without any thrusting or pulling, the bhaga is gently churned.

431. Passionate women living in the land of Persia,
     Can reach satisfaction using this technique alone;
     There it has been given the name 'the Perfumed Garden,'
     In Arabic, it is called *kel a kar*.[412]

432. A man with little strength, or one who is hot and tired,
     By a woman whose passion is extremely great,
     Riding on that man, engages in sexual union;
     The work is famously done by the woman, not the man.

433. Old men in India, taking a wife who is quite young,
     Not able to deal with the toil required by their bellies,[413]
     Therefore, for the most part, follow that tradition;
     Many other countries have a similar custom.

434. The supine man spreads his thighs and fully extends his legs,
     The woman lies above, with her calves held close together,
     Joining the root of the vajra, to her closed thighs and bhaga,[414]
     As the man's upper arms are tightly held by the hands,

---

412 This is not Arabic. Perhaps it is an Arabic rendering of some Sanskrit word. There may
   be a reference to *The Perfumed Garden*. Since Gendün Chöpel is said to have been very
   careful about foreign terms, most of the transcription errors we find in the text were
   probably mistakes by copyists.

413 The point seems to be that that old husband does not have sufficient strength and energy
   to do the needful.

414 The vajra is also stimulated outside of the bhaga.

The woman circles her hips, with strongly grinding motions;
This position is widely-known as the "way of a mare."

435. With the woman as above or riding the man like a horse,
The mouth of the bhaga is joined to the very root of the vajra;[415]
The lower bodies lean strongly together as they join.
Thrusting and pulling back are not engaged in here.

436. Then, in turns, to the right and left, and above and below,
The woman should rapidly waggle her pelvis then circle it;
This is called *bhramaraka*, 'the manner of a bee,'
Or 'the way of a bee, when it is gathering honey.'[416]

437. Like a millstone with its central hole,[417] the tip of the linga
Stirs in the cave of the bhaga and circles all about,
The supine man inserts his penis in the woman;
With her two feet extended to the surface of his chest,
Both, with joined hands, are rocking like a palanquin.[418]
This is called "the action of riding in a boat."

438. The woman, face down, is above the man as he lies supine,
With her hands and feet on the ground, she bends down and
    rides him;
With every thrust and withdrawal, she admires his long, thick vajra,
Of her partner, as it enters inside of her.
This ecstatic activity being performed by a woman,

---

415 They go all in.

416 This behavior is commonly observed in the two waggle and circle dances through which bees tell other bees where nectar may be found.

417 *rang thag*, specifically a millstone that is self-powered by wind or water.

418 A palanquin or sedan chair rocks when the bearers lift and carry it by its poles.

Is known in Sanskrit as *gatāgata,* coming and going.[419]

439. The woman sits on the penis of her partner,
     Her two legs are stretched until they are under his armpits,
     Her hands are placed to the right and left, upon the ground;
     They do, as they like, the movements of mortar and pestle, and
       palanquin.
     This is known as 'the melody of a palanquin.'

440. With the woman's two legs behind the back of the man,
     As their chests are joined, she embraces the shoulders of her partner;
     The supine man's upper body is leaning on a pillow.[420]
     This is called *rodhanika,* 'the reverse approach,'
     The movements of both a pestle and palanquin are done.

441. With the pair well and truly united, the two legs of the man,
     Wrap around his partner's spine, as women are wont to do;
     This has been given the name, 'the way of holding a bag.'
     Here, thrusting and pulling are difficult, so the palanquin motion
       is done.
     In other wondrous means of sexual union as well,
     Using the way of the palanquin is entirely blissful.

442. The man is lying supine with both thighs spread apart,
     Both of his knees are bent, most of the way that they can be;
     Facing him, the woman puts her buttocks over his penis,

---

419 Forgive a bad Sanskrit pun. A person who attains Buddhahood is a *tathāgata,* one who goes "that way," where "that" refers to suchness. If a woman pursued this ecstatic activity all the way to liberation, would she not be a *tathāgatāgatā,* "one who goes this way and that way," to all levels of phenomena, as she likes?

420 That created space for the woman to get her legs behind him.

Steadying her two feet to the right and left of him.

443. The woman, leaning back on the thighs of the man,
Performs the alternate actions of thrusting and pulling back;
In this way, the liṅga enters into her deeply,
Repeatedly coming in contact with the gate of the womb;

444. This technique is contraindicated for pregnant women,
It is called rodhanika, 'having a reversed manner.'
In a man, there is a little of a woman's nature,
Just as in a woman there is a little of a man's.

445. And so, when she rides a man, on the face of a woman,
There may be a fierce expression he has not seen before;
In any case, when a couple wants to have a baby,
And the woman wants to be pregnant, it is good to avoid this style.

447. The woman, presenting her back, is lifted to the man's lap,
Stretching out her hips, she joins him with her buttocks;
With one hand the man is holding the woman at her breast,
With the other hand he squeezes her bhaga, from the side.

448. Maintaining just the right tension, the vajra goes in and out,
The woman may, sometimes, steady her hand against a wall;
While this technique of sexual union is being performed,
If his finger rubs the lips above and beside the bhaga,
And both caress softly, below the cheeks of their partner's buttocks,
At the roots of their partner's thighs, their bliss will increase
   without measure.

449. The woman lies on her side and pushes her buttocks backward,
     The man, lying behind her, is thus made to meet her bhaga;
     By reaching with his head, under the woman's arm,
     He should kiss the tops of her breasts and nuzzle them.

450. As the man, sitting on a chair, is leaning back,
     Extending her buttocks from his left side, the woman meets him;
     Her legs, over his left thigh, are stretched out to the left,
     With one of her hands, she embraces the neck of her partner.

451. The woman, supine, places a cushion beneath her buttocks,
     Her feet are drawn up in the air by the man pulling a rope;
     The man takes hold of her knees from the front, and they unite.
     After the union is over, if the woman remains,
     For a short space of time, in the position described,
     It is said to improve the chances of the womb conceiving.

452. The man is sitting on a chair and leaning back,
     Both his feet, well-extended, are placed on the floor in front,
     With his buttocks on the edge of the seat, he spreads his thighs;
     The woman, facing backwards, sits on the lap of the man,
     As she stretches her buttocks outward, his liṅga enters her bhaga.

453. The woman's two feet are braced at the bottom of a wall,
     Fiercely thrusting her bhaga on the liṅga of her partner,
     The woman rubs and circles around it with her buttocks;
     Sometimes, leaning her hands on a ladder-rung in front of her,
     She repeatedly pulls her buttocks back and presses them forward.

454. Or also, leaning her hands, against a wooden rod,
     She presses down to the root of the liṅga, as before;
     Or exchanging chairs of different heights, they couple on them,
     While the woman performs the greater part of the rhythmic motion.

455. The woman kneels down and leans upon the bed,
     She bends her waist and stretches her pelvis to the back;
     Positioned by spreading his thighs, the man enters from behind;
     This is called *dhenukā*, 'the posture of a cow.'
     With the man's hand reaching forward, underneath the torso,
     He massages the swollen lips of her bhaga repeatedly.

456. For a change, the woman may stand up from her bent position,
     Leaning down to place her hands on the bed, she drops to her
         elbows;
     Again, she rotates her waist to keep her buttocks stretched backwards.
     For women who feel tormented by a ruthless passion,
     Of all positions for union, this is said to be the best,
     And so its use is an institution in many countries.

457. In another alternative, the woman, as before,
     Places her knees on the bed and then presents her buttocks,
     She lies on a pillow that slightly raises her upper body,
     The rhythmic motion is done by the man and woman equally;
     The man, by an embrace, with his hands in front of her,
     Rubs her torso, moving upward from her belly

458. With the woman's two hands staying clasped behind her,
     She lies on him supine, so that she may present her buttocks;
     They unite from behind her, using the palanquin motion,
     To grant themselves the taste of intoxicating joy.

459. From behind the woman, the man's two legs face forward,
They are stretched forward, underneath the woman's thighs;
Sometimes the woman turns her buttocks to the side,
Stretching out both her legs to the left of the man;

460. Sometimes she also turns them to the right like that.
This is an excellent way to keep her from getting pregnant;
All the standing and seated positions are also useful.

461. The woman, after placing her buttocks on a chair,
Spreading her feet wide apart, plants them on the floor;
As she lifts her upper body as high as she can,
The man stands up in front of her, and they unite.

462. This and similar positions for sexual union,
Are very useful for preventing pregnancy.
In brief, positions where the birthplace is facing downward,
And the liṅga enters into the woman from below,
And the woman's waist is not bent to the front,
Are ways of union good for preventing pregnancy.

463. If the woman stands, right after the man emits his semen,
Then stamps the soles of her feet repeatedly on the ground,
And after that, washes out her bhaga with warm water;
This is like a drug for avoiding being with child.

464. The woman places a pillow underneath her belly,
    Extending her arms and legs, she lies face down on the bed;
    Spreading his thighs,[421] the man then mounts her from behind,
    He steadies his cheek in the middle of the woman's spine.

465. With his two hands, from the root of the woman's thighs,
    Pulling her buttocks repeatedly to his penis, he enters;
    Sometimes with the fingers of his right and left hands,
    He squeezes the lips of the bhaga, as he pierces inward.

466. This and other techniques of entering from behind,
    Can be exchanged in various different sequences;
    Thus, the woman might stretch her buttocks outward and shake,
    Rubbing and massaging her partner's lower torso.

467. After the man has bent his head downward,
    He should kiss above the pelvis of the woman;
    Likewise, after sucking at the sides of her belly,
    He should slide his tongue beneath her arms and breasts.

468. Moreover, these various kinds of intoxicating activities,
    Should be done whenever you feel inspired to do them;
    By enjoying the woman from behind, as the lotus anthers,
    By direct touching and rubbing, can be completely awakened,
    The woman can be satisfied with intense, joyful passion,
    And that bestows exceeding pleasure on a woman.

---

421 This way he can bend his knees to reach the required height.

470. This refined delight existing as your indestructible nature,[422]
This taste of honey created from your self-risen body,[423]
Pervading to the tips of your hundred thousand pores,[424]
Is not experienced by even celestial Indra's tongue.[425]

471. An old man who has done it all, might say anything,
If he had to do it in secret, he might disparage everything;
This realm of desire has many pleasures of the senses,
But what could be better than the vagina of a woman?

That was the chapter on various means of sexual union.
The profound meaning of these virtuous qualities and final
aspirations:

557. That which attracts the entirety of the third thousand-fold world
realm,
As if to a lodestone that can be neither seen and touched,
If we really think about it, is the space of great bliss,

---

422 Since your relative human nature is only too destructible, this can only refer to your
absolute nature. A momentary delight of sexual union is actually a glimpse of the great
bliss of Sugatagarbha and it can be expanded through proper practice as described in
Part Four of this book.

423 Similarly, the body in question cannot be the impermanent human body that arises
from interdependent causes. It must be the indestructible vajra body of enlightenment.
As this too is identified with Sugatagarbha, the point is the same as before.

424 "Spreading what is spread," as described by Rinpoché regarding the final stages of sexual union.

425 The Buddhist teachings explain that enlightenment can be fully attained only when
practicing the proper path as a human being. As the gods of the god realms, for example,
taste celestial amṛita, and innumerable delights of the senses, this distracts them from
exploring the possibility of the ultimate bliss of enlightenment. Extended explanations
for this can be found in many traditional texts and in Rinpoché's *Unveiling Your Sacred
Truth — Book One*

Known to be the field where apparent existence dissolves.

558. Unsatisfied even by gaining the wealth of the
         third thousand-fold world realm,
     Famed for the blazing covetice of its limitless ambition,
     Really, this mind, this aphasic child, this knower of nothing,
     Wants to go back to its homeland, the space of bliss-emptiness.

559. You reveal the pure, true nature of things to holy beings,
     You just play funny tricks upon bewildered children;
     Among your defining qualities is indefinability;
     I prostrate to you, the deity of self-risen joy!

560. You appear in the minds of fools and those who never meditate,
     You are a friend to all, and everyone is your friend;
     Though you are seen by all, you are understood by none;
     I prostrate to you, the deity of self-risen joy!

561. You dance naked in space, free from relative garments,
     All your miraculous forms have no worldly colors and shapes;
     You shoot the star of experience that no awareness can grasp;
     I prostrate to you, the deity of self-risen joy!

562. To you where the various rainbows of elaboration dissolve,
     Where the ocean of illusion is calm and free from waves,
     Where even distracted motions of mind are unwavering,
     I prostrate to you who are the self-arisen great bliss!

563. You are seen by the Buddha eye that never blinks;
     Learned ones experience you when speech is broken;
     You meet with unfixated minds as non-elaboration;

I prostrate to you, the self-arisen space of bliss!

564. Here there is no proclamation of the secrets,
      Of profound secret tantra's practice and terminology;
      Though that is so, as this practice can be embarrassing,
      Tantrikas should try to keep it secret from other people.[426]

573. After we put our hopes in saṃsāric phenomena,
[c-d] It is true that experience finds in them no wondrous essence.

574. Still, as the numbers of men and women are similar,
      With candidates easily found, if they desire each other,
      As frustrated lust is worse karma than outright fornication,
      To indulge in sexual enjoyment is surely the better course.

575. If we keep the company of anything long enough,
      Everything in this life will sadden us, in the end;
      'The only cure for that sadness is the holy Dharma,'
      We will surely think that thought one time at least.

576. Fools who guard their false appearances from change,
      And learned scholars who generate fabricated thoughts
      Follow different paths from the crossroads of their births,[427]

---

426 We could interpret this in at least two ways: Traditional tantric texts should not be displayed to everyone in all circumstances, as they are beneficial only when specific conditions are met; furthermore, when tantrikas are passionately and "shamelessly" engaging in the Path of Desire, it is best to keep their activities secret, so as not to disturb social norms of a particular region and time. See Appendix II with quotes from the *Kālachakra*.

427 The scholars are from the relative point of view better than fools, but most of them still cling to conceptual thoughts. They have separate ways of life, but neither of them transcends saṃsāra and death, so the two are said to meet on the banks of the Ganges at death because of the traditional Indian belief that it is auspicious to die there with one's

But meet once more to die, on the banks of the three-fold Ganges.[428]

577. Yet if, on seeing the depths of the ocean of saṃsāra,
You simply cannot bear your disillusioned sadness,
Please wear a renunciate's saffron robes upon your body,
And strive for nothing but the peace of the holy Dharma.

578. The Tibetan scholars who came to this noble land of India,[429]
In the auspicious times of bygone centuries,[430]
Possessing the three trainings,[431] controlling the three gates,
Would find my present discourse quite difficult to hear.

579. I am one with little shame, but limitless faith in women;
I am the sort who chooses the bad and rejects the good;[432]
My vows have not guided my head since quite a long time ago,
But faking them in my innards was only recently smashed.[433]

---

cremated ashes becoming part of the river.

428 There are said to be three Ganges rivers, 1) the celestial Ganges flowing from Śhiva's topknot; 2) the one in this world; and 3) the Ganges of the Land of Death below the earth.

429 Where Gendün Chöpel resided at the occasion of writing.

430 Presumably he is thinking primarily of the origins of the later translation schools about the 11th - 13th centuries.

431 The three higher trainings of ethics, meditative absorption, and wisdom.

432 Because Gendün Chöpel eventually chooses to follow his innate faith in women and the Path of Desire, he is aware that he will be considered a "bad" person by his tradition.

433 Referring to no longer focusing on individual liberation vows as his main ethical conduct.

580. The proficiency of fish in water runs quite deep,
We are all most familiar with what we have experienced;
As I considered that, it seemed to be my destiny,
To expend a great deal of effort in writing this present treatise.

581. Though monks may revile it, that is only to be expected;
Though tantrikas may praise it, that is hardly forbidden;
It may not do very much for doddering Lugyal Bum,
But to young Sonam Tar it will be of great benefit.[434]

582. The author of the present treatise is Gendün Chöpel,
The place it was composed is the city of Mathurā;
An old brahmin explained to me the difficult passages,
A Muslim girl provided me with direct instruction.

583. The basis of explanation comes from the Indian texts;
I wrote in Tibetan verses for easier understanding.
The assembly of causes leaves nothing incomplete;
I expect a fine fruition, as the certain result.

584. The monk called Mipham[435] wrote about sex after reading books;
The rake called Chöpel wrote from personal experience;
The difference in their power to grant the essential blessings,
Will be known by passionate men and women in their practice.

---

434 These are common Tibetan names, so it is like an American saying, "...Joe Schmidt... Al Jones...," that is, this treatise may not help old people much, but young people will know what to do with it. (We could also interpret "old" here as referring to closed-mind persons rather than an exact age.)

435 Ju Mipham, see glossary.

585. If there seem to be many faults of excess or omission,
  Like seeming to say too little from the heat of passion,
  Such faults that are mistakes of additions or omissions,
  Confessing with regret, I hide and conceal nothing.

586. I am one who destroyed his life as a virtuous friend;[436]
  I lost my religious costume and all pretension to goodness.
  So whatever your faults may be as an individual person,
  Don't load them on the head of a lowly one like me![437]

587. By this merit, may all companions of the same family,
  Traverse the misty gloom that conceals the path of passion,
  Until, from the peaks of the mountains of the sixteen joys,
  They see the cloudless sky of true reality.

588. Yutrön, Gangā, Asali, and the rest of you,
  You ladies I related with, as we made free with our bodies,
  Continuing on our path that goes from bliss to bliss,
  May you reach Dharmakāya, the ultimate great bliss!

589. May all the humble people who live on this wide earth,
  Be set free from the prison pit of ruthless laws!
  May they be able to know, with ordinary freedom,
  The little enjoyments they need, that are so rightfully theirs.

---

436 A monk who is a good spiritual friend.

437 In the sense that he is already "disgraced" and there is no use trying to tear him down further.

Colophon by Gendün Chöpel on the good qualities of the teachings of desire:

This Kāma Śhastra by Gendün Chöpel who reached to the other shore of the ocean of fields that are knowable by the insight of oneself and others and cut through exaggerated statements about the passion of desire through seeing, hearing, and direct experience was completed in the later part of the second month of winter of the Tiger year, [January 1939,] in the great city of Mathurā in Magadha near the banks of the Glorious Yamunā as a light like the radiance of a spring dawn descended in the house of Gangādeva, where I was accompanied by Pañchāla, a woman who was a companion in the same practice. May it be auspicious! Sarva mangalaṃ.

Concluding Verses by the Author

All is well, whether reality is proclaimed or not.
Yet, in this realm of desire, we live only through our passion.
By not knowing how to make passion into the path,
By fighting it like poison or an enemy,
How afflicted we are!

The passion of some is the cause of saṃsāric suffering,
And others' passion, the path to wisdom and great bliss.
From abandoning kleśhas, transforming them, or using them
on the path,

Not to abandon — but use them — is a delight without precedent.
Something being essentially poisonous is impossible,[438]
Knowing how to use poison as medicine is sufficient.
There are no more enemies within saṃsāra.
Knowing how to turn foes to friends is the height of wisdom.

Great[439] *passion is the path of the Ḍākinī of Great bliss;*
Great anger the path of the Ḍāka with a tiger-skin skirt;
Great jealousy that of the troops of wrathful perseverance;
Great pride is the pride of victory over warfare in the
three realms.[440]

---

438 For example, cyanide being poisonous depends not only on its own nature, but the nature of beings that are its victims. It exists naturally in certain plants, and they are not poisoned by it. Similarly, the three mental poisons, attachment, aversion, and ignorance are toxic only in the conceptual environment of saṃsāra. In the environment of non-conceptual wisdom they become beneficial aspects of that wisdom.

439 "Great" here and in the following lines means passion and the other kleśhas as they are perceived from the viewpoint of absolute wisdom.

440 The three realms of saṃsāra are experienced as an endless war between dualities of

Additional Verse

This awareness holder, a child attached to his noble family,
By venerating the deities without such a family lineage,
And analyzing the limits of the family of good sense,
Is freed within the pure field of awareness holders, KYE! [441]

happiness and suffering, knowledge and delusion, etc., and all actual warfare is a consequence of that. When enlightenment is attained there is the "Great pride" of victory
over that warfare.

441   Rinpoché is poetically telling us that he is not merely a wandering beggar without resources. He has loyalty and well-founded pride in his family as a tantra practitioner and
Vajra Master of the Buddhist lineage. He has faith and respect for the deities who have
no such human family, meaning that their outlook is universal, not biased. Moreover,
by analyzing human experience with common sense, he has been able to develop an
understanding of ways of practice that are right or wrong, in the sense of them being
workable or not. By all that, may liberation be attained!

The Kālachakra statue at Dzokden Kalapa, Austria.

[Kālachakra Tantra Quotes]

Introduction

Below are a few passages taught by the Buddha in the *Kālachakra* in a form we can access on our Earth. Unfortunately, the full root tantra and its commentary written by Dharma King Suchandra are now accessible only in Śhambhala. The tantric text of the *Abridged Kālachakra* by Kalkī Mañjuśhrī Yaśhas is presented below in Tibetan, then in English — with the tantric text marked in bold, and a commentary by Ju Mipham written in plain text. Words in square brackets and footnotes to his commentary were added by us to facilitate understanding.

The author, Khentrul Rinpoché, did not include any of these passages and explanations in the original manuscript. As they might provide clarity regarding the differences between tantric practice in ancient times from what is done today, this appendix was added by the translator with Rinpoché's consent. Only a very small selection of passages of the *Kālachakra* concerned with the gift of desire and literal sexual practice is quoted below. You can read the whole tantra and its commentaries if you want to know the vast range of subjects that are covered there. However, none of this reading is a requirement for entering into and progressing on the Path of Desire.

Generally speaking, the Buddha gives students as much of the Dharma as they can bear to hear and no more. When he taught the second turning of the wheel of Dharma with its profound teachings of emptiness, he cautioned his bodhisattva followers not to speak of these Great Vehicle teachings to new students or followers of the individual liberation vehicle because they would accumulate bad karma by rejecting these teachings with aversion. When he taught the wish-fulfilling miracle of ultimate reality in the tantras, it was the bodhisattvas' turn to be shocked. This is why Rinpoché addressed the secrecy of tantra in Part One chapter 2 of this book. Thus, if you are in doubt as to whether you have the proper requirements for reading such tantric texts, you should consult the authorities of your lineage first.

Giving the Most Excellent Gift of Satisfying Desire, Kāma Dāna

བ་ལང་སྦྱིན་དང་ས་གཞི་སྦྱིན་པ་དེ་བཞིན་གཞན་ཡང་མི་ཡི་འཇིག་རྟེན་དུ་ནི་ལོངས་
སྤྱོད་སྦྱར་ར་འོང་ཉ་ (4.206.1)
Gifts of cattle and gifts of land, and likewise other gifts of food, clothing, and so forth, in this human world, bestow abundant fruitions of enjoying food, clothes, and so forth.

སྨན་དང་ཀ་ཟས་ལའཡིན་པ་དག་ནི་མཐའན་དག་ནད་འཕོག་བཀྲེས་པ་དག་ནི་སྐོམ་པ་
དག་ཀྱང་འཕྲོག་ར་འོང་འ (4.206.2)
Gifts of medicine and food take away all sickness and also take away hunger and thirst respectively. [...] However, these gifts do not bestow the fruition of bliss-equanimity.

འདོད་པའི་སྦྱིན་པ་ཐམས་ཅད་དུ་ནི་བདེ་བས་མཉམ་འཛུས་རྟེར་འཕོར་བའི་དུས་སུ་
རོ་ཀྱང་ཅི་ཞིག་དགོས། ར་འོང་འ (4.206.3)
On the other hand, if the gift of desire is given, the fruition of being of one taste with changeless great bliss and equanimity is bestowed on all occasions. In particular, at the time

of empowerments, and gaṇachakras, **what need is there to say** that such a gift should be offered to the Vajra Master.[442] [...]

སློན་ཚེ་སངས་ཨེགཡཨས་རྣམས་ཀྱིས་འརྗིན་མ་དན་ནི་སྨང་ཆེན་ཆུ་དང་ཞིང་ཏུ་ཏུ་མ་ཕ་གསེར་ཀྱི་བགུརྲ་ཞ་༢༠༤༘༡ (4.208.1)

In **former lives, the Buddhas** themselves gave **land** to others, **and elephants, horses, chariots, and many** other kinds of things. They gave these and great **loads of gold.**

སངས་རྒྱས་ཉིད་ཀྱི་སྨད་ཏུ་ཉིན་ཞིང་སྨར་ཡང་མགོ་དང་ཁྲག་དང་ཤ་རྣམས་དག་ཀྱང་རབ་ཏུ་སྨིན། ཞ་༢༠༦༘༡ (4.408.2)

And these were **given for the sake of attaining Buddhahood.** Again the giver's own **head, blood, and flesh were also totally given,** over and over.[443]

འདི་རྣམས་ཀྱི་ནི་བཞིན་པའི་སངས་རྒྱས་ཉིད་ཏུ་མ་གྱུར་ཏེ་ནས་འདོད་པའི་སྨིན་པ་རབ་ཏུ་སྨིན། ཞ་༢༠༤་ཞ་ (4.208.3)

However, **these** former Buddhas, **as they said** themselves, **did not become enlightened** by giving such gifts. **Then, they fully gave the gift of desire.**

གསང་བཟའི་སྨིན་པ་དེ་ཡིས་སྐྱེས་བུ་རྣམས་ནི་རྒྱལ་བ་སྐྱེ་ཉིད་རིགས་ལ་སངས། རྒྱས་ཉིད་ཏུ་འབྲངས། ཞ་༢༠༤་ཞ་ (4.208.4)

By those secret gifts,[444] **persons** who were bodhisattvas, de-

---

442 Offering various consorts; the practice in ancient times included offering the male student's family members as consorts.

443 These great acts of generosity are described in the mahāyāna sūtras. In the case of the tantric path today, more often such offerings of "head, blood, and flesh" are a metaphor for offering devotional service to the Guru.

444 Like a compassionate mother or father, the Buddha always communicates with his chil-

pending on the **producer of Victorious Ones,** Mahāmudrā, or Prajñāpāramitā possessing all the supreme aspects, were born **in the family** of inseparable bliss-emptiness, and by that, they were **born into Buddhahood.**

How a Karma Mudrā Should be Employed to Bestow the Four Higher Empowerments of Kālachakra[445]

དཔལ་ལྡན་ཤེས་རབ་ཅུ་མ་ཡང་དང་པོར་རིག་པ་གང་ཡིན་སྦྱམ་པའི་དབང་ནི་དེ་
ཉིད་དོ་ར་ $JJ(ʻʼ$ (3.119.1)

With **a glorious prajñā** consort, or śhakti, **also,** there is then the **first** of the higher empowerments. By the student **touching** the consort's **breasts** with his hands, there is the bliss of the moving white element, **which is** like the occasion of a growing child; this is the **actual Vase Empowerment.**[446]

---

dren in a way suited to their limitations. These tantric teachings were skillful means meant to produce the best possible results for a specific audience in strongly patriarchal times when women were regarded as men's possessions. Requiring practitioners to offer their family members and so forth as consorts to the Vajra Master was then a powerful means of overcoming attachment. Such a method suited the audience of that specific time.

445 According to Rinpoché, originally, the higher empowerments were done literally as described here, including the actual offering of a human consort to the Guru and the practice of the student with a consort. Nowadays, Vajra Masters perform symbolic empowerments, as described in Part One chapter 10 above; students can experience today the joy and bliss formerly transmitted by these actual empowerments by elevating their already existing sexual activity into the private tantric practice with their own partners as described in Part Four and Appendix I of this book. Rinpoché teaches a number of other cases where good results occur when we do not stick rigidly to the apparent literal meaning of scripture. Otherwise, we might be repelled by thinking that a literal interpretation of scripture that reflects the patriarchy of its time is the point, and it is not at all. Because today we have more suitable means of transmitting the experiences that were transmitted in actual empowerments in the past, we can say on that basis that the essence of the actual empowerments can still be transmitted in today's practice.

446 "Actual Vase Empowerment" is said here presumably to differentiate this *Kālachakra*

གསང་བ་དག་ལས་རེ་ཞིང་འཇིན་པ་སྐྱོང་བ་དག་ནི་བལྟ་བ་དག་གིས་གསང་བའི་
དབང་དུ་འགྱུར༔ ༣༡༡༩༢ (3.119.2)

Then, after, the master, according to the liturgy, performs the secret offering,[447] the student, with eyes covered by a blindfold, receives on the tongue amṛita bodhichitta **from** the consort's **secret** place and the **rabbit-imaged** moon[448] is given into the students' mouth by the master's left hand with joined thumb and ring finger. The student **tastes these, and** then the blindfold is removed. The mudrā's bhaga is also made to be clearly seen, **by** the student **viewer**, producing the moving bliss, which is like the occasion of youth. This **is the Secret Empowerment.**

ཤེས་རབ་ཡེ་ཤེས་དབང་ལ་མཆན་དག་རྒྱལ་བའི་རིགས་ཀྱི་ཡང་ལག་ཐམས་ཀྱི་སྦྱར་
བ་བྱས་ནས་ནི་༣༡༡༩༣ (3.119.3)

Then, in the **Knowledge-Wisdom** or **Prajñājñāna Empowerment,**[449] all the **aspects of the families of the Victorious One** are touched to the student's body, referring, as will be explained, to OM and so forth, the seed syllables of the five families, and the four letters **of the** deity's **faces**[450] and, **when** the student **has**

---

higher empowerment from *The Seven Empowerments of a Growing Child* which is an extensive Vase Empowerment of *Kālachakra* preliminary to this similar higher one.

447 Here, during the second higher empowerment, the master would enter into sacred union with the consort offered by the student. The resulting bodhichitta would be used as an empowerment substance ("secret offering.") Afterward, in the third higher empowerment, the master would give the consort to the student so that they enter into union.

448 Meaning "moon," which Tibetans say has the image of a rabbit on it, but the literal meaning here is the master's coarse thiglé.

449 Shortly, "Wisdom Empowerment," the third higher empowerment.

450 Syllables for visualization are commonly painted on cards, in the case of present-day symbolic empowerments. Some Vajra Masters additionally use special sacred objects to enhance the student's experience.

been purified[451] with these syllables,

རྒྱལ་བ་དག་ཀྱང་འདིར་ནི་བླ་མས་དབང་པོར་བྱས་ནས་སློབ་མ་ལ་ནི་ཕྱག་རྒྱ་སྦྱིན་
པར་བྱ། ར་ཅ✦ (3.119.4)

at this time, when he has witnessed[452] the Guru, as the **pure
Victorious One** Vajrasattva,[453] **the mudrā** consort **should be
given** back **to the student** so that they may hold hands[454] and
embrace. [...]

Such an empowerment is not for the benefit of the master who
teaches the tantras, draws maṇḍalas, and so forth. However,
for the student, by [...] mudrā consort and so forth, a variety of

---

451 According to David Reigle in an April 2023 letter, the Sanskrit of the *Vimalaprabhā* (or
Stainless Light, the commentary on the *Kālachakra* written by Kalkī Puṇḍarīka) here is
śodhayitvā, "having purified." This indicates that *sbyar ba* (joined) in the copy of our
Tibetan text may be an error for *sbyang ba* (purified).

452 Both Mipham and the Tibetan *Vimalaprabhā* have here *dbang por byas nas*, "empowered." According to David Reigle, *ibid.*, the Sanskrit of the *Vimalaprabhā* here is
sākṣiṇam, a witness. That implies that the Tibetan should be *dpang por byas nas*. However, it is possible that the translators of the *Vimalaprabhā* thought that there was a
mistake in the Sanskrit here when they translated *dbang por byas nas*. Then the translation would be, "at this time, when he has been empowered by the Guru, as the pure
Victorious One Vajrasattva..."

453 This is reminding the importance of pure perception of the Guru for the empowerment to be effective. In this case here the Guru is referred to as being inseparable from
Vajrasattva, the head of the sixth Buddha family of *Kālachakra*, unifier of all its enlightened maṇḍala. According to Khentrul Rinpoché, it also means that the Guru is doing what the Buddhas of the past did. Moreover, this makes it possible for the Guru to
empower the students with the same qualities so that they can perform the same sacred
activities as the Guru.

454 According to David Reigle, *ibid.*, the Sanskrit of the *Vimalaprabhā* here is *pāṇi-vyāpti*,
"holding hands," *bcangs* in the Tibetan version. This indicates that *lag pa bcings*, "with
bound hands," in the present copy of Mipham's commentary should presumably be *lag
pa bcangs*, "to hold hands." According to D. Reigle, *pāṇi-vyāpti* describes sexual relations for one class of gods. This is one of several passages that use terms referring to the
sexual union of certain classes of gods.

illusory displays of bliss is made to manifest. By that, the four
joys are recognized, and the view of suchness is made inseparable from the student. [...] This is explained extensively in the
fifth chapter [of the *Kālachakra*].[455]

How Male and Female Tantrikas Living in Villages Communicate Using Secret Signs to Avoid Trouble with Outsiders Who Might Otherwise Harm Them[456]

མཆོད་མོ་བསྐུན་ན་ལྷགས་པར་འོངས་སམ་དག་ཀྱང་ངེས་པར་བརྟོད་པར་འགྱུར་
ཏེ་རྣལ་འབྱོར་པ་ལ་ཡང་ངX་ྱ་ (3.186.1)

Now, [secret] mudrās[457] used for communication when heroes
and heroines meet each other are taught. When the yogīs first
meet the yoginīs, the **index fingers** formed in a vajra fist are
[are extended and] **shown** upward, with [thumbs covered by
the fingers so that the fingers covering the] the thumbs [are]
on the outward and [on] visible side; **when the** index fingers

---

455 The *Kālachakra* also describes the fourth higher empowerment, "Word Empowerment," the transcendental, ultimate wisdom empowerment that goes beyond the worldly and qualifies the students to enter the completion stage of the *Kālachakra* Six Vajra Yogas. When Rinpoché wrote the booklet *The Four Higher Empowerments — A Guidebook for Entering the Kālachakra Completion Stage*, he addressed this for the sake of students qualified by him to receive these higher empowerments. This booklet includes high pith instructions for personal meditation practice and, following Rinpoché's wishes, it should not be publicly displayed.

456 This selection was included to give a sense of what life as a tantric yogin was like, when tantra first spread. Practitioners were afraid that others would punish them for their "outrageous" worship through sacred feasts, involving "forbidden" foods and drinks, and sexual union beyond social norms, for example mixing castes or beyond patriarchal norms of their societies.

457 Here the word mudrā refers not to consorts but to particular gestures.

are shown joined like that,[458] "You all are welcome here" is certainly expressed by that mudrā. It is also done like that by the yoginīs for the yogīs.

གཉིས་ཀྱིས་ཉེན་ཏུ་ལེགས་པར་འོངས་དང་སྣལ་བཟང་ས་དགོ་ནི་ཧེ་ཕོ་བཅེངས་
པས་རབ་ཏུ་བརྗོད་པར་འགྱུར། ༣༡༨༦༢ (3.186.2)

By also extending the two middle fingers,[459] they answer, "You are very welcome," [...]

སོར་མོའི་སེ་གོལ་འདེབས་པ་རྐྱེན་ནི་འདི་ར་སྤྱག་པ་མཆོག་ཅེས་ངེས་པར་འགྱུར་
པ་སྟེ། ༣༡༨༦༣ (3.186.3)

Likewise, when the thumb and index fingers make a finger snap, the meaning is, "You here are excellent tantrikas;" or, sometimes too, tantrikas being very worthy is certainly expressed.

མཐེ་པོ་དང་ནི་སྲིང་མེད་དག་གིས་དམ་ཚིག་བཅས་པའི་ཆང་གིས་བྱིན་ནི་ཆོས་པར་
བྱེད་མོའི། ༣༡༨༦༤ (3.186.4)

If they snap like that, with the thumb and ring finger, it means, "With liquor and food of samaya substances, [the five types of flesh and amṛitas,] in a vajra feast,[460] we will satisfy you.

---

458 Presumably the two hands are brought closer together, so that the two tips of the index fingers touch each other.

459 Along with the index fingers, which are already extended.

460 The five types of "flesh" refers to human, elephant, ox, dog, and horse, all of which were considered as inappropriate to eat for the audience of that time. If these beings die a natural death, their flesh becomes a suitable samaya substance. The five amṛitas, often translated as "nectars," are to be partaken of as samaya substances without saṃsāric aversion or craving in order to eradicate bias. These are feces, urine, blood, marrow, and semen. The practitioner first dissolves the coarse meats and amṛitas, purifies them by meditation on emptiness, then has them reappear, and finally transforms them into actual amṛita. However, unless the practitioner has the ability to actually perform this transformation, these substances do not contribute to the attainment of enlightened qualities. These and other teachings on the subject can be read in *Perfect Conduct*, page

ཚེ་གནས་དག་ལ་རེག་པས་གཙོ་བོ་མཆུ་དཉཕ་ནུ་མ་བྱང་དང་ཏེས་པར་སེན་མོ་
འདེབས་པ་ཀྱང་ན་གའོ་ན་ (3.187.3)

By touching her **birth place,** a yoginī says, "You will be my **main man**" or husband. Likewise, by a yoginī **grasping her lips and nipples,** and these **particular places being scratched by the nails,** being her main [man or husband] is **also expressed.**[461]

སོར་མོ་ཕན་ཚུན་བཅིངས་ཤིང་གྱང་མོ་དང་ནི་མཐེ་བོ་བཀྱང་བས་དས་ཚོག་བཙོད་
པར་བྱེད་པ་ཡིན། ན་གའོ་ན (3.187.4)

When the **fingers** of both hands have been **mutually** joined and **clasped,**[462] and so connected, **by extending** from that **the middle finger and thumb,** that there is going to be **a samaya** [or vajra] feast gathering **is expressed.**

Up to this point, these are relaxed and joyful mudrās.
Now, [assertive] mudrās used by the yoginīs are taught.

116, or in *Buddhist Ethics,* 472-473. It is worth mentioning that advanced practitioners combine small amounts of these samaya substances into small, hard pills. Nowadays, for the vast majority of practitioners in monasteries and lay practitioners in the West, it is common to employ meat and alcohol that can be purchased in stores. These two serve as symbolic substitutes for the ten substances mentioned above. When practitioners cling to these symbolic substitutes and to their own personal preferences, they may defeat the purpose of the practice. According to Rinpoché, practitioners without higher realization need not worry much about literally practicing with the ten traditional substances, pills, or even these two common substitutes. To overcome grasping, it is beneficial to practice with any food or drink that one may have an aversion to. For example, strict vegans can try cheese, vegetarians can try a piece of ham, habitual meat-eaters can try potato; people attached to vodka can try juices, and so on.

461 These and some other passages that follow convey the character of empowering women at that time so that they are independent in relation to their own choices in the field of sexuality.

462 Folded into a two-handed fist.

མཆེ་བའི་དབུས་སུ་མཐེ་ཆུང་དང་ནི་སྙིང་ཁ་རུ་མཛུབ་མོ་འཛིགས་པ་རབ་ཏུ་ གསལ་བར་བྱེད། ༼༣.༡༨༨.༢༽ (3.188.2)

If, in the middle of the woman's own upper and lower canine teeth, the little finger is put and the index finger placed and shown at the heart and mouth, that very clearly means, "Danger!"[463]

ལག་པའི་རྒྱབ་ཀྱིས་སིང་ཆིག་ཅེས་པར་རབ་ཏུ་བརྗོད་དེ་མདོང་དུ་ཕྱོགས་པས་ འཇོག་ཆིག་འདུག་ཆིག་གོ། ༼༣.༡༨༩.༡༽ (3.189.1)

Bȳ [raising the forearms and] showing the backs of the hands, "Don't stay here, go away!", is certainly expressed, but, by [raising the forearms and] facing the palms frontward, "Stay, stay!"

རྐང་པ་རབ་ཏུ་སྐྱོང་པས་གཉིད་དང་ཕུས་མོ་བྱང་དག་སྐྱོང་ལ་བདག་ལ་ཤིན་ཏུ་དགའ་ བ་བྱིས། ༼༣.༡༨༩.༣༽ (3.189.3)

By fully extending the leg, "You may sleep here," is certainly meant, and by extending both knees, "I am very joyful."[464]

ཡན་ལག་ཀུན་ལ་རེག་པར་བྱེད་ཅིང་ཁ་རུ་ལག་པ་གནས་པ་དག་ལ་འདུས་པ་མིན་ པའི། ༼༣.༡༨༩.༤༽ (3.189.4)

All her limbs being touched by the left hand and the left hand resting on the mouth, covering it, means "I am being watched by the authorities and other people [who suspect that I am a tantrika], so I had better not go to the feast gathering."

ཕན་ཚུན་ལག་པ་བཅིངས་པས་བདག་གི་ཁྱིམ་དུ་དེ་རིང་འཁོར་མོ་འདུས་པ་དག་ནི་ རྟོད་པར་བྱེད། ༼༣.༡༩༠.༡༽ (3.190.1)

However, by clasping and folding the hands together, with the

---

463 This secret sign was likely used when enemies might overhear a verbal warning.
464 The secrecy implies that she may be joyfully anticipating more than sleep.

thumb and index finger sticking out from the center, "Today, at my house, there is a [vajra] feast gathering, and you should come," is said.

གནང་པ་ལ་ནི་འཕུག་པར་བྱེད་ན་དེ་བཞིན་དུ་ནི་ཕྱི་རོལ་འདུས་པ་དག་ལ་འགྲོ་བ་ ཡང་ན་ར་ཀྱ(◌་ན་ (3.190.3)

If the legs are scratched, through doing such an action, "I am going to a feast gathering, outside the village, and you should come too," is said.

That was the ascertainment of samaya feast gathering mudrās. Then wrathful mudrās are taught.

སྐུ་ནི་རང་གི་སོ་ཡིས་གཅོད་ན་མི་ཡི་ཕྱགས་ཀྱང་འདིར་ནི་སྦྱང་བར་བྱ་བ་ཀྱེད་པར་ བྱེད་ན་ར་ཀྱ(◌་ར་ (3.191.1)

Here when a yogī disrespects any of the messenger ladies out of inappropriate pride or one who has not attained power shows his own mantra to dispute a yoginī's wrathful one, if a powerful messenger lady cuts her own hair with her teeth, that means, "You [stupid] cow, you should fall by my hands here and now!"[465]

---

465 This and the next passage display some "self-defense" strategies for early female tantrikas. These remind us of the need to provide women with a way to protect themselves
from the social bias of their society, in the tantric context of an egalitarian approach at
many levels. It is interesting that when Kalkī Mañjuśhrī Yaśhas abridged this section of
the tantra, he made a point of keeping this section for yoginīs, probably because at that
time Śhambhala was still starting a broader process of transformation as he was the
first Kalkī, "holder of the (vajra) caste", who unified the Śhambhala inhabitants beyond
bias such as castes and so forth. The next two verses 3.191.2 and 3.191.3 are similar.

མཆུ་ལ་སོ་ནི་འདེབས་པར་བྱེད་ན་ཁྱོད་ཀྱི་རྒྱ་མ་ཚོ་བར་གནས་འདི་བདག་གིས་
བཟའ་བར་བྱ། ན་ཇ(ཇ་༔ (3.191.4)

If her teeth hit her lips, that means "KYE! What are you doing, you stupid cow! **The entrails abiding in your belly should be eaten by me.**"

If a powerful yoginī shows one of these wrathful signs, a yogī without corresponding realized power of his own had better not show a mantra in answer or dispute her in other ways. Placing the palm of his left hand on his heart, turning his body to the left, he should completely turn around; and then, with his left hand going upward in a submissive manner, he should leave. [...]466

---

466 The threat of killing them could be literal if the ultimate results for all concerned are good. Such wrathful activity is connected to one aspect of tantric samayas which says that we should not be loving to malevolent beings in the sense of facilitating their evil activity, but should be loving in the sense of helping them improve. This is best performed through the power of meditative concentration that sees clearly the results of the karma of others in order to know the exact ramifications of this act of liberation. As explained in *Perfect Conduct*, the secret samaya of "killing" while *liberating the mind* of an obstructor corresponds to the pure nature of hatred as the samaya of the vajra family of the Buddha Akṣhobhya. With prerequisites being complete — one possesses the specific power acquired through the depth of meditative realization or has received permission from the deity or the root Lama and has the motivation of great compassion and so forth — *wrathful concerned activity* liberates the consciousness of a great obstructor to the Dharma who could not be benefitted or tamed through peaceful means. One specific example of this wrathful activity is when a Vajra Master is preparing the ground and eliminating obstacles for the bestowing of an empowerment. If unseen beings are not willing to collaborate for the smooth performance of the ritual, the Vajra Master, after making peaceful offerings and requests to them, will warn them of the consequences of their disturbing behavior. In case they prefer to not listen to such warnings, the Vajra Master will either separate them from their protectors, sending them far away from each other, or directly liberate them, as described above. Such compassionate activities through wrathful means for the sake of sentient beings also appear in the sūtric teachings of the Great Vehicle, such as the *Sūtra of Skillful Means* (BDRC e-text UTIE00P16440489A_10951_bo pp. 605-607) where the Buddha tells the following story,

[605] Once five hundred merchants who desired profit were sailing in the midst of a

great ocean. With them on their journey at that time was a doer of bad deeds, a doer of evil deeds, proficient with archery and weaponry, who was secretly there to steal the others' wealth. [606] He was on that ship planning to attack and overcome those merchants. That criminal thought, 'Then, I will carry off all the wealth of these people and go back to Jambuling [India].' Also among those travelers at that time was a captain named Great Heart. While he was sleeping, the gods abiding in the midst of that great ocean told him what follows in a dream. "Among your fellow travelers on this ship is a man with such and such a name who is thinking, 'I will steal the wealth of all these others. I will kill all these merchants, carry off their wealth, and go back to Jambuling.' Because of those actions, this man will be excruciatingly struck. For his corruption, he will experience an unbearable retribution. Why so? These five hundred merchants are all abiding in enlightened awareness. They are irreversible bodhisattvas. If this man kills these irreversible bodhisattvas, [...] he will have to remain in the great hells for as long as it takes each and every one of these bodhisattvas to attain perfect enlightenment, consecutively. Captain, find some means by which he will not go to hell and all these people will not be killed." Then the captain awoke and pondered [607] for seven days. [...] He concluded, 'There is no means of preventing this man from slaying the merchants and going to the great hells but to kill him.' Then he thought, 'If I report this to the merchants, they will kill that man while thinking angry thoughts. Then they will all go to the great hells. [...] If I kill him, I will burn in the great hells myself. ... Nevertheless, I will kill him to achieve a good result for all the others involved.' Accordingly, Captain Great Heart, [...] kept those five hundred merchant bodhisattvas and that evil person from going to the great hells by deliberately stabbing that would-be robber to death with a spear.

The Buddha reveals that this is a story of one of his former lives and tells the good results for all concerned of this compassionate killing by Captain Great Heart,

'For me, that skill in means and great compassion blocked saṃsāra for one hundred thousand eons. The thief who died was reborn in the celestial realms. The five hundred merchants will now be the five hundred future Buddhas of this good eon. Son of good family, what do you think? Should blocking birth and death for one hundred-thousand eons through that skill in means and great compassionate wisdom [...] be regarded as an obstacle caused by my past deeds? [...] Do not view it in that way! View it as that [...] skill in means itself.'

In the definitive meaning of the tantric samaya of "killing," where beings' true Self, or Sugatagarbha, can never be destroyed, the samaya of "killing" means cutting off the dualistic mind by cutting off the flow of the saṃsāric winds moving in the side channels of the subtle body to become wisdom winds, to the central channel (Jamgön Kongtrül, *Buddhist Ethics*, p.253-254.) The definitive meaning of this samaya for individual meditative practice is related to the completion stage practices of the Six Vajra Yogas of *Kālachakra*, and it is not suitable to say more about them here.

Vajravega, a wrathful manifestation of Kālachakra

Glossary

ABHIDHARMA, *mngon chos:* One of the Three Baskets (*Tripiṭaka*) of the BUDDHA's teachings, emphasizing Buddhist psychology and philosophy. It contains a description of the universe, the different kinds of beings, the steps on the path to ENLIGHTENMENT, mistaken views, and so on in terms of truly existing phenomena or dharmas.

ABSOLUTE TRUTH, *don dam bden pa:* A.k.a. ultimate truth or definitive truth. One of the TWO TRUTHS, the other one being the RELATIVE TRUTH. It is defined differently by the different Buddhist Tenet Systems. 1) *Vaibhāṣhika:* uncompounded, indestructible phenomena, some of which are material and all of which are dualistic; 2) *Sautrāntika:* dualistic dharmas with their own intrinsic natures, known by perception, hence established by valid cognition without depending on imputed meanings; 3) *Chittamātra* (Mind Only): conceptually describable "absolute" mind and pure phenomena perfectly established by reasoning and the awareness of pristine WISDOM; according to higher MADHYAMAKA schools, the logic of these three has limitations; 4a) *Prāsaṅgika* Madhyamaka (RANGTONG, the GELUGPA view, for example): as no phenomena bear logical examination for absolute truth, there are, in that sense, no absolute phenomena. If there were, they would be conceptual; 4b) *Zhentong* Madhyamaka (JONANGPA view): the wisdom of the BUDDHAS, SUGATAGARBHA, absolute mind, and the phenomena perceived by it are what is truly existing and absolute — the statements about the pure relative are justified by realization of nondual or nonconceptual pure perception. As such statements do not bear analysis for absolute truth, the truth of realization is said to transcend concept and expression. In this sense, absolute truth refers to 1) BUDDHAHOOD; 2) the ultimate nature of reality known as "sublime EMPTINESS;" 3) the wisdom that directly realizes that emptiness; 4) phenomena perceived by that BUDDHA WISDOM; 5) our BUDDHA NATURE, fundamental true nature or potential for ENLIGHTENMENT, and so forth. Such statements are justifiable for Madhyamaka because they are useful in accomplishing the purposes of the world, the greatest of which is attaining enlightenment.

AFFLICTIVE OBSCURATIONS (or **EMOTIONS**): See KLEŚHAS.

AKṢHOBYA, *mi bskyod pa:* A BUDDHA who is the lord of one of the FIVE [tantric] BUDDHA FAMILIES. He is the chief of the VAJRA family.

AMITĀBHA, *'od dpag med:* A BUDDHA who is the lord of one of the FIVE [tantric] BUDDHA FAMILIES. He is the chief of the *padma* or LOTUS family.

AMOGHASIDDHI, *don yod grub pa:* A BUDDHA who is the lord of one of the FIVE [tantric] BUDDHA FAMILIES. He is the chief of the KARMA or action family.

AMRITA, *bdud rtsi:* Death-conquering food or drink of the gods, elixir of "immortality" that confers realization of the eternal NATURAL STATE. It can refer to any blissful substance, such as the seminal fluids in the context of the Path of Desire. Commonly translated as "nectar."

ANTIDOTE, *gnyen po,* pratipakṣha:[467] Remedy, means of suppressing or abandoning, especially the KLEŚHAS, employed in Buddhist SŪTRA tradition. For example, to abandon sexual desire, a practitioner might think of repulsive parts of the body, or how sexually desirable bodies will become rotting corpses. Antidotes for anger include thoughts of how anger can lead to rebirth in the lower realms.

ANUTTARA / ANUTTARAYOGA-TANTRA, *bla na med pa'i rgyud:* HIGHEST YOGA TANTRA. Tantric class that contains the Path of Desire. See also FOUR TANTRIC CLASSES.

ANUYOGA: Second of the three inner yogas and eighth of the nine vehicles (yānas), according to the classification of the NYINGMA school. It emphasizes MEDITATION on the CHANNELS, inner WINDS, and SUBTLE ESSENCES.

ARHAT, *dgra bcom pa:* One who has completely vanquished the enemy or KLEŚHAS, the highest level attained by the followers of the vehicle of INDIVIDUAL LIBERATION.

ATIŚHA, *a ti sha:* A.k.a. Dipaṃkara, a great Indian scholar who arrived in Tibet in 1042 and caused a major purification of the BUDDHISM present at that time, during which he founded the *Kadampa* school.

ATIYOGA: The highest of the three inner yogas and last of the nine vehicles (yānas), according to the NYINGMA school. It is also called DZOGCHEN.

ATTACHMENT, *zhen pa:* Inability to separate from a desired person, thing, or emotion, usually exaggerating the good qualities of the object. It

---

467 In the glossary, most terms in Sanskrit are not italicized to differentiate them from Tibetan ones.

eventually leads to SUFFERING.

AVALOKITEŚHVARA, *spyan ras gzigs:* Name of a BODHISATTVA, *Chenrezig* in Tibetan, representing the COMPASSION of all the BUDDHAS.

BARDO, *bar do:* 1) Most commonly, the intermediate state of existence between lives known as the "bardo of becoming;" 2) any period of transition included in the SIX BARDOS.

BHAGA: Womb or vagina, in Buddhist TANTRA symbolizing the primordial space that is the source of phenomena.

BODHICHITTA, *byang chub sems:* Absolute bodhichitta is the mind (*chitta*) of ENLIGHTENMENT (*bodhi*), the WISDOM that directly knows the nature of reality. Relative bodhicitta is the attitude dedicated to attaining BUDDHAHOOD in order to help all SENTIENT BEINGS. Relative Bodhichitta is either of *aspiration* only or of *application*. Application bodhichitta (*'jug pa'i byang chub kyi sems*) is the bodhichitta held by the BODHISATTVA PLEDGES, which includes entering into actual practice of the SIX PERFECTIONS, as opposed to aspiration bodhichitta (*smon pa'i byang chub kyi sems*). Other meanings of bodhichitta related to THIGLÉ are explained extensively in Part Four chapter 6.

BODHISATTVA, *byang chub sems dpa':* 1) A warrior of ENLIGHTENMENT, a being who strives for BUDDHAHOOD in order to be of utmost benefit to all SENTIENT BEINGS — here, the warrior nature is related to the attitude of never giving up in the face of difficulties, until full ENLIGHTENMENT is attained; 2) in general, someone who has taken and upholds the BODHISATTVA PLEDGES, or who acts in accordance with them with the LIBERATION of all beings as their highest priority; 3) more specifically, a being who has previously taken that pledge and has also already attained at least the indestructible, relative BODHICHITTA of the First Bodhisattva Level.

BODHISATTVA PATH / BODHISATTVA VEHICLE: A.k.a. GREAT VEHICLE, or MAHĀYĀNA. Unlike the INDIVIDUAL LIBERATION VEHICLE, Great Vehicle practitioners' primary motivation is to end the SUFFERING of all beings by bringing them to ENLIGHTENMENT. They accept the EMPTINESS of both a personal SELF and relative phenomena.

BODHISATTVA PLEDGE(S) / VOW(S), *byang chub sems dpa'i sdom pa:* DHARMA commitment to benefit oneself and others by ENLIGHTENMENT. The pledge involves a strong sense of responsibility to lead all SENTIENT BEINGS without exception to ENLIGHTENMENT or strive to attain it for the purpose of leading them to the same realization. There are eighteen root and forty-six secondary BODHISATTVA pledges that orient this highest altruistic commitment.

BÖN, *bon:* The native religion of Tibet, often considered shamanic in nature. It was first allegedly promulgated by Shenrab Miwo (*gshen rab mi bo*), Bön's founder in Zhang Zhung, an ancient name of the province of Gugey in western Tibet, west of lake Mānasarovar. He is considered a BUDDHA by Bön followers. Many elements of Tibetan Buddhist rituals are taken from Bön. Modern Bön has much in common with tantric BUDDHISM and the NYINGMA school in particular.

BUDDHA, *sangs rgyas:* Enlightened/Awakened/Omniscient One. One who has purified all OBSCURATIONS and developed all good qualities and the two kinds of omniscience: knowing directly the ultimate nature and extent of all phenomena. "The Buddha" usually refers to the historical being called ŚHĀKYAMUNI BUDDHA, yet there is an infinite number of Buddhas in the limitless THREE TIMES who have attained or will attain ENLIGHTENMENT.

BUDDHA-DHARMA, *sangs rgyas kyi chos:* 1) BUDDHA's teachings (the DHARMA of scripture); 2) the inner REALIZATIONS achieved by practicing the Buddha's teachings (the DHARMA of realization).

BUDDHAHOOD, *sangs rgyas [nyid]:* Complete ENLIGHTENMENT or omniscience, free from the extremes of both SAMSĀRA and the individual peace of NIRVĀṆA, also called non-abiding nirvāṇa; highest level of development of a being, having forever eliminated all OBSCURATIONS and karmic imprints and having developed all good qualities and WISDOM to their fullest extent.

BUDDHA NATURE, *[khams] de bzhin gshegs pa'i snying po:* Sugatagarbha or Tathāgatagarbha. The innate potential of all SENTIENT BEINGS to become a BUDDHA.

BUDDHISM, *sangs rgyas kyi chos:* Religion "established" by ŚHĀKYAMUNI BUDDHA. There is a great diversity of Buddhist traditions, they can be categorized as SŪTRA or TANTRA, or as part of one of the THREE VEHICLES.

BUDDHIST, *nang pa sangs rgyas pa:* A person who has taken REFUGE in the Three Jewels, and follows at least one of the THREE VEHICLES. In a broader sense, anyone who has the BUDDHA-DHARMA as the main reference for their spiritual path.

CHAKRASAMVARA, *bde mchog ['khor lo sdom pa]:* TANTRA of the HIGHEST YOGA TANTRA class, and its yidam showing the stages of the path and fruition of accomplishing the WISDOM of MAHĀSUKHA.

CENTRAL CHANNEL, *dbu ma*, avadhūti: Main energy channel in the SUBTLE BODY or its central axis. It starts at the forehead in the space between the eyebrows, going backward and up under the skull and then down to the level of the navel (and secret palace or lower). Its exact description varies according to the particular practice or school. See CHANNEL.

CHAKRA, *'khor lo:* Wheel, circle. A focal center where secondary (energy) CHANNELS branch out from the CENTRAL CHANNEL.

CHANNEL, *rtsa, nāḍi*: Energy channel in which subtle energy or inner WIND circulates. The "left" and "right" principal channels run from the nostrils to four fingers below the navel, where they join the CENTRAL CHANNEL.

COGNITIVE OBSCURATIONS, *she's grib:* A.k.a. OBSCURATION OF KNOW-ABLES. These include all dualistic concepts of subject, object, and action and other more subtle stains or ideas which prevent omniscience. For example, the thought that our own SUFFERING is separate from everyone else's suffering is a wrong dualistic idea that can be overcome by practicing the BODHISATTVA PATH. One of the TWO OBSCURATIONS with the obscuration of AFFLICTIVE EMOTIONS/KLEŚHAS, *nyon sgrib*. Both are overcome with the attainment of BUDDHAHOOD.

COMPASSION, *thugs rje*: The wish that others may be free from SUFFERING and its causes.

COMPLETION STAGE, *rdzogs rim:* Final stage in the practice of HIGHEST YOGA TANTRA using skillful methods to attain BUDDHAHOOD. In KĀLACHAKRA, this stage can be divided into six branches called the SIX VAJRA YOGAS.

CONSORT, *rig ma*, a.k.a MUDRĀ, *phyag rgya ma*. In a tantric context, a "partner" with whom one enters into union in order to experience the nature of reality. It can be a human being, a non-human being, or a visualized/generated consort. See also VIDYĀ CONSORT and detailed explanation in Part Four chapters 8 and 9.

CONTINUUM, *[sems] rgyud:* The stream of phenomena in an individual being's mind, including unconscious karmic propensities.

CYCLIC EXISTENCE, *'khor ba:* The cycle of death and rebirth, taking uncontrolled rebirths under the power of KARMA. This process arises out of IGNORANCE and is characterized by SUFFERING. It can be overcome by attaining NIRVĀṆA or full BUDDHAHOOD.

ḌĀKA, *dpa' bo:* Male equivalent of ḌĀKINĪ.

ḌĀKINĪ, *mkha' 'gro ma, dpa' mo:* Usually a non-human tantric female being, who protects tantric teachings and genuine practitioners; they can be worldly or highly realized beings. It can also refer to women in general who have achieved direct realization of EMPTINESS with the CLEAR LIGHT MIND or have strong propensities of doing so.

DEITY, *lha:* The symbolic form of a pure divine being, manifested from BUDDHA's WISDOM. Meditational BUDDHA form or WISDOM BEING. Sometimes this term refers to a wealth deity or DHARMA PROTECTOR.

DESIRE REALM, *'dod khams:* One of the THREE REALMS within CYCLIC EXISTENCE, where beings desire and enjoy the five external sense objects (form, sound, smell, touch, and taste) and where the resulting SUFFERING is experienced. It consists of the SIX REALMS (including the desire realm gods).

DHARMA, *chos:* Doctrine, law, truth. 1) What prevents SUFFERING, usually referring to BUDDHA-DHARMA; 2) any phenomena or objects of knowledge (in this book written without capital letters as "dharma"); 3) religion or religious knowledge (written as "Dharma"); 4) realization of the path and the consequent cessation of SUFFERING.

DHARMADHĀTU, *chos dbyings:* The all-pervading space or ground of awareness for all beings that is the source of all phenomena of SAMSĀRA and NIRVĀNA. The KĀYAS of ENLIGHTENMENT manifest from this reality as well as all conventional phenomena.

DHARMAKĀYA, *chos sku:* "Truth Body" of a BUDDHA, embodying the DHARMA of realization. The pure, omniscient MIND of a BUDDHA, resulting from the full transformation of the MIND. It is the enlightened aspect of DHARMADHĀTU and the source of all enlightened activity. Also refers to the OTHER-EMPTINESS aspect of BUDDHAHOOD. See also KĀYAS.

DHARMA MUDRĀ, *chos kyi phyag rgya:* Defined in Part Four chapter 8.

DHARMA PROTECTOR, *chos skyong:* Guardian of the BUDDHA's teachings, protecting their transmission from becoming diluted or distorted; they also protect genuine practitioners. 1) Worldly protectors: ordinary GODS, spirits, and so forth bound with oaths by a tantric VAJRA MASTER; 2) non-worldly wisdom protectors: manifestations of BUDDHAS or BODHISATTVAS in wrathful form.

DHARMARĀJAS, *chos rgyal:* Dharma Kings in general; in particular, the title of the first seven or eight Dharma Kings of Śhambhala before the first Śhambhala Kalkī.

DIVINE PRIDE, *lha'i nga rgyal:* Non-deluded pride that regards oneself as having the pure and indestructible BUDDHA NATURE. In the GENERATION STAGE in particular, divine pride is directly related to visualizing the YIDAM or DEITY and identifying oneself with it, rather than with one's saṃsāric form; this includes perceiving surroundings and enjoyments as those of the DEITY and its MAṆḌALA. It is a powerful method to purify ordinary conceptions.

DOLPOPA SHERAB GYALTSEN, *dol po pa shes rab rgyal mtshan:* (1292 – 1361), highly accomplished master and the most significant lineage holder of the JONANG Tradition of Tibetan BUDDHISM. He was responsible for establishing the union without contradiction of the ZHENTONG sūtric teachings and the KĀLACHAKRA TANTRA practice lineages.

DOWNFALL, *lhung ba:* A fault due to transgression of a VOW, pledge, or SAMAYA. The purification process varies greatly depending on each vehicle, level of practice, and so forth.

DROPS: See SUBTLE ESSENCE and THIGLÉ.

DZOGCHEN, *rdzogs chen:* Profound practice of the NYINGMA tradition, also known as the *Great Perfection.*

DZOKDEN: 1) Perfect Age, a period of peace and harmony at the beginning of time; 2) a Second Golden Age on Earth as prophesied in the KĀLACHAKRA TANTRA (see GOLDEN AGE); 3) Dzokden Practice Community, an international network of individuals, practice groups, training institutes, and retreat centers under the leadership of the author.

EMPOWERMENT, *dbang,* abhiṣheka: Bestowal of permission and a special potential power to practice a specific part of TANTRA given by a tantric master or VAJRA MASTER by means of a ritual, usually involving a pledge to uphold specific tantric SAMAYA or commitments. There are different levels of empowerment. It is also commonly translated as "Initiation." In essence, empowerment helps the students connect with their own BUDDHA NATURE.

EMPTINESS, *stong pa nyid:* There are many categories depending on the teaching and context. The most important for this book is the distinction between: 1) Self-Emptiness / RANGTONG in Tibetan — emptiness of relative phenomena of their own INHERENT EXISTENCE; and 2) Other-Emptiness / ZHENTONG in Tibetan — emptiness of anything else other than absolute SUGATAGARBHA (See ABSOLUTE TRUTH). Both refute all conceptualized and dualistic phenomena. Moreover, both say that full realization of emptiness is ENLIGHTENMENT. Their description of enlightened reality is less different than it might seem from their distinctions alone, but the sense of "emptiness" is different. For Zhentongpas, absolute truth or BUDDHAHOOD is not considered empty of itself.

EMPTINESS MUDRĀ, *stong pa nyid kyi phyag rgya:* A kind of tantric CONSORT defined in the Part Four chapter 8.

EMPTY-FORM, (or Body of Empty-Form), *strong gzugs [kyi sku]:* Specific to the KĀLACHAKRA practice, it refers to the direct perception of visionary forms, sounds, and so forth that are not perceived as conventional objects. They are regarded as aspects of BUDDHA NATURE. Starting during the experience of the FOUR HIGHER EMPOWERMENTS, or through the yogic practice of the SIX VAJRA YOGAS, there are different stages and levels of perception of empty-forms. In tantric contexts, "Body of Empty-Form" usually refers to a nonmaterial "body" which manifests through diligent practice and is developed into the "form body" (*rupakāya*) of a BUDDHA. See KĀYAS. Sometimes it is compared to the rainbow body of other tantric practices.

ENLIGHTENMENT, *byang chub:* see BUDDHAHOOD.

EON, *bskal pa:* "Great eon" means the lifetime of a single universe, from creation to destruction. "Small eon" means one twentieth of a great eon.

FEAST OFFERING, *tshogs kyi 'khor lo* (or *"tsok"*), gaṇachakra: A tantric feast in which one blesses, offers, and consumes food and drink as AMṚITA or wisdom nectar. As described in many tantras and as practiced in the original tantric tradition, some feast offerings included practices such as dances, songs of realization, and sexual union as part of the Path of Desire. The last does not occur in the Tibetan monastic tradition or among lay SAṄGHAS in the West, at least in public knowledge. See more details in footnote 460 and Appendix II.

FORMLESS REALM, *gzugs med khams:* Highest meditation realms of CYCLIC EXISTENCE. Beings there have renounced form and ATTACHMENT to form pleasures and exist only within their own mind stream. Their MIND is still bound by subtle desire and attachment to mental states and a personal SELF. So, when the good KARMA of these beings' meditative concentration is exhausted, they are reborn in lower realms of SAṂSĀRA.

FORM REALM, *gzugs khams:* State of CYCLIC EXISTENCE where no SUFFERING of suffering is experienced. Beings there have renounced the enjoyment of external sense objects but still have ATTACHMENT to the internal form of their own bodies and MIND.

FOUNDATIONAL VEHICLE: See INDIVIDUAL LIBERATION PATH / VEHICLE.

FRUITION, *'bras bu:* 1) Effect of a cause; 2) ENLIGHTENMENT as the result or goal of practicing the BUDDHIST path. According to the GREAT VEHICLE, the enlightenment of the ARHATS of the path of INDIVIDUAL LIBERATION is incomplete. Moreover, the stages leading to full ENLIGHT-

ENMENT as a vajra holder on the TANTRA path are a little different than those of BODHISATTVAS on the SŪTRA path.

GAṆACHAKRA*:* See FEAST OFFERING.

GELUG(PA), *dge lugs [pa]:* "Yellow-hats." School in the Tibetan tradition founded by TSONGKHAPA. Its main emphasis is on ethics and sound scholarship prior to serious MEDITATION, including detailed study and practice of the GENERATION STAGE. Its huge monastic SAṄGHA has been linked to political power in Tibet for many centuries. Philosophically they advocate Self-Emptiness of the second turn of the wheel of Dharma, rather than Other-Emptiness.

GENDÜN CHÖPEL: Born in Amdo (1903-1951), he was recognized as an incarnate Nyingma Lama and became a monk in his teens, excelling in scholarship. In the 30's he went to India and gave up his ordination vows. He was interested in India's attempts to gain its freedom from Britain, and its art and culture. He wrote many works on these topics and created paintings and poems, but most of all, what caught his intention was its erotic tradition. He studied both the relevant texts and the techniques they described. His *Treatise on Desire* was written in 1939 but not published until 1967. He is one of the most original thinkers in Tibetan history.

GENERATION STAGE, *bskyed rim:* In HIGHEST YOGA TANTRA, stage of practice wherein one mentally visualizes oneself as an enlightened DEITY and one's surroundings as the deity's MAṆḌALA. One meditates on forms, sounds, thoughts, and so forth as having the pure nature of the deity's form, mantra, and wisdom, respectively. See DIVINE PRIDE and PURE PERCEPTION.

GOD, deva, *lha:* In BUDDHISM, it refers to a long-lived, but mortal, being in CYCLIC EXISTENCE, temporarily abiding in a "heavenly state" as a result of virtuous KARMA.

GOLDEN AGE [OF ŚHAMBHALA], *sham bha lha'i rdzogs ldan dus:* A period of peace and harmony on Earth which, according to a literal understanding of the Outer KĀLACHAKRA, will last more than 1,000 years following the "defeat of the barbarians" by the twenty-fifth KALKĪ of ŚHAMBHALA Raudra, in which the the KĀLACHAKRA TANTRA teachings will flourish.

GREAT BLISS: See MAHĀSUKHA.

GREAT VEHICLE, *theg pa chen po*: See BODHISATTVA VEHICLE / PATH and THREE VEHICLES.

GURU, *bla ma:* In BUDDHISM, Guru is typically used only for high tantric teachers or VAJRA MASTERS. In Tibet, often referred to as Lama, or "my Lama." They act as very important SPIRITUAL FRIENDS or teachers. Indeed, not all Lamas are considered qualified to be a root or main Guru, students' principal tantric teacher or VAJRA MASTER who gives them the empowerments and experiential transmissions. A practitioner can have more than one root Guru, although it is more common to focus one's devotion on a specific qualified VAJRA MASTER as a root Guru who introduces the students to the tantric path and guides them along the path.

GURU YOGA, *bla ma'i rnal 'byor*: Practice of seeing one's GURU as a BUDDHA — or, more specifically, as the embodiment of all the BUDDHAS — and devotedly merging one's mind with the GURU's mind. This practice is considered the gateway to the TANTRA path. It is a preliminary to the GENERATION STAGE.

HEROES AND HEROINES, *dpa' bo dpa' mo:* It can refer to ḌĀKAS and ḌĀKINĪS respectively or to genuine or accomplished male and females tantrikas.

HIGHEST YOGA TANTRA, *bla na med pa'i rgyud:* A.k.a. Anuttarayoga-Tantra, Anuttara Tantra, or Anuttara. Highest tantric class that contains the Path of Desire. Buddhist TANTRAS such as *Kālachakra, Chakrasaṃvara,* or *Guhyasamāja* belong to this tantric class. See also FOUR TANTRIC CLASSES.

HĪNAYĀNA: "Lesser Vehicle." See INDIVIDUAL LIBERATION VEHICLE.

IGNORANCE: Two kinds of ignorance are fundamental to the BUDDHA-DHARMA: 1) *ma rig pa,* the obstruction of knowables is ignorance of the non-dual NATURAL STATE and leads beings to see phenomena as separate from an apparently independent existing self that perceives them; 2) *gti mug,* also translated as "stupidity" or "ignoring," is a KLEŚHA. With desire and aversion, it is one of the THREE POISONS. When phenomena do not engender either desire or aversion which motivate normal human activity, *gti mug* ignores them as irrelevant or without significance.

INDIVIDUAL LIBERATION [Path/Vehicle], *so so thar pa'i [lam/theg pa]:* A.k.a. Foundational Vehicle, Personal Liberation Path, Hīnayāna, or Śhrāvakayāna. BUDDHIST path leading to INDIVIDUAL LIBERATION from CYCLIC EXISTENCE, which forms the basis of all the BUDDHA's teachings. It accepts truly existing phenomena, but the EMPTINESS of an individual self. Accomplishing this path is enough to attain freedom from CYCLIC EXISTENCE but not to reach full ENLIGHTENMENT.

INHERENT EXISTENCE, *rang bzhin bden grub:* Existence that is true, objective, self-powered, self-sufficient, independent, intrinsic, and so forth,

a misconception projected onto relative phenomena. Such alleged existence would be independent of causes and conditions, parts, or the mind
imputing it which is self-contradictory for relative phenomena.

INNER WINDS, *nang gi rlung*: see WINDS.

JÑĀNA, *ye shes*: Primordial or pristine WISDOM that perceives the non-
dual, non-conceptual reality of ENLIGHTENMENT. Unlike PRAJÑĀ, it is
never worldly or conceptual. There are many divisions like the five or six
wisdoms (see footnote 91) of the FIVE or six tantric BUDDHA FAMILIES,
the wisdoms of the nature and extent of phenomena (*ji lta ba mkhyen
pa'i ye shes* and *ji snyed pa mkyen pa'i ye shes*), and the two wisdoms of
MEDITATION and post-meditation (*mnyam bzhag gi ye shes* and *rjes thob
kyi ye shes*).

JÑĀNASATTVA, *ye shes sems dpa'*: An actual WISDOM being, or DEITY,
who is invited to descend and unite with one's visualized deities called
"commitment-beings" (SAMAYASATTVA).

JONANG(PA), *jo nang [pa]*: Tradition or school of Tibetan BUDDHISM
which combines the study of the ZHENTONG MADHYAMAKA view with
the practice of the SIX VAJRA YOGAS of the KĀLACHAKRA COMPLETION
STAGE. Its main lineages masters are DOLPOPA SHERAB GYALTSEN and
Jetsün TĀRANĀTHA. Due to centuries-long political persecution and other
reasons, it remained a small school in comparison with the other schools
of Tibetan Buddhism.

JU MIPHAM: Important Tibetan master born in Derge (1846-1912) in eastern Tibet. At fifteen he undertook eighteen months of intensive retreat on
Mañjuśhrī. He later said that from then on he had always been able to understand any text. He also received and mastered innumerable teachings

and transmissions from masters of the non-sectarian (*Rimé*) movement Jamyang Khyentsé Wangpo and Jamgön Kongtrül, and other masters of all traditions throughout Tibet.

KAGYÜ, *bka' brgyud*: School of Tibetan BUDDHISM, founded by Marpa Chökyi Lodrö and Khyungpo Nyaljor (11th century). Called the "Practice Lineage," its special COMPLETION STAGE practice is MAHĀMUDRĀ.

KĀLACHAKRA, *dus kyi 'khor lo:* Literally, "Wheel of Time." Name of the principal DEITY of a TANTRA of the same name in the HIGHEST YOGA TANTRA class. It forms the basis of the main practice of the JONANG tradition, the KĀLACHAKRA SIX VAJRA YOGAS. This tantra was taught by the BUDDHA and upheld in the BODHISATTVA PURE REALM of ŚHAMBHALA before appearing in India and Tibet around the 10th century.

KALKĪ, *rigs ldan:* "Possessor of the [Vajra] Caste," a special title for some of the DHARMARĀJAS or Dharma Kings and Queens of ŚHAMBHALA. According to the KĀLACHAKRA, the brahmin ṛiṣhis of Śhambhala were empowered as members of a single, unbiased vajra caste by Dharma King Mañjuśhrī Yaśhas, who became the first of the line of Kalkī kings. All subsequent Dharma Kings and Queens are considered Kalkīs. The Kalkī Kings are prophesied in the Kālachakra and the Kalkī Queens in visions and transmissions received by the author.

KARMA, *las:* Action, impulse. Also, the imprint which the action leaves on one's mind-stream and the consequences thereof. "The law of karma:" the teaching that all experiences are results of propensities imprinted on our mind-streams of previous actions. Virtuous actions lead to happiness, negative actions to SUFFERING and unpleasant states, in this and subsequent lives.

KARMA MUDRĀ, *las kyi phyag rgya:* A human or a non-human real being acting as a CONSORT, who assists in generating great bliss so that the practitioner can dissolve the karmic inner WINDS and realize absolute WISDOM. See also CONSORT, VIDYĀ CONSORT, and Part Four chapters 8 and 9.

KĀYA, *sku:* Body (honorific). KĀYAS are different spheres of manifestation of a BUDDHA. The most common classification includes three kāyas, NIRMĀṆAKĀYA, SAMBHOGAKĀYA, and DHARMAKĀYA. The first two are classified under Rūpakāya, *gzugs sku,* the form body of a BUDDHA. Nirmāṇakāya can be perceived by all sentient beings and Sambhogakāya by tenth level BODHISATTVAS. The last, DHARMAKĀYA, is perceived only by the Buddhas. A further classification speaks of four kāyas adding "Svabhavikakāya," the "nature body" representing the inseparability of the other three kāyas.

KLEŚHAS, *nyon mongs:* Mental afflictions, afflictive or obscuring emotions. Defiled mental functions, which cause SUFFERING. When not tamed, they disturb our mental peace and propel us to act harmfully to others and ourselves. When brought to the path, they are put to work as part of the skillful means of TANTRA. The main afflictions are listed as being three, five, or six. These AFFLICTIVE OBSCURATIONS are distinct from the more subtle COGNITIVE OBSCURATIONS. All obscurations are abandoned when ENLIGHTENMENT is attained. See THREE POISONS, FIVE POISONS, and SIX ROOT KLEŚHAS.

LAMA, *bla ma:* 1) Literally means someone who is "heavy" with good qualities; 2) in Tibet, it mainly refers to one's GURU or root Guru, for example, "my Lama"; 3) it can also mean a monastic or lay practitioner who has spiritual realization beyond that of ordinary monastics and scholars (like a *Geshe*) and can guide students on the TANTRA path. Usually, the term is used for male masters, female masters are given other names to represent this status such as *Khandrola* or *Jetsunma*, but there are exceptions; 4) commonly refers also to the main leader ("the Lama") of a spiritual community even if there are other Lamas in the same community; 5) in some lineages, all practitioners are called Lamas after they have completed certain long-term practice commitments such as a three-year retreat. In the JONANG tradition, this is not accepted since all monks usually participate in a three-year retreat at least once in their lifetime.

LESSER VEHICLE: See INDIVIDUAL LIBERATION VEHICLE / PATH.

LIBERATION: See NIRVĀṆA and ENLIGHTENMENT for the different meanings according to INDIVIDUAL LIBERATION VEHICLE and GREAT VEHICLE respectively.

LIṄGA, *liṅga:* A.k.a. VAJRA. The penis in tantric contexts.

LOTUS, *padma:* Specifically in the Path of Desire, a reference to the vagina and labia.

MADHYAMAKA, *dbu ma:* Middle-way school. According to SŪTRA, profound philosophical view of EMPTINESS, either Self-emptiness (RANG-TONG) or Other-emptiness (ZHENTONG), depending on the school.

MAHĀMUDRĀ, *phyag rgya chen po:* Great seal, the great consort of EMP-TY-FORM. The FRUITION of tantric practice according to the new translation schools.

MAHĀSIDDHA, *grub thob chen po:* Great SIDDHA.

MAHĀSUKHA, *bde ba chen po:* The great bliss of the FRUITION of the TANTRA PATH.

MAHĀYĀNA, *theg pa chen po:* Great (mahā) Vehicle (yāna). See BODHISATTVA VEHICLE.

MAṆḌALA, *dkyil 'khor:* Literally, center and surroundings. The center is the essence, while that which surrounds is the representation of that meaning among phenomena: 1) in the sense of enlightened maṇḍala, it is a symbolic representation of an enlightened reality through a meditation visualization, usually in the form of a palace with one or more DEITIES present. The different circles of ornament or areas of the "palace" represent different degrees of the truth of reality, and the DEITIES represent the pure awareness of these realities. It is a model to understand the different ways BUDDHA NATURE manifests. When practitioners receive an EMPOWERMENT, the VAJRA MASTER introduces them to the specific enlightened maṇḍala of that empowerment. It helps them develop a great awareness of the various enlightened aspects of the maṇḍala; 2) in other contexts, as in the Maṇḍala Offering practice, a universal maṇḍala means a symbolic representation of the entire wordly universe or of how the universe is perceived by SENTIENT BEINGS; 3) sometimes it means realms or spheres, as in "the maṇḍalas of body, speech, and mind;" 4) in Guru Maṇḍala, it means the teaching environment created by the GURU.

MANTRA, *sngags:* 1) Prescribed syllables in Sanskrit to protect the mind or accomplish particular actions. They are associated with specific energies. Recitation of mantras is typically done with specific visualizations; it is fundamental for the GENERATION STAGE practice; 2) "Secret Mantra" is used as a synonym for VAJRAYĀNA, TANTRA, or TANTRAYĀNA. See subchapter 2.2 for deeper meanings.

MĀRA, *bdud:* 1) Anything which interrupts the attainment of LIBERATION such as a harmful influence that creates obstacles for practice and ENLIGHTENMENT; 2) mythologically, a powerful god who dwells in the highest abode in the DESIRE REALM and his minions; a master of illusion who attempted to prevent the BUDDHA from attaining enlightenment at Bodhgaya; 3) māra symbolizes ego-clinging and the EIGHT WORLDLY CONCERNS.

MEDITATION, *sgom:* Literally, "habituating" or "familiarizing." Habituating ourselves to virtuous states of mind, especially the unveiling of the enlightened mind. It can be divided into ŚHAMATHA (calm abiding meditation that prepares the mind to experience deeper levels of reality) and VIPAŚHYANA (clear seeing, or insight meditation, employing analysis or direct perception of emptiness as an antidote to IGNORANCE for attaining LIBERATION).

MERIT, *bsod nams:* Gathering of pure virtuous actions, or positive potential. Imprints of positive actions in the mind stream, leading to happiness or good conditions in future rebirths, making the mind more open to wisdom, and eventually leading to ENLIGHTENMENT. The accumulations of MERIT and WISDOM are the two accumulations of the path to ENLIGHTENMENT.

MESSENGER LADY, *pho nya ma*: A poetic name for a tantric CONSORT or MUDRĀ who transmits the message of realization through bliss.

MIND, *sems*: The mind is an eternal continuity of experience of non-physical character. It operates at different levels of subtlety: gross and subtle — both being relative and conceptual — and very subtle. Being a non-physical phenomenon, it has gross aspects that are closely linked to the brain but subtle and very subtle aspects that are not. It can be divided into primary minds — what we use to describe *what* is appearing to the mind — and secondary minds which are used to describe *how* we relate to those appearances. There are eight forms of primary minds: five types of sensory consciousness (related to the five senses) and three types of mental consciousness — gross mental consciousness, deluded consciousness, and the foundational consciousness where karmic imprints are stored. The relative mind can be described as an awareness with thoughts of the variety of phenomena regarded as mental objects that views them as real and gathers karmic seeds of such perception in the foundational consciousness. The very subtle mind whose nature for JONANAGPAS is BUDDHA NATURE goes beyond the foundational consciousness and is related to the pristine awareness of enlightened reality.

MUDRĀ: 1) Seal; 2) Tantric consort; 3) Tantric gesture (usually with hands). Regarding the second meaning, see also CONSORT, VIDYĀ CONSORT, and detailed explanation in Four Part chapters 8 and 9.

NĀLANDĀ UNIVERSITY, *na len dra:* Important BUDDHIST University in Magadha, present-day Bihar, India, destroyed by Muslim invaders in the twelfth century. It was among the world's first universities.

NATURAL STATE, *gnas lugs:* The way things really are. Natural state of phenomena before delusive conceptual distortions were imposed on it.

NIRMĀṆAKĀYA, *sprul sku:* "Emanation Body" of a BUDDHA that can be experienced by ordinary beings. An emanation of the SAMBHOGAKĀYA in ordinary physical form. Nirmāṇakāyas are phenomenal manifestations to aid beings, like a big fish in a famine or lights for someone lost in a dark forest. The Nirmāṇakāya is seen as it is by those with enough MERIT, others see merely an ordinary being. SHĀKYAMUNI BUDDHA is an example of a supreme Nirmāṇakāya. Tibetan Rinpochés are said to be born Nirmāṇakāyas. See also KĀYAS.

NIRVĀṆA: State beyond SUFFERING. State outside CYCLIC EXISTENCE attained by practicing the INDIVIDUAL LIBERATION PATH. This is distinct from full BUDDHAHOOD or "non-abiding nirvāṇa," which is a much more profound experience of full ENLIGHTENMENT.

NYINGMA, *rnying ma:* Oldest Tibetan Buddhist tradition, established by PADMASAṂBHAVA. Nowadays, the main emphasis is on DZOGCHEN practice.

OBSCURATIONS, *sgrib:* Misconceptions and their resultant afflicted states of mind, including both AFFLICTIVE OBSCURATIONS (or obscurations to NIRVĀṆA) and more subtle COGNITIVE OBSCURATIONS (also known as obscurations to BUDDHAHOOD).

PADMASAṂBHAVA, *padma 'byung gnas,* a.k.a. "Guru Rinpoché:" Great Indian VAJRA MASTER, who came to Tibet in 817AD and spread tantric teachings. With his powerful SIDDHIS he dispelled evil forces which obstructed BUDDHISM in Tibet and made inimical local deities into DHARMA protectors. He is said to have been born on a lotus flower in Uḍḍiyana *(o rgyan),* a country northwest of ancient India, now Pakistan.

PRAJÑĀ, *shes rab:* Superior knowledge, discriminating awareness of reality, including 1) ordinary practical knowledge, logical reasoning, and scientific understanding; and 2) direct non-conceptual perception of EMPTINESS as the way things are in enlightened realization by the perfection of prajñā. One of the SIX PERFECTIONS. See WISDOM.

PRAJÑĀPĀRAMITĀ, *shes rab kyi pha rol tu phyin pa:* Perfection of PRAJÑĀ. Also, the name of a female DEITY.

PRĀTIMOKṢA, *so so thar pa:* Goal of the Lesser Vehicle, with precepts and VOWS established by the BUDDHA for nuns, monks, and lay practitioners. See INDIVIDUAL LIBERATION.

PŪJĀ, *mchod pa:* Ceremony of worship, with extensive physical or mental offerings to the GURUS, DEITIES, BUDDHAS, BODHISATTVAS, and so forth.

PURE REALM, *dag pa'i zhing:* A BUDDHA pure realm is a realm outside CYCLIC EXISTENCE where BUDDHAS, BODHISATTVAS, and practitioners with sufficient MERIT and indestructible FAITH abide. Conditions are conducive for practicing BUDDHA-DHARMA and attaining ENLIGHTENMENT. "Pure-Land Buddhism" is a MAHĀYĀNA tradition emphasizing methods to be reborn in realms like Sukhāvati, the pure realm of Amitābha. ŚHAMBHALA is a bodhisattva pure realm where tantric practitioners pray to be reborn if they do not achieve LIBERATION in this lifetime or in the BARDOS. There, all the conditions for rapidly progressing towards enlightenment in a single lifetime through the KĀLACHAKRA teachings are at hand. A bodhisattva realm is still part of cyclic existence and this allows SENTIENT BEINGS to be reborn there more easily than in a Buddha realm.

PURE PERCEPTION, *dag snang:* Sacred outlook fundamental to all aspects of TANTRA, including attitude toward the GURU and one's own companions in the tantric path (VAJRA BROTHERS AND SISTERS), visualization of DEITIES, and so forth. On the highest level, the practitioner learns to perceive the entire world and its contents as a pure enlightened realm, displaying the KĀYAS and FIVE WISDOMS. First, sufficient stabilization in pure perception is attained through devotional practice towards the GURU, then, after receiving EMPOWERMENT, one practices by visualizing oneself and all other beings as enlightened deities, the outer world as its enlightened MAṆḌALA, all sounds as its MANTRA, all thoughts as the deity's enlightened mind and so forth.

RANGTONG, *rang stong:* Self-emptiness or intrinsic EMPTINESS.

RED AND WHITE ESSENCES, *khams dmar po dang, khams dkar po*: 1) The male and female contributions to existence, in general, such as in the occasion of generating an embryo, referred to in a generalized form as se-men and (menstrual) blood; 2) male and female subtle essences or drops present in the CHANNELS of the SUBTLE BODY, especially the left and right channels beside the CENTRAL CHANNEL. The left carries primar-ily the white masculine energy and the right the red feminine energy. In some teachings, the left and right positions of these two channels are said to be reversed in women. Mastery of these essences is part of advanced practices of the COMPLETION STAGE. See THIGLÉ.

REFUGE, *skyabs:* Taking refuge means entrusting one's spiritual develop-ment and protection from CYCLIC EXISTENCE to the Three Jewels. In a fundamental sense, this means the BUDDHA as the teacher, the DHARMA as the teachings, and the SAṄGHA as the community that practices and embodies the qualities of the teachings. In TANTRA in particular, taking refuge in the GURU is the root of the path; in addition, one takes refuge in the enlightened DEITIES, BODHISATTVAS, ḌĀKINĪS, ḌAKAS, and DHAR-MA PROTECTORS. On the absolute level, taking refuge means unveiling one's own BUDDHA NATURE and achieving full BUDDHAHOOD as the na-ture of things. The traditional objects of refuge are sacred representations of various aspects of one's own BUDDHA NATURE.

RELATIVE TRUTH, *kun rdzob:* Conventional or delusive truth (as opposed to ABSOLUTE TRUTH) as it appears to the six senses of SENTIENT BEINGS, involving a duality of *self* and *other* and the causal interdependence of phenomena.

356 TANTRIC PATH OF DESIRE

RENUNCIATION, *nges 'byung:* Determination to be free or emerge out of the SUFFERING of CYCLIC EXISTENCE, no longer having ATTACHMENT or craving to the pleasures of CYCLIC EXISTENCE which lead to suffering and AFFLICTIONS. Originally, the BUDDHA's teachings focused on the monastic path of renunciation. In other teachings of the GREAT VEHICLE and TANTRA, he taught how full ENLIGHTENMENT could be attained by lay practitioners, implying deeper levels of renunciation, as the author discusses in this book.

RINPOCHÉ, *rin po che:* Jewel, Precious One, referring often to an important reincarnated LAMA, or sometimes just a title of respect towards the spiritual teacher.

ROOT GURU: See GURU.

SĀDHANA, *sgrub thabs:* Tantric method to actualize oneself as the BUDDHA figure for which one has received EMPOWERMENT; also a tantric ritual text which sets out a particular MEDITATION practice, as a solid guideline or proper frame for practice. The formal sādhana practice supports the tantrika to stabilize and increase the experience of one's own true nature perceived during EMPOWERMENT. When the different aspects and meanings of the sādhana are integrated into the practitioner's continuum, one is able to apply similar principles in different life experiences beyond formal practice as in the case of the Path of Desire.

SAKYA, *sa skya:* School of Tibetan BUDDHISM, founded by Khon Könchok Gyelpo (11th century). Their main practice is *Lamdré*. Sakyas ruled in Tibet for over 100 years before the secular power was handed to the Dalai Lamas of the GELUG tradition.

SAMĀDHI, *ting nge 'dzin:* Generally speaking, meditative stabilization or concentration. One-pointed involvement in MEDITATION where the meditation object and the practitioner are experienced as inseparable and indistinguishable. As there are many types of samādhi, the term does not imply high REALIZATION or accomplishment on the part of the practitioner. Also the name of the sixth of the SIX VAJRA YOGAS of KĀLACHAKRA.

SAMAYA, *dam tshig:* In TANTRA, sacred link or bond, or commitment between GURU and student, and also between students (VAJRA BROTHERS AND SISTERS), emphasizing PURE PERCEPTION. It is often referred to as the "secret samayas" or "secret tantric commitments" that one establishes with the Guru during EMPOWERMENT. They must be kept as pure as possible to benefit oneself and others. The author lists the samayas of KĀLACHĀKRA in *Unveiling Your Sacred Truth — Book 3* (Often translated as "tantric vows.")

SAMAYA FEAST, SAMAYA GATHERING: See FEAST OFFERING.

SAMAYA MUDRĀ, *dam tshig gi phyag rgya:* Explained in Part Four chapter 8.

SAMBHOGAKĀYA, *longs spyod rdzogs pa'i sku:* "Enjoyment Body,", or bliss body, of a BUDDHA, which only BODHISATTVAS who have achieved the Tenth Bodhisattva Level can perceive, and from which NIRMĀNAKĀYA forms emanate for the benefit of other sentient beings. The tangible form of a Buddha's WISDOM, the result of the transformation of speech. The Buddha taught the *Kālachākra Tantra* in the Sambhogakāya form of the KĀLACHĀKRA DEITY. See also KĀYAS.

SAMSĀRA, *'khor ba:* See **CYCLIC EXISTENCE.**

SAṄGHA, *dge 'dun*: Spiritual community. One of the Three Jewels of BUD-DHISM along with BUDDHA and DHARMA. There is no full attainment of BUDDHAHOOD without the support of a Saṅgha and each individual joins the level of Saṅgha suited to her or his current stage of spiritual development: 1) in the broadest sense, the whole community of BUDDHISTS, including nuns, monks, and lay people up to high level BODHISATTVAS; 2) ordained Saṅgha: nuns and monks (at least four monks are needed for a gathering to be considered Saṅgha); 3) Ārya Saṅgha, realized beings who have experienced EMPTINESS and stabilized that realization, such as ARHATS or BODHISATTVAS who have attained at least the First Bodhisattva Level; 4) in a modern context, a Saṅgha often means a group of practitioners connected to a specific teacher, a specific lineage, or a specific Buddhist Center; they gather for practice, to volunteer in organizational activities, and so forth.

SĀṄKHYA, *grangs can*: School of Indian philosophy. It is said that in the *Kālachakra Tantra,* the BUDDHA borrowed terms from Sāṅkhya in his teachings so that they would be more accessible to his Vedic audience in Śhambhala. Sāṅkhya views reality as composed of two independent principles, *puruṣha* (witness-consciousness) and *prakṛiti* (matter or nature), but including many aspects of mind. Unmanifest prakṛiti is an inactive, unconscious balance of three *guṇas* (qualities), *sattva* (light or spiritual power), *rajas* (energy), and *tamas* (darkness or inertia). When prakṛiti comes into contact with puruṣha, prakṛiti evolves into twenty-three *tattvas*, aspects of being: intellect (*buddhi, mahat*), ego (*ahamkara*), mind (*manas*), the five sensory capacities, the five action capacities, and the five subtle elements (*tanmatras*) from which the five "gross elements" (earth and so forth) develop. In a living being, *jiva*, puruṣha, is bonded to prakṛiti.

SECRET MANTRA, *gsang sngags:* The most common Tibetan term for TANTRA, TANTRAYĀNA, or VAJRAYĀNA. See TANTRAYĀNA and footnote 1.

SELF, *bdag:* The delusive self or ego of saṃsāra. Like all dualistic phenomena of CYCLIC EXISTENCE, it does not truly exist. ZHENTONG adherents like DOLPOPA state that while the saṃsāric self lacks true existence, the "true Self," SUGATAGARBHA or BUDDHAHOOD truly exists.

SELF-GENERATION, *bdag bskyed:* Practice in TANTRA whereby one visualizes and generates oneself as an enlightened DEITY.

SENTIENT BEING, *sems can, 'gro ba:* (Trans)-migrator. Beings that possess a MIND that is contaminated by AFFLICTIONS or their karmic imprints, living lost within CYCLIC EXISTENCE without any control over their future rebirths.

ŚHĀKYAMUNI BUDDHA, *sangs rgyas shā kya thub pa:* Name of the historical BUDDHA, living in India in the 6th century BC.

ŚHAMBHALA, *sham bha la:* Subtle pure human realm which contains the fullness of the KĀLACHAKRA teachings. King SUCHANDRA of ŚHAMBHALA requested ŚHĀKYAMUNI BUDDHA to teach this TANTRA; since then, the KĀLACHAKRA teachings have transformed this realm into a subtle place of perfect peace and happiness. See PURE REALM.

SHÉPÉ DORJÉ or **LELUNG SHÉPÉ DORJÉ**, *sle lung bzhad pa'i rdo rje* (1697-1740): Important master of both the GELUG and NYINGMA schools, well-known for living a tantric lifestyle. He is most famous for his writings on the origin of various DHARMA PROTECTORS, entitled *Life Stories of an Ocean of Oath-Bound Protectors of the Teachings.* He was among the earliest masters to reveal practices related to *Gesar of Ling.*

SIDDHA, *grub thob:* Accomplished or realized person who has attained significant SIDDHIS.

SIDDHI: In general, a common term for significant spiritual realizations. Ordinary or common siddhis are relative siddhis or miraculous powers that usually cannot be explained by logical understanding. While there are traditional lists of ordinary siddhis, their actual number is far from being limited to these lists. These accomplishments can be attained by practicing different traditions. Extraordinary or uncommon siddhi means the attainment of ENLIGHTENMENT through practicing the BUDDHA-DHARMA.

SPIRITUAL FRIEND, *dge ba'i bzhes gnyen*: A GREAT VEHICLE term for a BUDDHIST teacher linked to students by friendship and common values. The requirements for being a true spiritual friend include having more good qualities than the student and honestly caring about others among many more. However, there are fewer requirements to be an authentic spiritual friend than to be an authentic tantric GURU or VAJRA MASTER.

STHAVIRA, *gnas brtan:* 1) Elder or venerable monastic; 2) *gnas brtan pa*: Sthavira school, one of the basic four schools of the followers of the INDIVIDUAL LIBERATION vehicle. It was divided into a number of branches, only one of which, called THERAVĀDA, is still extant.

SUBTLE BODY: *phra ba'i lus*: The apparatus of CHANNELS, WINDS, and SUBTLE ESSENCES or DROPS (*rtsa, rlung, thig le*) employed in the yoga practice of the COMPLETION STAGE, as presented in chapter 2 of the *Kālachakra Tantra*, the "Inner Chapter." This includes various self-existing seed syllables and MAṆḌALAS of DEITIES. It is said that all aspects of the external world such as the five elements and the cyclical motions of the planets and stars have their inner equivalents such as the subtle elemental principals and the cyclical motions of the inner winds through different chakras that govern different stages of life and the coming of death at its end. Moreover, the mental body of the BARDO is also sometimes called a subtle body.

SUBTLE ESSENCE, bindu, *thig le:* See RED AND WHITE ESSENCES and THIGLÉ.

SUFFERING, *sdug bsngal:* Any unsatisfactory condition, referring to physical and mental pain. All problematic situations and unsatisfactoriness that is part of the changing and conditioned nature of CYCLIC EXISTENCE. Suffering is overcome by attaining NIRVĀṆA and FULL ENLIGHTENMENT.

SUGATAGARBHA, *bde gshegs snying po:* In the third turning of the wheel of DHARMA and in TANTRA, it means the absolute and truly existing nature of mind and phenomena, with its innumerable BUDDHA qualities that are also truly existing. Sugatagarbha is often used to refer to BUDDHA NATURE. Realizing it fully means complete ENLIGHTENMENT.

SŪTRA, *mdo:* Discourse, speech, etc. of the BUDDHA registered in written form by his followers.

SŪTRAYĀNA, *mdo'i theg pa:* SŪTRA vehicle, also "exoteric or common path." It refers both to the INDIVIDUAL LIBERATION and GREAT VEHICLES combined, thus excluding and opposed to TANTRAYĀNA (the "esoteric or uncommon path").

TANTRA, *rgyud:* Literally, "continuity" or "stream." Continuity or weaving together is maintained throughout the practice that does not use ANTIDOTES to eliminate any mental phenomena: 1) it refers to the systems of MEDITATION described in the tantric texts with esoteric teachings that are not found in SŪTRAYĀNA and require EMPOWERMENT by a tantric GURU or VAJRA MASTER; 2) more specifically, a tantric scripture.

TANTRA PATH / TANTRA VEHICLE : See TANTRAYĀNA.

TANTRAYĀNA, *rgyud kyi theg pa:* A.k.a. TANTRA, SECRET MANTRA, and VAJRAYĀNA. The tantric vehicle or path. Tantric practitioners have the same goal as the practitioners of the BODHISATTVA VEHICLE of attaining full ENLIGHTENMENT for the sake of all SENTIENT BEINGS. The tantric path offers skillful means for achieving this goal much more swiftly. See also TANTRA.

TANTRIC VOWS, *dam tshig sdom pa:* See SAMAYA.

TANTRIKA, *sngags pa, gsang sngags 'dzin pa:* Tantra practitioner.

TĀRANĀTHA: Highly accomplished yogī, master, and scholar of the JONA-NG tradition (1575-1635). One of the most important references in Tibetan BUDDHISM, his writings are considered incomparable by lineage masters of various schools. He wrote about the history of Buddhism in India based on the memory of his past life as the Indian MAHĀSIDDHA Kṛishṇāchārya (Kānhapa). As a result of his *Rimé* (non-sectarian) approach, he was able to uphold multiple lineages of different schools of Tibetan Buddhism.

THANGKA, *thang ka:* Tibetan-style painting on cloth that can be rolled up like a scroll. Traditional Tibetan temples display various thangkas of tantric deities on their walls.

THERAVĀDA: Literally "the tradition of the Elders." Buddhist school from the INDIVIDUAL LIBERATION VEHICLE that is widespread in Southeast Asia and Shrī Laṅka. See STHAVIRA.

THIGLÉ, *thig le:* It usually refers to SUBTLE ESSENCES or drops with various degrees and classifications depending on the context. See detailed explanation in Part Four chapter 6.

TILOPA, NĀROPĀ, MARPA, AND MILAREPA, *ti lo, mar pa, mi la:* Early highly accomplished figures in the succession that was to become the KAGYÜ school. Each has a well-known biography.

TORMA, *gtor ma:* Offering cake used in tantric rituals.

TRANSMISSION, *ngo sprod:* In a higher sense, pointing out by whatever means the experiential meaning of a certain teaching; for example, the GURU pointing out the NATURAL STATE to the student during the fourth higher empowerment of HIGHEST YOGA TANTRA. In English, the term often refers merely to an *oral transmission* of DHARMA texts (in this case, not necessarily done by the Guru). Transmissions are considered authentic if the teacher has previously received the same transmission from an unbroken lineage or through direct revelation.

TRULKHOR, *yantra yoga, 'khrul 'khor:* Special yogic exercises of TANTRA to support swift spiritual achievements. They are found in the COMPLETION STAGE practices, but some teachers teach some of these practices as part of general yoga practice outside the context of the completion stage.

TSOK, *tshogs [kyi 'khor lo]:* See FEAST OFFERING.

TSONGKHAPA, *rje tsong kha pa:* Great Tibetan scholar and master (1357-1419), founder of the Tibetan GELUG school.

TUMMO, *gtum mo:* Special inner heat generated in tantric yoga practice of the CHANNELS, WINDS, and SUBTLE ESSENCES. For JONANGPAS, this practice is one of the aspects of the SIX VAJRA YOGAS OF KĀLACHAKRA.

ULTIMATE, *mthar thug:* The final state, viewpoint, or realization attained by the BUDDHIST path, the understanding of which varies with different schools. ZHENTONGPAS say that the ultimate viewpoint perceives the phenomena of ABSOLUTE TRUTH. PRĀSAṄGIKAS who do not accept phenomena of absolute truth might say that the ultimate viewpoint perceives enlightened reality beyond distinctions of appearance and EMPTINESS and so forth.

ULTIMATE TRUTH: see ABSOLUTE TRUTH.

VALID COGNITION, *tshad ma,* pramāṇa: A.k.a. "valid reasoning." Means of experiencing or establishing knowledge as true and certain, said to be, 1) mngon sum tshad ma, direct perception based on the six consciousnesses or yogic insight; 2) rjes dpag gi tshad ma, logical reasoning or inference; and 3) lung tshad ma, scriptural authority or other reliable testimony.

VALID REASONING, *tshad ma,* pramāṇa: See VALID COGNITION.

VICTORIOUS ONE: *rgyal ba:* A BUDDHA who has accomplished the goal of the path by overcoming or being victorious over defilement by the KLEŚHAS and the TWO OBSCURATIONS.

VAJRA, *rdo rje:* Indestructible, diamond, adamantine. In particular, a ritual scepter *(dorjé)* symbolizing the BUDDHA's mind, the FIVE WISDOMS, great bliss, and the masculine quality of ENLIGHTENMENT. Together with the bell, it symbolizes the union of method and wisdom, immutable bliss and empty-form, and masculine and feminine. In particular tantric contexts, it means also the liṅga or penis.

VAJRA BROTHERS AND SISTERS: A.k.a. "vajra siblings," those who took EMPOWERMENT from the same VAJRA MASTER or GURU, regardless of whether it was taken at the same time or not or whether it was the same empowerment or not. There are many levels, and the importance of the relationship increases depending on the type of empowerment.

VAJRA FEAST: See FEAST OFFERING.

VAJRA MASTER: A.k.a. "tantric master." The highest level of a spiritual teacher or master, qualified to guide followers on the complete tantric path to full enlightenment. See GURU.

VAJRASATTVA, *rdo rje sems dpa':* A BUDDHA represented as a white tantric DEITY with various ornaments, usually related to purification practices such as the recitation of the hundred-syllable MANTRA with visualizations. The KĀLACHAKRA is unique in presenting the Vajrasattva Buddha family as the sixth Buddha family that represents the inseparable nature of all FIVE BUDDHA FAMILIES; in this context, Vajrasattva is blue in color and is connected to the sexual CHAKRA.

VAJRAYĀNA, *rdo rje theg pa:* Indestructible (vajra) vehicle (yāna). Synonym for TANTRA, TANTRAYĀNA, and SECRET MANTRA. See TANTRA.

VIDYĀ CONSORT, *rig ma:* A.k.a. MUDRĀ. Spiritual consort. Literally, "knowledge consort," but *vidyā* has a unique range of meanings. Like *prajñā*, it may mean either ordinary worldly knowledge or spiritual knowledge. It may also refer to either seeking or teaching knowledge, in which sense a vidyā is a learning or teaching consort who embodies the knowledge learned or taught. See detailed explanation about MUDRĀS or CONSORTS in Part Four chapters 8 and 9.

VINAYA, *'dul ba:* Monastic discipline. Rules governing the conduct of nuns and monks.

VIRTUE, *dge ba:* Good deeds that lead to positive outcomes in this life or in future rebirths, according to karmic cause and effect. By nature they exclude selfishness. Virtues are defiled or impure when good deeds of body, speech, and mind are performed without a proper understanding of the nondual nature of reality. In this case, the positive outcome will be limited to short-term results. Practicing virtuous actions leads to the accumulation of MERIT.

VIŚHVAMĀTĀ, *vishva ma ta:* Female aspect of the KĀLACHAKRA union or YAB-YUM DEITY, representing WISDOM and EMPTY-FORM, known in short as KĀLACHAKRA's ultimate CONSORT.

VOW, *sdom pa:* A holy commitment to benefit ourselves and others, divided into three levels or THREE VOWS: PRĀTIMOKṢHA or INDIVIDUAL LIBERATION vows, BODHISATTVA pledges, and TANTRIC SAMAYA commitments.

WINDS, *rlung,* prāṇa: Patterns of energies flowing in the inner CHANNELS of the SUBTLE BODY.

WISDOM: As opposed to information, knowledge, or technique, wisdom is defined as the ability to use knowledge to contemplate and act productively. BUDDHISM distinguishes provisional, conceptual worldly wisdom and the ultimate non-conceptual wisdom of enlightened realization. The highest worldly wisdom is said to be that of the path leading to ultimate wisdom. That includes the reasoning that establishes EMPTINESS and techniques and conduct that produce enlightened realization of emptiness as the way things are. However, when practitioners cling to reasoning and yogic conduct as ends in themselves, they do not lead to long-term realization; in that case, they are faults, rather than wisdom. Wisdom is commonly used to translate PRAJÑĀ (*shes rab*) and JÑĀNA (*ye shes*).

WISDOM MUDRĀ, *ye shes phyag rgya:* A visualized or generated tantric consort. Described in Part Four chapter 8.

YAB YUM, Father-mother tantric DEITIES depicted in sacred sexual union representing non-duality or the inseparability of masculine and feminine aspects such as skillful means and prajñā, or great bliss and emptiness, and so forth.

YIDAM, *yi dam:* Abbreviation for *yid kyi dam tshig*, "mind SAMAYA." Enlightened DEITY or BUDDHA in SAMBHOGAKĀYA form used in tantric MEDITATION such as KĀLACHAKRA, CHAKRASAMVARA, and so forth.

ZHENTONG, *gzhan stong:* Also known as Zhentong MADHYAMAKA or Great Middle Way. It is regarded by JONANGPA masters and some masters of other Tibetan schools as the highest of all BUDDHIST philosophical approaches. Literally, it means "other-emptiness" or "emptiness of other," since all delusive phenomena are empty of themselves but BUDDHA NATURE is full of truly existing enlightened qualities and empty of any phenomena *other* than those. Zhentong madhyamaka does not reject Rangtong madhyamaka in the sense of their shared understanding of RELATIVE TRUTH but differs from it mainly in the sense that for Zhentongpas, BUDDHA NATURE, ENLIGHTENMENT, enlightened qualities, and so forth truly exist as ABSOLUTE TRUTH.

Glossary lists

EIGHT GREAT MASTERIES, *dbang phyug chen po brgyad:* Eight "ordinary" good qualities: 1) good qualities of subtle form, *gzugs phra ba'i yon tan;* 2) good qualities of coarse form, *gzugs rags pa'i yon tan;* 3) buoyancy, *yang ba'i yon tan;* 4) pervasiveness, *khyab pa'i yon tan;* 5) becoming sincere and genuine, *yang dag thob pa'i yon tan;* 6) brilliant clarity, *rab tu gsal ba'i yon tan;* 7) stability, *brtan pa'i yon tan;* 8) the arising of total satisfaction, *'dod dgu 'byung ba'i yon tan.*

EIGHT WORLDLY CONCERNS, *jig rten chos brgyad:* A.k.a. "eight worldly dharmas." *Attachment* to: 1) gain or wealth; 2) pleasure, comfort, or enjoyment; 3) recognition or status; 4) praise; and *aversion* to: 5) loss; 6) pain or hardship; 7) being ignored or insignificance; and 8) criticism or disgrace.

EIGHTEEN SCIENCES [of ancient India], *rig gnas bco brgyad:* 1) music, *rol mo;* 2) **sexual techniques, *'khrig 'thabs;*** 3) ways of livelihood, *so tshis;* 4) enumeration, *grang can;* 5) grammar, *sgra;* 6) medicine, *gso ba;* 7) religious systems, *chos lugs;* 8) crafts and manufacturing, *bzo ba;* 9) archery, *'phong spyod;* 10) logical argument, *gtan tshig;* 11) logical proof, *sbyor ba;* 12) entailment, *rang gi bcas pa;* 13) remembering what is heard, *thos pa dran pa;* 14) astronomy, *skar ma'i dpyad;* 15) astrology, *rtsis;* 16) illusions, *mig 'phrul;* 17) former lives, *sngon rabs;* 18) history, *sngon byung brjod.*

EIGHTY KINDS OF CONCEPTUALIZED AND EMOTIONAL STATES: Classification of KLEŚHAS according to TANTRA. According to Longchenpa's commentary (*sems nyid ngal gso*), after the four elements have dissolved into each other in the process of dying or in meditative absorption, finally the mind experiences the luminosity of pristine WISDOM at the heart center. At that time the four luminosities of DHARMAKĀYA arise, the pristine wisdoms of (1) shining forth, (2) increase, (3) attainment, and (4) full attainment. By the wisdom of "shining forth," **thirty-three thoughts arising from aversion** cease. According to the *Abbreviated Lamp of Action* (Āryadeva, chap. 4, f78A4), these are: 1) non–passion, '*dod chags dang bral ba*; 2) intermediate non–passion, '*dod chags dang 'bral ba bar ma*; 3) extreme non–passion, *shin tu 'dod chags dang 'bral ba;* 4) mental going, *gang yid kyis 'gro ba dang*; 5) mental coming, '*ong ba*; 6) suffering, *mya ngan*; 7) intermediate suffering, *mya ngan bar ma*; 8) extreme suffering, *shin tu ma ngan tu 'gyur pa;* 9) peace, *zhi ba*; 10) discursive thoughts, *rnam par rtog pa*; 11) fear, '*jigs pa*; 12) intermediate fear, '*jigs pa bar ma*; 13) extreme fear, *shin tu 'jigs pa*; 14) craving, *sred pa;* 15) intermediate craving, *sred pa bar ma*; 16) extreme craving, *shin tu sred pa*; 17) clinging, *nye bar len pa*; 18) non–virtue, *mi dge ba*; 19) hunger, *bkres pa*; 20) thirst, *skom pa*; 21) feeling, *tshor ba*; 22) intermediate feeling, *tshor ba bar ma*; 23) extreme feeling, *shin tu tshor ba*; 24) the apprehender, *rig pa po*; 25) the apprehended, *rig pa*; '*dzin pa'i gzhi* [this is presented as a separate listing, but makes more sense as part of the last or omitted, as by Longchenpa]; 26) discrimination, *so sor rtog pa*; 27) shame, *ngo tsha shes pa*; 28) loving-kindness, *brtse ba*; 29) intermediate loving-kindness, *brtse ba bar ma*; 30) extreme loving-kindness, *shin tu brtse ba;* 31) anxiety, *dogs pa dang bcas pa*; 32) hoarding, *sdud pa*; 33) jealousy, *phrag dog*. Then the wisdom of *shining forth* dissolves into the *wisdom of increase*. By that wisdom, the **forty thoughts arising from passion cease.** According to the *Abbreviated Lamp of Action* (f78A6) they are: 1) desire, *chags pa*; 2) yearning, *kun tu chags pa*; 3) joy, *dga' ba*; 4) intermediate joy, *dga' ba 'bar ma*; 5) extreme joy, *shin tu dga' ba*; 6) rejoicing, *rangs pa*; 7) extreme gladness, *rab tu mgu ba*; 8) wonder, *ngo mtshar;* 9) laughing, *dgod pa*; 10) satisfaction, *tshim pa*; 11) embracing, *'khyud pa';* 12) kissing, *'o byed pa*; 13) sucking, *'jib pa*; 14) steadfastness, *brtan pa*; 15) perseverance, *brtson pa*; 16) arrogance, *khengs pa*; 17) action, *bya ba*; 18) befriending, *dbrog pa*; 19) power, *stobs*; 20) enthusiasm, *spro ba*; 21) undertaking what is difficult, *dka ba la sbyor ba*; 22) undertaking what is of intermediate difficulty, *dka ba la sbyor ba bar ma*; 23) undertaking what is of supreme difficulty, *shin tu dka ba la sbyor ba*; 24) wrath, *drag pa*; 25) flirtatiousness, *rnam par sgeg pa*; 26) animosity, *'gras pa*; 27) virtue, *dge ba*; 28) clear words, *tshig gsal*; 29) truth, *bden pa*; 30) untruth, *mi bden pa*; 31) certainty, *nges pa*; 32) not clinging, *nye bar mi len pa*; 33) being a giver, *sbyin pa po*; 34) encouraging others, *bskul ba*; 35) bravery, *dpa ba*; 36) shamelessness, *ngo tsha med pa*; 37) deceptiveness, *sgyu zin pa*; 38) attractiveness, *gdug pa;* 39) mischief, *mi srun pa*; 40) great dishonesty, *gya gyu che ba*, making exactly forty. Then the wisdom of increase dissolves in the *wisdom of attainment*. By that wisdom, **seven thoughts arising from ignorance** cease. According to the *Abbreviated Lamp of Action* (f78B:2) they are: 1) intermediate passion/attachment *chags pa bar ma* [Longchenpa has "dullness," *bying ba*]; 2) forgetfulness, *brjed ngas pa*; 3) confusion, *'khrul pa*; 4) having nothing to say, *mi smra ba*; 5) sadness, *skyo ba*; 6) laziness, *le lo;* 7) doubt, *the tshom*. [These 80 disappear as the inner winds dissolve, corresponding to three absorptions of white appearance, red increase, and black attainment.]

ELEVEN VIRTUOUS MENTAL FACTORS, *dge ba bcu gcig*: 1) faith; śhraddhā; *dad pa*; 2) moral shame or dignity; hri; *ngo tsha shes pa*; 3) fear of unwholesomeness or propriety; apatrāpya; *khrel yod pa*; 4) non-attachment; alobha; *ma chags pa*; 5) non-aggression or non-hatred; adveṣha; *zhe dang med pa*; 6) non-ignorance or non-delusion; amoha; *gti mug med pa*; 7) diligence; vīrya; *brtson 'grus*; 8) pliancy of mind or flexibility, praśhrabdhi; *shin tu sbyang ba;* 9) Conscientiousness or introspection;

apramāda; *bag yod pa*; 10) equanimity; upekṣhā; *btang snyoms*; 11) non-violence; avihiṃsā; *rnam par mi 'tshe ba.*

FIFTY-ONE MENTAL FACTORS, *sems byung nga gcig*: **Five omnipresent mental factors:** 1) sensation or feeling; vedanā; *tshor ba;* 2) perception or discrimination; saṃjña; *'du shes;* 3) intention; chetanā; *sems pa;* 4) contact; sparśha; *reg bya;* 5) mental engagement or attention; manaskāra; *yid byed.* **Five object-determining factors:** 1) aspiration or interest; chanda; *'dun pa;* 2) belief or appreciation; adhimokṣha; *mos pa;* 3) mindfulness; smṛiti; *dran pa;* 4) concentration or meditative absorption; samādhi; *ting nge 'dzin;* 5) wisdom or superior knowledge; prajñā; *shes rab.* **Six root mental afflictions or kleśhas:** 1) ignorance; avidyā; *ma rig pa;* 2) attachment or desire; rāga; *'dod chags*; 3) aversion or anger; pratigha; *kong khro*; 4) pride; māna; *nga rgyal*; 5) doubt; vichikitsā; *the tshom*; 6) wrong views; dṛishṭi; *lta ba.* **Twenty derivative or subsidiary mental afflictions or kleśhas:** 1) fury or rage; krodha; *khro ba;* 2) resentment; upanāha; *'khon du 'dzin pa;* 3) hostility or spitefulness; pradāśha; *'tshig pa;* 4) harmfulness or cruelty; vihiṃsā; *rnam par 'tshe ba;* 5) jealousy; īrśhya; *phrag dog;* 6) deceat or deception; śhāṭhya; *g.yo;* 7) hyprocrisy or pretense; māyā; *sgyu;* 8) personal lack of shame; āhrīkya; *ngo tsha med pa;* 9) Lack of conscience or disregard for others; anapatatrāpya; *khrel med pa;* 10) concealment; mrakśha; *'chab pa;* 11) miserliness, mātsarya; *ser sna;* 12) self-infatuation; mada; *rgyags pa;* 13) lack of faith, āśhraddhya; *ma dad pa;* 14) laziness; kausīdya; *le lo;* 15) heedlessness; pramāda; *bag med pa;* 16) forgetfulness; muṣhitasmṛtitā; *brjed ngas;* 17) non-introspection or inattention; asaṃprajanya; *shes bzhin min pa;* 18) lethargy; styāna; *rmug pa;* 19) excitement; auddhatya; *rgod pa;* 20) distraction; vikṣhepa; *rnam par g.yeng ba.* **Eleven virtuous mental factors:** see the previous list. **Four variable mental factors:** 1) sleep; middha; *gnyid;* 2) regret; kaukṛitya; *'gyod pa;* 3) gross detection or conception; vitarka; *rtog pa;* 4) Discernment; vichāra; *dpyod pa.*

(FIVE) BUDDHA FAMILIES, *rigs lnga:* 1) Padma Family (lotus), ruler Amitābha who embodies the primordial wisdom of discrimination; 2) Vajra Family, ruler Akṣhobhya, mirror-like wisdom of primordial awareness; 3) Ratna Family (jewel), ruler Ratnasambhava, primordial wisdom of equality; 4) Karma Family (action), ruler Amoghasiddhi, all-accomplishing wisdom; 5) Buddha Family, ruler Vairochana, pristine wisdom of DHARMADHĀTU. Their colors vary depending on the tantric system.

FIVE CHAKRAS, *'khor lo lnga:* In tantric Buddhism usually the following wheels of channels or energy centers, 1) the forehead wheel, *dpral bar bde ba'i 'khor lo*; 2) the wheel of great bliss at the crown, *gtsug tor du bde chen 'khor lo*; 3) the wheel of enjoyment at the throat, *mgrin par longs spyod rdzogs pa'i 'khor lo;* 4) the wheel of Dharma at the heart, s*nying gar chos kyi 'khor lo;* 5) and four finger widths under the navel, the wheel of emanation, *lte bar sprul pa'i 'khor lo.* Six chakras are used in the KĀLACHAKRA system, the above five, and 6) the wheel that maintains bliss at the secret place, *gsang gnas bde skyong 'khor lo.*

FIVE ELEMENTS, *'byung po lnga:* 1) earth, *sa*; 2) water, *chu*; 3) fire, *me*; 4) wind, *rlung*; and 5) space, *nam mkha'.* These elements have both gross and subtle qualities which determine how the body and MIND dissolves at the moment of death.

FIVE POISONS, *dug lnga*: 1) Attachment or desire, *'dod chags;* 2) aversion or anger, *zhe sdang;* 3) ignorance, *gti mug;* 4) pride, *nga rgyal;* 5) jealousy, *phrag dog.*

FIVE WISDOMS, *ye shes lnga:* see FIVE BUDDHA FAMILIES.

FOUR DEFEATS: The Four *Pārājikas* (Four Defeats) for which expulsion from the monastic SAṄGHA is compulsory and there is no way for monastics to restore their vows: 1) sexual intercourse; 2) theft; 3) murder; 4) false claims (of realization).

FOUR [HIGHER] EMPOWERMENTS, *dbang bzhi:* 1) Vase Empowerment, *bum dbang*; 2) Secret Empowerment, *gsang dbang*; 3) Wisdom Empowerment, *shes rab ye shes dbang*; 4) Fourth or Word Empowerment, *tshig dbang, bzhi pa'i dbang.*

FOUR JOYS, *dga' ba bzhi:* 1) Joy, *dga' ba*; 2) Supreme Joy, *mchog dga'*; 3) Special Joy, *khyad dga'*; 4) Innate Joy, *lhan skyes dga' ba.* See Part Four chapter 8.

FOUR KĀYAS: See KĀYAS.

FOUR MEANS OF GATHERING DISCIPLES (ATTRACTING OTHERS / STUDENTS), *bsdu ba'i dngos po bzhi:* 1) Being generous, *sbyin pa*; 2) speaking in an agreeable or pleasant manner, *snyan par smra ba*; 3) teaching beneficial conduct in accordance with individuals' needs, *don spyod pa*; and 4) sameness of purpose of acting in accordance with what one teaches, *don mthun pa.*

SIX CHAKRAS: See FIVE CHAKRAS.

SIX VAJRA YOGAS, *sbyor ba drug:* The KĀLACHAKRA system of Highest Yoga Tantra practice involving the energy CHANNELS, inner WINDS, and SUBTLE ESSENCES which is the basis for the COMPLETION STAGE as practiced by the JONANG tradition. These six yogas include six specific sets of profound yogic practices performed in sequence: 1) withdrawal; pratyāhāra, *sor sdud;* 2) meditative stabilization; dhyāna; *bsam gtan;* 3) life force control or power; prānāyāma; *srog rtsol;* 4) retention; dhāraṇā; *'dzin* pa; 5) recollection; anusmṛiti; *rjes dran;* and 6) meditative absorption; samādhi; *ting nge 'dzin*. This set of six should not be confused with the Six Dharmas of Nāropā or Niguma which are often translated as Six Yogas. See the author's *Sacred Truth — Book 3*, pp. 276-292.

SIX PERFECTIONS, *pha rol tu phyin pa drug:* 1) Generosity, *sbyin pa;* 2) ethical discipline, *tshul khrims;* 3) patience, *bzod pa;* 4) joyful effort or diligence, *brtson 'grus;* 5) meditative concentration, *bsam gtan;* and 6) wisdom, *shes rab.*

SIX ROOT KLEŚHAS /AFFLICTIVE EMOTIONS / MENTAL AFFLICTIONS; *rtsa nyon drug:* 1) ignorance; avidyā; *ma rig pa;* 2) attachment or desire; rāga; *'dod chags;* 3) aversion or anger; pratigha; *kong khro;* 4) pride; māna; *nga rgyal;* 5) doubt; vichikitsā; *the tshom;* 6) wrong views; dṛiṣhṭi; *lta ba.*

SIXTEEN JOYS, *dga' ba bcu drug:* The four joys are combined from 1.1 (Joy of Joy) to 4.4 (Innate Joy of Innate Joy.) See FOUR JOYS and subchapter 4.8.2.

TEN NON-VIRTUES, *mi dge ba bcu:* **three of body:** 1) killing, *srog gcod;* 2) stealing, *ma byin len;* 3) improper sexual conduct; *log g.yem;* **four of speech:** 4) lying, *rdzun smra ba;* 5) divisive words, *phra ma;* 6) harsh words, *tshig rtsub;* 7) worthless or idle chatter, *ngag 'chal';* **three of mind:** 8) covetousness, *brnab sems;* 9) ill-will or malice, *gnod sems;* 10) wrong view, *log lta.*

THIRTEEN OFFENSES WITH REMAINDER (of the vinaya precepts), *lhag ma bcu gsum gyi sdom khrims nyes pa:* They are called *Saṅghādisesa*, "involving the community (Saṅgha) in the initial (ādi) and subsequent (sesa) stages." Because the first five are sexual, they are relevant to the author's discussion in this book: 1) intentionally causing oneself to emit semen, or getting someone else to cause one to emit semen [through means other than sexual intercourse, which is one of the FOUR DEFEATS], except during a dream; 2) making lustful bodily contact with a woman whom one perceives to be a woman; 3) making a lustful remark to a woman about her lotus or anus, or about her performing sexual intercourse; 4) telling a woman that her having sexual intercourse with a male monastic would be beneficial in any way; 5) acting as a go-between to arrange a marriage, affair, or assignation between a man and a woman who are not married to each other; 6) building a plastered hut — or having it built — without a sponsor, destined for one's own use, without having obtained the monastic community's approval, in a place that is disturbed or without adequate space, or exceeding the standard measurements; 7) building a hut with a sponsor — or having it built — destined for one's own use, without having obtained the monastic community's approval, in a place that is disturbed or without adequate space, or exceeding the standard measurements. 8) making a false charge that a *bhikkhu* (full-ordained monk) has committed a defeat offense (*pārājika*) in hopes of having him disrobed; 9) without making false statements willfully distorting the evidence while accusing a *bhikkhu* of having committed a *pārājika* offense, in hopes of having him disrobed; 10) to persist — after the third proclamation of a formal rebuke in the monastic community — in taking a philosophical position, alone or with a group, that could lead to schism; 11) to persist — after the third proclamation of a formal rebuke in the monastic community — in supporting a potential schismatic; 12) to persist — after the third proclamation of a formal rebuke in the monastic community — in resisting admonishment; 13) to persist — after the third proclamation of a formal rebuke in the monastic community — in criticizing a banishment issued against oneself.

THREE POISONS, *dug gsum*: Kleśhas of 1) attachment or desire, *'dod chags*; 2) aversion, aggression, or anger, *zhe sdang*; and 3) ignorance, *gti mug*.

THREE REALMS, *khams gsum:* 1) DESIRE REALM, *'dod khams*; 2) FORM

REALM, *gzugs khams*; and 3) FORMLESS REALM, *gzugs med pa'i khams*.

THREE TIMES, *dus gsum*: 1) Past, *'das pa*; 2) present, *da lta ba*; and 3) future, *ma 'ongs pa*.

THREE TURNINGS OF THE WHEEL OF DHARMA, *chos kyi 'khor lo rim pa gsum:* 1) First turning emphasizing INDIVIDUAL LIBERATION VEHICLE teachings; 2) second turning emphasizing MAHĀYĀNA SŪTRA teachings of EMPTINESS of self and phenomena; 3) third and final turning emphasizing the definitive meaning sūtras and TANTRA teachings of truly existent BUDDHA NATURE empty of anything other than that. Some schools consider the second turning as being the definitive turning but this is rejected by DOLPOPA and his adherents.

THREE VEHICLES, *theg pa gsum*: 1) Vehicle of Hearers, Śhrāvakayāna (the same as INDIVIDUAL LIBERATION), *nyan thos kyi theg pa*; 2) Vehicle of Pratyekabuddhas, Pratyekabuddhayāna, *rang sangs rgyas kyi theg pa*; 3) the Great Vehicle (including MAHĀYĀNA and often also TANTRAYĀNA or VAJRAYĀNA), *theg pa chen po;* or 1) HINAYĀNA (the same as INDIVIDUAL LIBERATION), *theg chung*; 2) Great Vehicle (mahāyāna), *theg chen*; and 3) tantrayāna or vajrayāna.

THREE VOWS: 1) PRATIMOKṢHA (INDIVIDUAL LIBERATION) vow, *so so thar pa'i sdom pa*; 2) BODHISATTVA pledges or vows, *byang chub sems dpa'i sdom pa*; and 3) tantric SAMAYAS or vows, *dam tshig gi sdom pa.*

TWENTY SUBSIDIARY AFFLICTIONS (or KLEŚHAS), upa-kleśha, *nye nyon nyi shu*: See FIFTY-ONE MENTAL FACTORS.

TWO OBSCURATIONS, *sgrib gnyis*: 1) AFFLICTIVE OBSCURATIONS (of KLEŚHAS), *nyon mongs pa'i sgrib*; and 2) COGNITIVE OBSCURATIONS. See

OBSCURATIONS.

TWO TRUTHS, *bden pa gnyis:* 1) RELATIVE TRUTH (or conventional truth), *kun rdzob bden pa*; and 2) ABSOLUTE TRUTH (also ultimate or definitive truth), *don dam bden pa.*

Bibliography[468]

Tibetan Sources, Sūtras and Tantras[469]

Abridged Cakrasaṃvara Tantra,[470] *Rgyud kyi rgyal po dpal bde mchog nyung ngu, zhes bya ba Tantrarāja śrī laghusaṁbara nāma,* D0368 Kangyur, rgyud ka 213b1-246b7

Cakrasaṃvara Root Tantra: See *Abridged Cakrasaṃvara Tantra.*

Diamond Sūtra, *'Phags pa shes rab kyi pha rol tu phyin pa rdo rje gcod pa zhes bya ba they pa chen po'i mdo, Ārya vajracchedikā nāma prajñāpāramitā mahāyāna sūtra,* D0016 Kangyur, shes phyin, ka 121a1-132b7.

---

468 Abbreviations: BDRC Buddhist Digital Resource Center; D sde ge.

469 Most quotations in this book were translated as cited in the author's unpublished Tibetan version of this book.

470 Elsewhere in the book we edited "c" as "ch;" "ch" as "cch;" "ṣ" as "ṣh;" "ś" as "śh;" and "ṛ" as "ṛi" to aid pronunciation for those unfamiliar with Sanskrit diacritics. The same is not followed below in this bibliography.

Guhyasamāja Tantra, De bzhin gshegs pa thams cad kyi sku gsung thugs kyi gsang chen gsang ba 'dus pa zhes bya ba brtag pa'i rgyal po chen po, Sarvatathāgata kāya vāk citta rahasyo guhyasamāja nāma mahā kalparāja, D0443, rgyud, ca 90a1-157b7.

Lotus Sūtra, Dam pa'i chos pad ma dkar po zhes bya ba theg pa chen po'i mdo, Saddharma puṇḍarīka nāma mahāyāna sūtra. D0113 Kangyur, mdo sde, ja 1b1-180b7.

Minor Sayings of the Vinaya, 'Dul ba phran tshegs kyi gzhi, D0006 Kangyur, 'dul ba, tha 1b1-da 333a7.

Perfection of Wisdom Sūtra in Eighteen Thousand Stanzas, 'Phags pa shes rab kyi pha rol tu phyin pa khri brgyad stong pa zhes bya ba theg pa chen po'i mdo, Daśa sāhasrikā prajñāpāramitā sūtra, D0010 Kangyur, shes phyin, ga 1b1-206a7.

Sūtra of Skillful Means, 'Phags pa thabs mkhas pa zhes bya ba theg pa chen po'i mdo, Ārya *upāyakauśalya nāma mahāyāna sūtra,* D0261 Kangyur, mdo sde, za 283b2-310a7. BDRC Etext UTIE0OP16440489A_10951_bo, accessed March 27, 2023.

Vast Expanse of Play, 'Phags pa rgya cher rol pa zhes bya ba they pa chen po'i mdo, Ārya *lalitavistara nāma mahāyāna sūtra,* D0095, mdo sde, kha 1b1-216b7.

Treatises in Tibetan

Āryadeva, 'phags pa lha: *Abbreviated Lamp of Action, Spyod pa bsdus pa'i sgron ma, Caryāmelāpakapradīpa*, D1803 Tengyur, rgyud, ngi, 57a2-106b7.

Amoghavajra, Don yod rdo rje: *Oral Instructions on Entering Into the Yoga of Suchness through Passionate Union, Rjes chags kyi sbyor bas de kho na nyid kyi rnal 'byor la 'jug pa'i man ngag, Anukampopakramatattvayogā vatāropadeśa nāma*, D1745 Tengyur, rgyud, sha, 113b2-116a3. Adarshah. org etext, accessed March 8, 2023.

Lelung Shépé Dorjé, sle lung bzhad pa'i rdo rje:
  – *Treatise on the Protectors: Dam can bstan srung rgya mtsho'i rnam par thar pa cha shas tsam brjod pa legs bshad*, 2 volumes, Leh: T.S. Tashigang. BDRC scan W1kG9276 [s.l]: [s.n], accessed February 17, 2023.
  – *Eliminating the Torment of Peoples' Sexual Desire:* (Author listed as *'ol dga' rje drung 03 bzhad pa'i rdo rje), Rgyo 'dod skyes bu'i gdung sel*, BDRC scan W8LS19933, accessed Feb. 21, 2023.
  – *Clear Points of the Path of Means, Thabs lam gyi gnad 'ga 'zhig gsal bar byed pa'i man ngag thabs lam snying bcud khams khul nas 'tshol bsdu zhus pa'i pe rnying dpe dkon*, BDRC scan purl.bdrc.io/resource/ MW3PD982_D6A2D5. Accessed Mar. 20, 2023.

Longchenpa, *klong chen rab 'byams pa dri med 'od zer*:
  – *Snying thig ya bzhi* (dar thang glog klad par ma), BDRC: e-text UTIE0OPI7944B80B_I1KG12052, accessed Mar. 7, 2023.
  – *Theg pa mtha' dag gi don gsal bar byed pa grub pa'i mtha' rin po che'i mdzod*, BDRC e-text lccw.0424, vol 15, accessed March 7, 2023.

Nāgārjuna, klu grub: *Precious Garland, Rgyal po la gtam bya rin po che'i phreng ba, Rājaparikathāratnāvali,* D4158 Tengyur, spring yig, ge, 107a1-126a4.

Surūpa, gzugs bzang: *'Dod pa'i bstan bcos zhes bya ba, Kama* Śāstra *nāma,* D2500 Tengyur, volume 53, rgyud, zi, 274b7-277a7.

Tāranātha: *Brilliant Clarity of Union, Zab lam rdo rje rnal 'byor gyi rnam par bshad pa rgyas par bstan pa zung 'jug rab tu gsal ba chen po zhes bya ba bzhugs so.* BDRC scan W22276-v4, accessed Nov. 3, 2022.

Tsongkhapa, Jé, *Extensive Explanation of the Abridged Cakrasaṃvara Tantra, Clarifying all the Hidden Points, Bde mchog bsdus pa'i rgyud kyi rgya cher bshad pa sbas pa'i don kun gsal ba,* in *The Complete Works of Je Tsongkhapa, Rje tsong kha pa'i gsung 'bum,* 18 volumes, Adarshah.org etext, location 8.10.145a, accessed Mar. 12, 2023.

Non-Tibetan Sources

al-Nefzawi, Muhammad ibn Muhammad, *Perfumed Garden of Sensual Delight, Al-fī nuzhaï al-ḫāṭir:* Tr. Richard Francis Burton, 1886, available online at https://www.sacred-texts.com/sex/garden

Bailey, Cameron, *A Feast of Scholars: The Life and Works of* Sle lung Bzhad pa'i rdo rje, thesis, Faculty of Oriental Studies, Wolfson College Oxford, England, pdf available at https://www.academia.edu/68203543/A_feast_for_scholars_the_life_and_works_of_Sle_lung_Bzhad_pa_i_rdo_rje

Baker, Ian, *The Heart of the World: A Journey to the Last Secret Place.* New York: Penguin Press, 2004. (Contains a translation of Lelung Shépé Dorjé's *Account of a Journey to Pemakö.*)

Bhikkhu-vibhanga, English translation with vinaya rules: https://www.wisdomlib.org/buddhism/book/vinaya-pitaka-1.bhikkhu-vibhanga/d/doc227039.html

Battersby, Matilda, for the *Independent* [digital news] Monday 20 September, 2010 00:00: [based on] former *Independent* journalist Sarah Harris's documentary about India's temple prostitutes.

Bowker, John, *The Concise Oxford Dictionary of World Religions*, Oxford University Press: Great Clarendon Street, Oxford, OX2 6DP, United Kingdom, Print Publication Date: 2000 Print ISBN-13: 9780192800947. Online publication date: 2003, ISBN: 780191727221.

Dowman, Keith tr., *The Divine Madman: The Sublime Life and Songs of Drukpa Kunley, Brag-phug Dge-bśes Dge-'dun-rin-chen*, United States: Dawn Horse Press, 1980.

Gendün Chöpel, *The Passion Book, a Tibetan Guide to Love and Sex*, Lopez D.S. and Thupten Jinpa tr., Chicago; London: The University of Chicago Press, 2018.

Jamgön Kongtrül, International Translation Committee founded by the V.V. Kalu Rinpoche tr. ed., *Buddhist Ethics*, New York: Snow Lion Publications, 1998.

Ju Mipham, Note-commentary on the *Abridged Kālacakra Tantra*, BDRC scan W23468v17img231. 929, v18img3-977, accessed August 13, 2022, revised 2023, tr. Rime Lodrö (Ives Waldo), unpublished efile.

Lelung Shépé Dorjé, *sle lung bshad pa'i rdo rje*:
– *Journey to Pemakö*. For a translation, see Baker, Ian, 2004.
– *Life*: See Cameron Bailey, *A Feast for Scholars*.

Longchenpa, *The Great Chariot*, a Commentary on *The Great Perfection: The Comfort and Ease of Mind*, tr. Rimé Lodrö (Ives Waldo) unpublished e-file, electronic.

Nālandā Translation Committee under the direction of Chögyam Trungpa Rinpoche tr., *The Life of Marpa the Translator*, Shambhala Publications: Boulder CO, 1982.

Ngari Panchen and Pema Wangyi Gyalpo, *Perfect Conduct: Ascertaining the Three Vows*, Commentary by H.H. Dudjom Rinpoché, tr. Khenpo Gyurme Samdrub and Sangye Khandro, Wisdom Publications: Boston, 1996.

Padoux, André, *The Hindu Tantric World, an Overview*, University of Chicago Press: Chicago and London, 2017.

Robinson, James B. tr., *Buddha's Lions, the Lives of the Eighty-four Mahasiddhas*, Dharma Publishing: Berkeley CA, 1979. Translated from Smon grub shes rab tr, *grub thob brgyad cu rtsa bzhi'i chos skor*, New Delhi: Chophel Legdan, 1973, itself a translation of the *Caturaśitisiddhapravṛtti* by Abhayadatta. The book contains the Tibetan text.

Shar Khentrul Rinpoché (Jamphel Lodrö),
– *Empowerment Liturgy of the Dharma Kings and Kalkīs of Śhambhala in the North, along with the Kalkī Princes and Princesses, entitled "The Heroic Courage of Spiritual Warriors of Great Power,"* Dzokden: San Francisco, 2022.
– *The Four Higher Empowerments, a Guidebook for Entering the Kāla-*

chakra Completion Stage, first published by Tibetan Buddhist Rimé Institute: Belgrave, Australia, 2016. (This booklet is only accessible to those who have received these Higher Empowerments from the author).
– *The Hidden Treasure of the Profound Path*, Tibetan Buddhist Rime Institute: Belgrave Australia, second edition, 2016.
– *Ocean of Diversity*, Buddhist Rimé Institute: Belgrave Australia, 2015.
– *The Realm of Śhambhala: A Complete Vision for Humanity's Perfection*, Shambhala Press: Boulder CO, 2021.
– *The Seven Empowerments of a Growing Child — A Guidebook for Entering the Kālachakra Generation Stage*, Tibetan Buddhist Rimé Institute: Belgrave, 2016. (This booklet is only accessible to those who have received these Empowerments from the author).
– *Śhambhala Dharma Kings Sādhana*, Dzokden: San Francisco, 2022.
– *Unveiling Your Sacred Truth, Books 1-3*, Tibetan Buddhist Rimé Institute: Belgrave Australia, 2017.

Sleeman W.H., *The Thugs or Phansigars of India, comprising a history of the rise and progress of that extraordinary fraternity of assassins; Compiled by Original and Authentic Documents published by Sleeman, Superintendent of Thug Police,* Carey and Hart:Philadelphia, 1839.

The Hevajra Tantra, a Critical Study, volumes I and II, Oxford University Press:London, 1959.

Taylor, P. M., *Confessions of a Thug.* London: Richard Bentley, 1858.

Vātsyāyana, *Kāma Sūtra,* second or third century. The colophon says: "This treatise was composed, according to the precepts of scripture, for the benefit of the world, by Vātsyāyana, while leading the life of a religious student at Benares and wholly engaged in the contemplation of the Deity. This work is not to be used merely as an instrument for satisfying our desires. A person acquainted with the true principles of this science, who preserves his Dharma (virtue and religious merit), his Artha (worldly wealth), and his Kama (pleasure or sensual gratification), and who has regard for the customs of the people, is sure to master over the senses. In short, an intelligent and knowing person attending to Dharma and Artha and also to Kama, without becoming the slave of his passions, will obtain success in everything that he may do." English translation, *Complete Kāma Sūtra, the first unabridged modern translation of the classic Indian text*, tr. Alain Danielou, Park Street Press:Rochester VT, 1994.

About the Author

Shar Khentrul Rinpoché spent the first 20 years of his life herding yak and chanting mantras on the plateaus of Tibet. Inspired by the bodhisattvas, he left his family to study in a variety of monasteries under the guidance of over twenty-five masters in all the Tibetan Buddhist traditions. Due to his non-sectarian approach, he earned himself the title of *Rimé* (unbiased) Master and was identified as the reincarnation of the famous *Kālachakra* Master Ngawang Chözin Gyatso. While at the core of his teachings is the recognition that there is great value in the diversity of all spiritual traditions found in this world, he focuses on the Jonang-Shambhala tradition. *Kālachakra* (wheel of time) teachings handed down from the Kalkī Kings of Śhambhala, contain profound methods to harmonize our external environment with the inner world of body and mind. This tantra is connected directly to the karma of our earth to bring about the Golden age of Peace and Harmony (Dzokden). Khentrul Rinpoché has made it his life mission to spread these precious teachings in as many languages as possible globally so that we can truly transform our world, one person at a time from their inside out.

Shar Khentrul Jamphel Lodrö

Rinpoché's Vision

Dzokden was founded with the express purpose of supporting Khentrul Rinpoché in realizing his vision to bring about the Golden Age of peace and harmony in this world. As our community continues to grow and develop, more and more people are getting involved with this extraordinary effort.

To give you a sense of the scope of Rinpoché's vision, we can speak of eight goals that reflect Rinpoché's short and long term priorities:

Immediate Goals

Ultimately speaking, lasting, genuine happiness is only possible through profound personal transformation. Now more than ever, we need methods to develop our wisdom and actualize our greatest potential. It is for this reason that Rinpoche places such a heavy priority on the preservation of the Jonang Kālachakra Lineage. There are four ways in which Rinpoché proposes to do this:

1. **Create opportunities to connect with an authentic and complete Kālachakra lineage in close collaboration with dedicated meditators in remote Tibet.** Our goal is to create all of the supports for practicing Kālachakra in accordance with the authentic lineage masters who have upheld this tradition for thousands of years. We do this by commissioning statues and paintings, writing books and

giving teachings around the world. We place particular emphasis on ensuring the authenticity of our materials, drawing on the profound experience of highly realized meditators who are dedicating their lives to these practices.

2. **Establish international retreat centres for the study and practice of Kālachakra.** In order to integrate the teachings into our minds, it is crucial to have the opportunity to engage in periods of intensive practice. Therefore, we are working to create the necessary infrastructure that will support and nurture the members of our community to engage in both short and long-term retreat. This includes the purchase of land and the construction of everything that is needed to conduct group and solitary retreats. Our long-term aim is to develop a network of such centres around the world, forming a global community that supports a wide variety of practitioners.

3. **Translate and publish the unique and rare texts of Kālachakra masters.** The Kālachakra System has been the subject of countless texts over the course of Tibet's long history. So far, only a small fraction of these texts have been translated and made accessible in the West. While the theoretical texts are important, we aim to focus particularly on the pith instructions that will guide dedicated practitioners to a deeper experience of these profound teachings.

4. **Develop the tools and programs for a structured learning experience.** With pockets of students distributed throughout the world, we believe it is important to make the most of modern technologies to facilitate the process of learning for our students. Our aim is to develop a robust online educational platform that allows our international community to access quality study programs that are intuitive, structured and engaging.

Long-Term Goals

While we each work towards achieving ultimate peace and harmony in our own minds, we must not lose sight of the fact that we exist within the context of a world filled with a great diversity of individuals. These individuals give rise to a wide variety of beliefs and practices that in turn shape how we relate and interact with each other. In this interdependent reality, it is vital to find viable strategies for promoting greater tolerance and respect. To this end, Rinpoché proposes four specific areas of activity:

1. **Promote the development of a Rimé Philosophy through dialogue with other traditions.** With the desire to be constructive members of a pluralistic society, we need to learn ways of reconciling our differences. To this end, we aim to help people develop the positive qualities that promote an attitude of mutual respect, openness to new ideas and an inquisitive desire to overcome our ignorance.

2. **Develop highly realised role models by offering financial support to dedicated practitioners.** In order to ensure the authenticity of our spiritual traditions, it is imperative that there are people who actualize the highest of realizations. Therefore, we aim to create a financial scholarship program which facilitates genuine practitioners who wish to dedicate their lives to spiritual development, regardless of their system of practice. By helping people actualize the teachings, they become positive role models for those around them, inspiring and guiding the generations to come.

3. **Actualize the great potential of female practitioners by developing specialized training programs.** The Tibetan culture has a long history of cultivating highly realized masters through the intensive training of those who are recognized to have great potential. Unfortunately, all too often the search for potential was focused only on male candidates. Rinpoché believes that it is increasingly important

to have strong, highly realized, female role models who can help to bring greater balance into our world. For this reason, we are working to develop a unique training program for providing women with the opportunity to actualize their spiritual potential. It is our aim to design a specialized curriculum as well as the financial infrastructure to fully support all aspects of their education.

4. **Promote greater flexibility of mind and a broader understanding of reality through modern educational programs.** In a world that is rapidly evolving, we need to rethink the types of skills that we are teaching our children. The rigid structures of the past are often ill equipped to prepare students for the challenges that they will face during their lives. Therefore, we aim to develop a variety of educational programs that can help children to become more flexible and more capable of adapting to their context. An important part of these programs is the development of greater awareness of the role that our mind plays in our day-to-day experiences. We also aim to bring reforms into the monastic education system that would help make them more relevant for this modern world.

How can you offer your support?

The above will not be possible without your support and participation. A vision of this magnitude requires a great deal of merit and generosity from many benefactors over many years. If you would like to offer your support, please do not hesitate to contact us.

Dzokden
3436 Divisadero Street
San Francisco, California 94123
United States of America
www.dzokden.org

www.ingramcontent.com/pod-product-compliance
Lightning Source LLC
Chambersburg PA
CBHW021658120626
46545CB00004B/1303